Phenomenologies of Scripture

John D. Caputo, *series editor*

PERSPECTIVES IN
CONTINENTAL
PHILOSOPHY

ADAM Y. WELLS

EDITOR

Phenomenologies of Scripture

FORDHAM UNIVERSITY PRESS
New York ■ 2017

Bloechl, Jeffrey. "Inventions of Christianity: Preambles to a Philosophical Reading of Paul." In *Saint Paul between Ancient Philosophy and Contemporary Thought*, edited by G.-J. van der Heiden and A. Cimino. © 2017 by Brill. Portions reprinted by permission of Brill.

Hart, Kevin. *Kingdoms of God*. Pp. 115–38. © 2014 by Kevin Hart. Reprinted by permission of Indiana University Press.

Marion, Jean-Luc. Translated by Stephen E. Lewis. *The Reason of the Gift*. Pp. 69–90. © 2011 by the Rector and Visitors of the University of Virginia. Reprinted by permission of University of Virginia Press.

Visit us online at www.fordhampress.com.

Library of Congress Cataloging-in-Publication Data available online at http://catalog.loc.gov.

Printed in the United States of America

19 18 17   5 4 3 2 1

First edition

Contents

Phenomenologies of Scripture

Biblical Criticism and the Phenomenology of Scripture

ADAM Y. WELLS

What Can Phenomenology Do for Biblical Studies?

Science is central to the discourse of modern biblical interpretation: how should we study the Bible *scientifically*? Can we discover truths about biblical narratives with scientific rigor? Do recent scientific discoveries undermine or support biblical narratives? We tend to assume that science—for example, historical science, archaeology, etymology, and so forth—is the truer and more stable intellectual discourse, to which biblical interpretation must be conformed. Yet this veneration of *Bibelwissenschaft* (biblical science) is not simply a natural extension of our culture's regard for scientific and technological achievement. Rather, it is generated out of a particular historical nexus—namely, a convergence of the Enlightenment's regard for natural science and the Reformation's suspicion of ecclesial authority. Far from forming the stable center of biblical interpretation, science has functioned ambivalently *within* the historical discourse of biblical studies as both cure and disease. Accordingly, a phenomenological approach to scripture aims to shift the center of biblical studies from science to scripture itself. This approach is not unscientific or anti-scientific; it refuses to draw unreflectively from the methods of the natural sciences, for a true science of scripture must draw its methods from a concrete engagement with scripture.

The methods of modern biblical criticism have their roots in Spinoza's *Tractatus Theologico-Politicus* (1670), which establishes "the marching orders of biblical scholars over the next three centuries."[1] In chapter 7 of the *Tractatus*, Spinoza laments the lack of rigor commonly involved in the interpretation of scripture:

> to make Scripture appear more wonderful and awe-inspiring, [interpreters] explicate it in such a way that it seems diametrically opposed both to reason and Nature. . . . They ascribe to the Holy Spirit whatever their wild fancies have invented, and devote their utmost strength and enthusiasm to defending it. For human nature is so constituted that what men conceive by pure intellect, they defend only by intellect and reason, whereas the beliefs that spring from the emotions are emotionally defended.[2]

Against such fanciful and emotionally motivated hermeneutics, Spinoza seeks a "true method of Scriptural interpretation," which would allow us to "escape from this sense of confusion, to free our minds from the prejudices of theologians and to avoid the hasty acceptance of human fabrications as divine teachings."[3] This "true method," which avoids theological prejudice, is discerned by analogy with the natural sciences: "I hold that the method of interpreting Scripture is no different from the method of interpreting Nature, and is in fact in complete accord with it."[4] Just as natural science relies not on superstition, but looks to the natural world for the source of its data, so should the true method of scriptural interpretation look toward scripture itself (not theological prejudice) as the source of its data. Accordingly, conclusions about the meaning of scripture ought to be deduced from the study of scripture.

The analogy Spinoza draws between natural science and scriptural study is equivocal in an important way. On the one hand, we could read Spinoza's statement to mean that the true method of scriptural study should be *like* the natural sciences, related in some analogous fashion. On the other hand, we might understand Spinoza's statement to mean that the true method ought to be *drawn directly* from the methods of natural science. The underlying question is: should a true science of the Bible be *like* a natural science or should it *be* a natural science? Spinoza seems to imply the former, while his heirs in the field of biblical studies assume the latter, with "science" becoming roughly synonymous with "natural science."

Spinoza's emphasis on a scientific approach to scripture prefigures historical criticism, which became (and perhaps remains) the predominant mode of biblical criticism.[5] The scientific turn in biblical criticism, which grew out of the Enlightenment and took hold in the eighteenth and nineteenth centuries, opened up new intellectual avenues for the study of scripture, but it also engendered a crisis about the status of scripture *within* biblical studies. As George Marsden points out in his study of American fundamentalism, "The crucial issue seems rather to have been perceived as that of the authority of God in Scripture in relation to the authority of modern science, particularly science in the form of higher criticism itself."[6] By treating the Bible as a historical text, open to scientific inquiry like any other historical artifact, historical criticism seemed to call into question the sacred status of biblical texts.

Proponents of the historical-critical method were well aware of what was at stake in the scientific desacralization of scripture. Julius Wellhausen, for example, in his resignation from the Theology faculty at the University of Greifswald, noted that "scientific treatment of the Bible" is at odds with traditional modes of understanding scripture:

> I became a theologian because the scientific treatment of the Bible interested me; only gradually did I come to understand that a professor of theology also has the practical task of preparing the students for service in the Protestant Church, and that I am not adequate to this practical task, but that instead despite all caution on my own part I make my hearers unfit for their office. Since then my theological professorship has been weighing heavily on my conscience.[7]

Wellhausen sees his continuing commitment to biblical science as somehow antithetical to traditional religious commitment, and so he no longer considers himself fit to train students in an ecclesial setting. After his resignation from the Theology faculty, Wellhausen became a professor of philology at the University of Halle. The scientific spirit, it seems, was better accommodated in a secular setting.

Similarly, though a bit more polemically, Charles Augustus Briggs, an eminent biblical scholar, who was tried for heresy at the Presbyterian Church's 1893 General Assembly, speaks of traditional biblical interpretation as "rubbish" that must be cleaned out to uncover the real truths of the Bible:

> The valleys of biblical truth have been filled up with the debris of human dogmas, ecclesiastical institutions, liturgical formulas, priestly ceremonies, and casuistic practices. Historical criticism is digging through this mass of rubbish. Historical criticism is searching for the rock-bed of the Divine word, in order to recover the real Bible. Historical criticism is sifting all this rubbish. It will gather out every precious stone. Nothing will escape its keen eye.[8]

Briggs's sense of the superiority of historical criticism and inferiority of traditional modes of biblical interpretation is palpable. Particularly striking is the totalizing scope of historical criticism, which reflects the Enlightenment ideal of an all-encompassing objective science: "Nothing will escape its keen eye."

A more moderate understanding of the relation between scripture and science is present in the work of Abraham Kuyper, an early-twentieth-century Reformed theologian, who argued that Christianity fundamentally divided human consciousness into two types, Christian and non-Christian: "the Christian religion places before us this supremely important fact [that is, the fact that there exist two kinds of people]. For it speaks of a regeneration (παλιγγενεσία), of a 'being begotten anew' (ἀναγέννησις), followed by an enlightening (φωτισμός), which changes man in his very being."[9] For Kuyper, the "new birth" of Christianity is the birth of a new consciousness—one that sees, interprets, and evaluates the world differently. Accordingly, there are two types of science: one arising out of Christian consciousness and one arising out non-Christian consciousness:

> We speak none too emphatically, therefore, when we speak of two kinds of people. Both are human, but one is inwardly different from the other, and consequently feels a different content rising from his consciousness; thus they face the cosmos from different points of view, and are impelled by different impulses. And the fact that there are two kinds of *people* occasions of necessity the fact of two kinds of human *life* and *consciousness* of life, and two kinds of *science*; for which reason the idea of the *unity of science*, taken in its absolute, implies the denial of palingenesis, and therefore from principle leads to the rejection of Christian religion.[10]

Unlike Wellhausen, who abandoned the religious setting for a more secular and scientific one, and Briggs, who reduced all true understanding of the Bible to scientific understanding, Kuyper is uncomfortable with foisting the methods of natural science onto Christianity. For doing so leads to "the rejection of Christian religion." To avoid this consequence, Kuyper divides science into that which is appropriate to Christian consciousness and that which is appropriate to non-Christian consciousness. In doing so, however, Kuyper reinforces the very crisis that motivated both Wellhausen and Briggs to differentiate their work from traditional modes of biblical interpretation: higher criticism of the Bible, based on the methods of the natural sciences, seems incompatible with traditional understandings of the Bible *as scripture*. Academic or "scientific" approaches to the Bible are separate from (if not opposed to) the function, use, and understanding of scripture in ecclesial settings. Kuyper attempts to resolve this crisis by calling into question the universality of science, effectively breaking science in two—Christian science and non-Christian science—while Wellhausen and Briggs maintain the universality of science by rejecting any mode of biblical interpretation that does not cohere with the methods of natural science. In all three cases, the underlying assumption is that "science" is essentially synonymous with "natural science" and is therefore incompatible with any mode of understanding not based in the natural sciences.

Wellhausen, Briggs, and Kuyper's positions are different ways of responding to a crisis in biblical interpretation generated by a particular conception of science. By defining science as natural science, the relationship between religious and scientific modes of scriptural interpretation becomes agonistic, with few options for resolution: we may (1) reject religious modes of understanding in favor scientific modes (à la Wellhausen and Briggs); (2) reject scientific modes of understanding in favor of religious modes (à la fundamentalism); or (3) maintain that religious and scientific modes of understanding are somehow "separate but equal" (à la Kuyper and Stephen J. Gould). In each case, the understanding of science as natural science and the resulting agonism between religious and scientific modes of understanding goes unquestioned and largely unnoticed. Furthermore, it is important to note that this crisis in biblical interpretation is not simply an academic one. By assuming that science ought to privilege the methods of natural science and that religious and scientific modes of understanding are therefore incompatible, we open the door to fundamentalism and dogmatism (in both religious and secular spheres), with all the violence, injustice, and cultural solipsism that ensues.

Phenomenology, for its part, is no stranger to crises involving the boundaries and methods of science. Edmund Husserl sought to establish phenomenology as an absolute science—that is, a science upon which all other sciences might be grounded. In order to do so, according to Husserl, "we accept nothing given in advance, accept nothing as a beginning that has been handed down, nor allow ourselves to be blinded by any names, no matter how great, but rather seek to gain the beginnings through free devotion to the problems themselves and the demands radiating from them."[11] Phenomenology therefore rejects the widespread assumption that the natural sciences are the only sources of truth and validity (a view that Husserl calls "the natural attitude") and demands a "return to the things themselves." Science ought not to impose a method that predetermines the meaning and function of the objects it studies; rather, science should draw its method *from* its objects of inquiry—that is to say, a truly *scientific* method must be derived from a practical connection to the "things themselves." Phenomenology therefore provides a way to analyze the progress and goals of the sciences, to determine the boundaries of a particular science as it relates to its objects of inquiry, and to answer meta-theoretical questions about the methods and scope of various sciences. The phenomenology of scripture thus begins with the idea of science: what kind of science is appropriate to scripture? What scientific method would allow us to analyze and understand scripture without reducing its complexity?

Furthermore, phenomenology resolves the crisis of higher biblical criticism not by reinscribing (or reversing) the hierarchy of relations between science and religion (or between the academy and the church), but by reenvisioning the Spinozistic analogy between science and biblical interpretation. Biblical scholars of the eighteenth, nineteenth, and twentieth centuries often assumed that scientific approaches to scripture must draw their methods from the natural sciences. The problem with such an assumption is not that it is overly scientific, but that it is not scientific enough. Why, when it comes to biblical interpretation, should we assume without question that the methods of natural science are universally applicable? (We do not assume this in the case of geometry, for instance, which deals primarily with ideal figures rather than the real, empirically observable figures relevant to the natural sciences.) Why must we make the unscientific assumption that the truth or validity of scripture is restricted *in principle* to what can be established through natural scientific methods? Should science not avoid assumptions that predetermine its conclusions?

Accordingly, a phenomenology of scripture does not impose the methods of natural science onto scripture; rather, phenomenology starts with scripture itself, allowing scripture to "give" itself freely—even if it "gives" itself differently to different interpretive communities. For, if we want to know *what scripture means* or *how it works*, we cannot begin our investigation by assuming answers to those very questions. Much as Spinoza intended, a phenomenological approach to scripture tries to develop a method of interpretation by turning to scripture itself, allowing scripture—in the fullness of its many historical, philosophical, theological, social, literary, and religious contexts—to guide the methods used for scriptural analysis. Spinoza puts it nicely:

> In this way—that is, by allowing no other principles or data for the interpretation of Scripture and study of its contents except those that can be gathered from Scripture itself and from historical study of Scripture—steady progress can be made without any danger of error, and one can deal with matters that surpass our understanding with no less confidence than those matters which are known to us by the natural light of reason.[12]

In other words, the phenomenology of scripture must begin with a radical openness to scripture, rigorously avoiding the temptation to declare at the outset what scripture can or must mean.

The link drawn between phenomenology and Spinoza, the progenitor of modern biblical criticism, indicates quite a bit about the goals of this volume. By reenvisioning Spinoza's analogy between science and biblical interpretation, a phenomenological approach seeks to renew and reinvigorate higher biblical criticism, not by rejecting the insights of modern biblical scholarship, but by integrating those insights into an approach that places no restrictions on the truth, validity, meaning, and function of scripture. This is an enormous task. Historical criticism of the Bible is difficult enough. If we also include the literary, theological, ecclesial, secular, and other contexts of scripture—as a phenomenological approach must— biblical criticism becomes exceedingly complex. The essays in this volume therefore serve not as representative summaries of a mature intellectual enterprise, but as forays into new modes of biblical criticism informed by phenomenology. Ranging from reflections on how to read the Bible to explorations of sacrifice, fatherhood, community, law, grace, and unity, the essays in this volume demonstrate the broad fecundity of phenomenological approaches to scripture.

What Can the Bible Do for Phenomenology?

If phenomenology offers a scientific approach to scripture, it can do so only by developing tools and methods that allow scripture to give itself fully— tools and methods that do not place a priori restrictions on what scripture is or what it means. A phenomenological approach to scripture therefore involves rethinking the phenomenological method through hermeneutical engagement with scripture so that the method ultimately matches scriptural phenomena in all their complexity. It behooves us then to have some idea of the general goals and methods of phenomenology, if only to have a foundation for building new goals and methods.

While there have been many formulations of phenomenology, its guiding aim has remained more or less the same since Edmund Husserl first articulated the "principle of all principles": "that every originary presentive intuition is a legitimizing source of cognition, that everything originarily (so to speak, in its personal actuality) offered to us in 'intuition' is to be accepted as what it is presented as being, but also only within the limits in which it is presented there."[13] Everything that gives itself to be perceived (in whatever way it gives itself) ought to be accepted as being just what it is; phenomenology should place no restrictions on what appears or how it appears—any "presenting intuition" is fair game. Accordingly, phenomenology must be radically open to *any* phenomenon that manifests itself. It is, therefore, possible to construct a phenomenology of imaginary objects (which give themselves in the mode of fantasy) or perceived objects (which give themselves in the mode of temporal presence) or past experiences (which give themselves in the mode of memory). The crucial question is: how can phenomenology maintain radical openness? Better yet, how can we be *sure* that phenomenology is radically open? Aren't presuppositions and assumptions insidious and inescapable?

Husserl emphasizes phenomenology's openness by calling it a "presuppositionless science"; yet the goal is not to eliminate all presuppositions, but to recognize them, subject them to critical inquiry, and set aside (or bracket) those that are inappropriate to the task at hand. We cannot, for example, construct a phenomenology of unicorns if we presuppose that reality is restricted to the natural world; our naturalistic presuppositions would have to be set aside. In fact, much of Husserl's early work challenges naturalistic assumptions about the world. We normally take for granted that objects "out there" in the world exist independently of us, ready to be recorded by a camera or perceived by a person. We also tend to assume that the object-world is the ultimate arbiter of truth and value—that is, we can only make sense of what is "in here" (my subjective experience) by referring to what is "out there" (the object-world). Yet reality is not quite that simple.

Consider the experience of lighting a cigarette in a nonsmoker's house: "After a few puffs, the subject looks anxiously for a place to deposit his ashes. There are no ashtrays. The subject casts about, settles on a seashell or a nut dish, and, with a mixture of anxiety and relief, knocks off the ash."[14] Where did the ashtray come from? Was it simply "out there" in the object-world ready to be found by our smoker? Clearly not. He did not "find" the ashtray, as there were none to be found; rather, he constituted the ashtray through his actions.[15] Of course, "something" was there (a shell or a nut dish)—our smoker did not materialize an ashtray out of nothing—but there was nothing about that "something" that necessarily made it an ashtray. Its status as an object had to be conferred or constituted by our smoker. These sorts of experiences happen to us so often that we tend not to notice them. We simply see an ashtray, when in fact a whole host of constituting processes has gone into making it what it is. In actuality, the division between the experiencing subject and experienced object is not as clear as our commonsense naturalism would lead us to believe. Objects do not simply exist "out there." They are constituted as particular objects (for instance, a shell becomes an ashtray) by experiencing subjects. Thus commonsense naturalism, which presupposes that objects exist independent of experience, must be set aside in the course of a phenomenological investigation.

The method of setting aside presuppositions, so that phenomena give themselves in all their fullness, is known as "phenomenological reduction." It consists of two "moves": *epochē* and reduction. Husserl explores these "moves" in a thought experiment about the annihilation of the object-world.[16] Suppose that every regularity, every concatenation of experiences, every expectation we normally assume in our experience of the world were suddenly demolished: effect no longer follows cause; time no longer proceeds from past to future; the things that we perceive no longer have a stable meaning or identity. This would be tantamount to the destruction of the object-world, for even though the material world may continue to exist, its "raw material" could not be ordered into meaningful, regular experience, and so no meaningful object could ever be constituted. Yet what would this mean for the experiencing subject? Husserl argues that the subject would, of course, be changed (how could it not be?!) but it would not be eliminated:

> For an annihilation of the world means, correlatively, nothing else but that in each stream of mental processes . . . certain ordered concatenations of experience and therefore certain complexes of theorizing reason oriented according to those concatenations of experience would be excluded. But that does not mean that other mental processes and concatenations of mental processes would be excluded. Consequently no real being, no being which is presented and legitimated in consciousness by appearances, is necessary to the being of consciousness itself.[17]

If the world degenerated into the sort of chaos Husserl imagines, it would no longer consist of meaningful, stable objects. Consciousness would still be there, but it would not be able to make meaning out of the world's irregularity.

This thought experiment illustrates two important points: first, the object-world is dependent on consciousness, and not the other way around; this runs counter to the naturalistic assumption that the object-world is the ultimate arbiter of truth, meaning, and value. Second, consciousness normally interacts with the world in a *thetic* manner. That is to say, we observe regular occurrences in the world and form various *theses* about reality—for instance, effect follows cause, the sun will rise tomorrow. Some of these theses are so engrained in us that we hardly ever question them. Normally, this poses no problem, but if phenomenology is to be radically open, then it cannot be restricted by everyday assumptions about the way the world works. *Epochē* (that is, the first task of the phenomenological reduction) therefore involves identifying and setting aside any thetic stance that might affect our investigation. Husserl claims that the "natural attitude," which assigns epistemic priority to the object-world, is the fundamental thetic stance of modernity, though there are many other thetic stances that may need to be set aside, depending on the phenomena under investigation. For instance, when analyzing biblical texts, it may be necessary to bracket the thesis that there is a rigorous divide between the natural and the supernatural. The concept of "supernature," which was not operative in the ancient world, would undoubtedly distort an investigation of the Bible.

The second move of the phenomenological reduction involves an exploration of the residuum left after *epochē*. If we suspend the thesis of the natural attitude, what remains? For Husserl, the reduction points to consciousness, or the experiencing subject itself, as the constituting source of phenomenal objects. It is no accident that Husserl chose the word "reduction" to characterize this move. From the Latin *reducere*, meaning "to lead back," the reduction is a process of analysis that begins with a phenomenon and leads back to its constitutive origin.

In Husserl's early work, phenomena originate in transcendental subjective consciousness. His later work rejects the Cartesian subject-object schema and develops a subtler notion of the process by which phenomena are constituted. In *Formal and Transcendental Logic* and *The Crisis of European Sciences and Transcendental Phenomenology*, Husserl argues that the "objectness" of any given phenomenon is not bestowed by an individual consciousness, but develops over time through a historical process of generation. Take, for example, a mathematical truth like the Pythagorean theorem. Husserl suggests that the truths of geometry originated in concrete "lifeworld" situations.[18] Perhaps we have a triangular plot of land and need to know the length of each side. We figure out a method to measure our land and then induce from it a theoretical formulation, which we communicate to others for use in similar situations. The more general our theoretical formulation becomes, the more objective it is.

Writing plays an important role: "it makes communications possible without immediate or mediate personal address; it is, so to speak, communication become virtual."[19] The written text provides a high degree of generality by transmitting information across space and time without requiring personal, "word of mouth" communication. Once our geometrical theorem is written down—"$A^2 + B^2 = C^2$"—it becomes nearly universal in scope. There is, however, a danger in all this: the original lifeworld situation of phenomena is easily forgotten, hidden beneath the sediment of un-acknowledged layers of meaning that are passively synthesized into any given phenomenon. It is the phenomenologist's task to trace phenomena back to their origins in the lifeworld in order to "de-sediment" them. This is not a narrowly historical enterprise. We do not, for instance, need to know biographical details of Pythagoras's life to understand the Pythagorean theorem. Rather, phenomenologists look at the transcendental "conditions of possibility" that give rise to any particular phenomenon. In the case of the Pythagorean theorem, those conditions of possibility include a concrete need to quantify or measure.[20]

The origin to which the reduction leads is contested. For Martin Heidegger, the phenomenological reduction leads back to *Dasein* (that is, the transcendental conditions of possibility for human existence); for Eugen Fink, reduction leads back to the *meontic* Absolute; for Jean-Luc Marion, the reduction leads back to "givenness"; for Claude Romano, it leads back to "the event." These various formulations tend to reflect different conceptions of the transcendental status of consciousness itself. On the one hand, Husserlian phenomenology locates the origin of phenomena in the transcendental depths of consciousness, which always precedes (and forms the conditions of possibility for) whatever presents itself as an object for consciousness. Jean-Luc Marion, on the other hand, argues that transcendental depth develops as a response to that which gives itself: "Only the impact of what gives itself brings about the arising, with one and the same shock, of the flash with which its first visibility bursts and the very screen [that is, consciousness] on which it crashes."[21] For Marion, that which gives itself to consciousness is the origin of consciousness. "The given" essentially creates consciousness and influences the way that consciousness constitutes the object-world.

Husserl's notion of transcendental consciousness seems incompatible with any attempt to treat consciousness as something *produced*. Yet scripture may ultimately resolve phenomenology's collective uncertainty about the role of transcendence. Scripture certainly fits the Husserlian model: it is a textual phenomenon whose "conditions of possibility" must be sought in the lifeworld context(s) from which it originated. On the other hand, scripture has a transcendental function much like Marion's "given": it forms the "conditions of possibility" for the world-constituting activity of religious communities. That is to say, scripture is *both* the constituted result of transcendental processes (that is, a phenomenal object) *and*, for religious communities, the transcendental origin of the phenomenal world. As such, scripture can be studied both as the result of historical processes of constitution *and* as a source for contemporary philosophical reflection about the nature of the world, time, Being, human communities, the phenomenological method, and so forth. The essays in this volume attest to both possibilities.

Ultimately, the phenomenology of scripture is a pragmatic endeavor though which biblical studies and phenomenology mutually repair tensions and lacunae within and between their respective discourses. Phenomenology, for its part, offers biblical studies a scientific approach that is not restricted to the methods of the natural sciences. In turning to the Bible, phenomenology also has the chance to clarify its method and goals by resolving lingering questions about the role of transcendence in the process of constitution. More importantly, a phenomenological approach to scripture allows for a fruitful dialectical exchange between the fields of philosophy and biblical studies about the "big questions" of religious life and human existence.

What Are These Authors Doing with Phenomenology and the Bible?

This volume grew out of the "theological turn" in French phenomenology. While that turn has been opposed by some in the phenomenological tradition (notably Dominique Janicaud), its proponents have been largely successful in establishing religion as a legitimate area of phenomenological research.[22] Thus much of contemporary phenomenology has to do with religious phenomena. Although the theological turn originated with French Catholic philosophers, the field has become much more international and ecumenical. Contributors to this volume are both Protestant and Catholic and hail from the United States, Australia, and France.

Historically speaking, the phenomenological approach to religion is still in its infancy. Many questions remain: is the theological turn inherently Roman Catholic or Christian? Is its methodology or scope limited by a religious focus? Is the theological turn an enduring theological movement or simply a late-twentieth / early-twenty-first century discourse? One thing is certain: if phenomenology is going to have an enduring theological impact, it must eventually turn to scripture, which is the constitutive source (albeit historically complicated and without any static meaning) of theological reflection. This volume, then, is an important test case for the theological turn in phenomenology; it demonstrates that phenomenology can in fact turn to scripture in an intellectually fruitful way.

The essays in this volume offer different phenomenological approaches. They treat scripture both as a phenomenon, produced through a complicated process of historical generation, and as a touchstone for analyzing contemporary philosophical and theological issues. Robert Sokolowski's essay examines the nature of scripture in a Roman Catholic context, especially as it relates to the process of reading biblical texts. If scripture is God's word *and* a human text, how do we read it while preserving both aspects? This is not simply a hermeneutical issue; it reflects the mystery of the incarnation itself. God revealed godself at a particular time in a particular way, but with enduring significance—scripture is a Word revealed at a certain time for all time. In that sense, scripture functions like a sacrament: "[The words of scripture] are an analogue to the Eucharist, food for the intellect as the Eucharist is food for the soul, and both Scripture and the Eucharist find their place in the corporate community that is the Church." So, while historical and textual research is necessary, it must also be situated in the traditions of the church.

Jean-Luc Marion's "Sketch of a Phenomenological Concept of Sacrifice" uses the sacrifice of Isaac as a touchstone for philosophical reflection on the idea of the gift. Genesis 22 offers an important insight: if Abraham's actions on Mount Moriah amount to a sacrifice, then sacrifice is neither tantamount to destruction—after all, Isaac was not killed—nor is it a form of economic exchange, as if Abraham owed Isaac to God as a counter-gift in return for the God's promise. Rather, the sacrifice of Isaac ultimately reveals that Isaac is a gift *given* by God—that is, sacrifice shifts the focus from *what is given* to the *giver*: "For the function of sacrifice is only to allow the recognition of the giver and, through him, the entire process of givenness, by reducing the given." In other words, the sacrifice of Isaac makes apparent Abraham's (and Isaac's) proper relation to God, the *giver*.

Jean-Yves Lacoste's "To Exist without Enemies" offers a theologically rich reading of the Sermon on the Mount, particularly the antitheses (Mt 5:38–48), in which Jesus issues a series of seemingly impossible commands culminating in the order to "be perfect, as your heavenly Father is perfect." Lacoste argues that the antitheses are speech-acts that exceed Mosiac law without abrogating it, effectively calling Jesus's audience to enact (and creating in them the ability to practice) the exact sort of extra-moral perfection that Jesus demands, in the context of both a world (*kosmos*) where such acts make little sense and a kingdom (*Basileia*) where they will no longer be necessary. The antitheses challenge us to participate in the divine nature of the One whose love and mercy "rain on the just and unjust alike" (Mt 5:45). Just as God's love and mercy pervade creation, so are Christians commanded to love the "unjust" as much as the "just," not as we might love an enemy ("bless their hearts"), but as we love those closest to us—namely, our brothers, sisters, family, and friends.[23] Lacoste argues that the command to love gives us, first, a sense of place (we live "in a world where friends and enemies live side by side"); second, a sense of how we are to love ("by seeking reconciliation of all with all"); and third, a sense of our future ("a city where legislating will be unnecessary since the Law, more than being 'inscribed' on the hearts of the children of Israel, will be fulfilled, and will have purely and simply disappeared").

In "The Manifestation of the Father," Kevin Hart argues that Jesus's parables present (or phenomenalize) a type of phenomenological reduction from world (*kosmos*) to kingdom (*Basileia*). The goal of the parables, then, is to nudge readers to live according to the kingdom even while still in the world. More radical than Husserl's reduction, Jesus's reduction proceeds from *kenosis* (an "emptying out" of worldly meaning and value) to *epektasis* ("stretching out" toward God). Focusing on the character of the father (and Father) in the "Prodigal Son" (Lk 15:11–32), Hart maintains that compassionate fatherhood is an important aspect of the kingdom and is ultimately (and paradoxically, from a worldly perspective) inseparable from the realities of the cross and resurrection: "the preaching of the kingdom by the one person who can do so brings about the cross, and the resurrection is a vindication of the kingdom as the true teaching of God and how to live here and now so as to enter the eschatological kingdom of heaven, eternal life with God."

Robyn Horner's "Phenomenology as *Lectio Divina:* Jesus and the Woman Caught in Adultery" offers important methodological reflections on phenomenology while also examining the function of visibility in John 8:2–11. Horner juxtaposes the visibility of the woman with the "*invisability*" of Jesus. The text obscures Jesus even as it invites us to look at him: "As I listen, as I try to see, Jesus is over *there* somewhere, removed from me, not invisible exactly, but *invisable*—I cannot focus my intentional aim on him as such." Yet, while Jesus is ungraspable, the woman is extremely visible, perhaps too visible. In the course of the narrative, Jesus transforms the woman's pornographic visibility into a visible mirror of God's love and mercy.

Jean-Louis Chrétien's "Split Interpretations of a Split I" tracks various interpretations of Romans 7:7–25, focusing on the use of first-person pronouns in the passage. Does the "I/me" refer to Paul in a straightforward autobiographical sense? Is Paul inhabiting someone else's experience by speaking in character (*prosopopoiea*)? Does the text reflect both possibilities at once? Chrétien argues that the passage describes, or better *creates*, a Christian interiority that is inherently agonistic: "the inner space will never cease to be a battlefield, where the enemy's resistance increases in proportion to the territory conquered." The "I" is both Paul's and the reader's; the varying interpretations ultimately reflect the real existential dilemmas of Christian life.

Jeffrey Bloechl's "Love and Law according to Paul and Some Philosophers" examines 1 Corinthians 12 in light of recent works by Giorgio Agamben and Alain Badiou. While Agamben and Badiou see in Paul's letters a message of liberation from worldly political orders, Bloechl argues that their analyses fail to grasp Paul's conception of the community of faith. Focusing on Paul's analogy between the community and the body, Bloechl considers the "flesh": "His word 'flesh' designates something like a dynamism of our being, by which we are attached to the world and everything in it—and to that degree precisely not to the God of Jesus Christ." Paul's aim is not to negate the world, the flesh, or the law, but to reconstitute them within the horizon of faith. For Paul, the law is not a harbinger of political totalism to be overcome through messianic subjectivity (as is the case for Agamben and Badiou); rather, the law is reenvisioned within the horizon of faith: "the law itself can be uplifting and energizing, so long as we are alive to a sense that it is given in divine love." Similarly, Paul's community is politically ordered, but that order is transformed by the love of God. While Agamben and Badiou treat political order as something antithetical to human freedom and flourishing, Paul's transformation of the community reveals that there is, for the faithful, "no conflict between the complete exercise of one's freedom and a commitment to the love of God."

In "The Affects of Unity," Emmanuel Housset examines the affective dimensions of Paul's conception of community in Ephesians 4:1–4. According to that passage, Christians are called to live with "humility, gentleness, and patience." For Housset, those three affects constitute a Christian way of "being-thrown" into the world, "[constituting] an opening to the world [un pâtir] prior to all objective intentionality, before all constituting activity." Thus the affects are not normative virtues or subjective sentiments, but the very conditions of a Christian existence that exceeds the purely human possibilities of "social dispersion and violence." Through the affects of humility, gentleness, patience, love, and peace, "man becomes unified in the always fragile and on-going task of unifying all mankind."

Finally, Walter Brueggemann and Dale Martin, two well-known biblical scholars, respond to the essays in this volume. They are generally supportive, while offering important insights and criticisms from outside of phenomenology. Brueggemann likens phenomenology to the methods of "close reading" and "thick description" advocated by George Lindbeck and Gilbert Ryle based on Clifford Geertz's anthropological method. He argues that such approaches have an important political function: they resist our culture's totalizing impulse to master and control meaning by exploring the richness of texts: "the text and its reading constitute a welcome (and deeply unwelcome!!) act amid societal totalism that wants to monopolize imaginations, administer all possible meanings, and so control all economic goods." Brueggemann also helpfully situates phenomenology as "readings from and in a third place." First, there are the canonical readings of scripture, reflecting the church's practices of reading. Second, there are the reading practices of the critical academy, which are often in tension with the church. Phenomenology offers a third mode of reading, drawing from both the church and the academy while in thrall to neither: "Reading in the third place 'from elsewhere' permits the text to be transgressive about what is possible and invites the reader well beyond the familiar to new awarenesses and new possibilities."

Brueggemann offers two important criticisms. First, he notes that many of the authors, who are experts in phenomenology, do not cite relevant developments in the field of biblical studies. A phenomenological approach to scripture is an interdisciplinary endeavor that has enormous potential but also may be limited by the realities of academic life. In some sense, it is no surprise that phenomenologists and biblical scholars do not keep up with each other's fields. (Who has time?) Yet mutual engagement is necessary if a phenomenological approach to scripture is to be successful. Second, Brueggemann points out that the method of phenomenology is not completely spelled out here.[24] That is a fair point. A phenomenological approach to scripture ought to have an explicit and well-defined methodology. On the other hand, it is important not to let methodology predetermine a given phenomenon's meaning or value. A phenomenology of scripture develops its methods through concrete engagement with scriptural phenomena; the method cannot be spelled out beforehand. Nonetheless, more a posteriori reflection on the phenomenological method is certainly warranted.

Like Brueggemann, Dale Martin appreciates that many of the essays "offer fresh readings of scripture that, though informed by modern historical criticism, go beyond that ascetic, and sometimes dry and narrow, discipline." Martin is concerned, however, that the rhetoric of "letting texts give themselves" erases the agency of the interpreter, as if readers are simply "passive receptors" of objective textual meaning. Martin argues that such rhetoric raises both moral and philosophical concerns; texts cannot *make* readers act in any particular way, nor can texts tell readers how to interpret them: "no text has ever 'meant' anything apart from some kind of interpretation." In a sense, Husserlian phenomenology agrees: there is no object "out there" in the world that exists in complete isolation from human consciousness; objects are always *objects for*. In fact, the original insight of phenomenology consists in recognizing the complex processes that go into constituting phenomenal objects *as objects*. Martin acknowledges this, but nonetheless wonders about the rhetoric of givenness in many of the essays: "But then why all this talk about letting texts 'speak for themselves,' 'supplying for us' the methods of interpretation we are then supposed to use to interpret them? Why not put the agency where it belongs, with us human beings, rather than where true agency can never reside: in 'things themselves'?"

In answer, the rhetoric of "givenness" serves two purposes: first, it directs our attention back to scripture, encouraging us to think about the ways that our methods of reading limit, predetermine, or otherwise reduce complexity and meaning.[25] To say that scripture gives itself is not to say that it gives itself outside of a hermeneutical context. As Robyn Horner puts it, "what is given must somehow be contextualized in order for it to be given as such." A phenomenology of scripture therefore considers (or *should* consider) all the complex hermeneutical and historical processes that go into constituting scripture.

Second, the rhetoric of givenness gestures toward the "counter-intentionality" of scriptural texts.[26] In reading scripture, our intentions and expectations—based on our personal experiences, affiliation with historical communities, and so forth—often meet with resistance. That is to say, texts "act" on readers *within* the process of interpretation. Scripture, in particular, is so saturated with meaning that readers can be "pulled up short." Interpretive agency, with all its intentions and assumptions, can be so overwhelmed by scripture's surplus of meaning that the conscious life of the interpreter (and her interpretive community) is altered. To put it differently, reading scripture is a hermeneutical interaction—a back-and-forth—between text, interpreter, and religious community, which are bound together within a particular horizon of experience and interpretation. While there are ethical reasons for emphasizing the agency of the interpreter (particularly over and against literalist or foundationalist denials of interpretive agency), too narrow a focus on the interpreter distorts the hermeneutical process by ignoring the counter-intentionality of the text.

While I ultimately disagree with some aspects of Martin's characterization of phenomenology, his criticism highlights important tensions within phenomenology regarding givenness (grace, the gift) that may ultimately affect phenomenological approaches to scripture.[27] It is my hope, however, that a scriptural turn will shed light on the very questions that Martin, Brueggemann, and others within the phenomenological tradition have raised about the goals and methods of phenomenology.

Notes

1. James Kugel, *How to Read the Bible* (New York: Free Press, 2007), 31. For a summary of Spinoza's influence on biblical criticism, see Walter E. Stuermann, "Benedict Spinoza: A Pioneer in Biblical Criticism," *Proceedings of the American Academy for Jewish Research* 29 (1960–61): 133–79.

2. Benedictus de Spinoza, *Theological-Political Treatise*, trans. Samuel Shirley (Indianapolis: Hackett, 1998), 86f.

3. Ibid., 87.

4. Ibid.

5. On Spinoza's place in the history and development of biblical criticism, see Roy A. Harrisville and Walter Sundberg, *The Bible in Modern Culture: From Baruch Spinoza to Brevard Childs*, 2nd ed. (Grand Rapids: Eerdman's, 2002).

6. George Marsden, *Fundamentalism and American Culture* (New York and Oxford: Oxford University Press, 1980), 120.

7. Cited in Robert J. Oden Jr., *The Bible without Theology* (New York: Harper and Row, 1987), 20.

8. Charles Augustus Briggs, *General Introduction to the Study of Holy Scripture: The Principles, Methods, History, and Results of Its Several Departments and of the Whole* (New York: Charles Scribner's Sons, 1899), 531.

9. Abraham Kuyper, *Sacred Theology* (Lafayette, Ind.: Sovereign Grace, 2001), 50.

10. Ibid., 51.

11. Edmund Husserl, "Philosophy as a Rigorous Science," trans. Marcus Brainard, *New Yearbook for Phenomenology and Phenomenological Philosophy* 2 (2002): 293.

12. Spinoza, *Theological-Political Treatise*, 87. N.B.: Phenomenology is not committed to the particular method developed by Spinoza, but it shares Spinoza's desire to investigate scripture in a way that is both intellectually responsible and free from *unquestioned* assumptions about scripture's meaning, truth, and validity. Presuppositions are of course inevitable; the goal is to recognize them and investigate their genesis.

13. Husserl, *Ideas Pertaining to a Pure Phenomenology and to a Phenomenological Philosophy*, trans. F. Kersten (The Hague and Boston: Nijoff, 1983), 44 (§24).

14. Erazim Kohák, *Idea and Experience: Edmund Husserl's Project of Phenomenology in "Ideas I"* (Chicago: University of Chicago Press, 1978), 11.

15. Ibid., 11.

16. Husserl, *Ideas Pertaining to a Pure Phenomenology*, 109 (§49).

17. Ibid., 110 (§49).

18. See Husserl's "Origin of Geometry," in *The Crisis of European Sciences and Transcendental Phenomenology*, trans. David Carr (Evanston, Ill.: Northwestern University Press, 1970), 353–78.

19. Ibid., 361.

20. This sort of "genetic" phenomenological approach is relatively widespread in contemporary biblical scholarship, due in large part to the influence of Michel Foucault.

21. Jean-Luc Marion, *Being Given: Toward a Phenomenology of Givenness* (Palo Alto, Calif.: Stanford University Press, 2002), 265.

22. For more on the origins of the theological turn, see Dominique Janicaud, ed., *Phenomenology and the "Theological Turn": The French Debate* (New York: Fordham University Press, 2001).

23. Lacoste's vision of "enemy love" reminds me of the climactic scene in Flannery O'Connor's short story "A Good Man Is Hard to Find," in which the chauvinistic Southern grandmother tells the murderous Misfit, "Why you're one of my babies. You're one of my own children"; see O'Connor, *A Good Man Is Hard to Find and Other Short Stories* (New York: Harcourt, 1992), 22.

24. I have added material about the phenomenological method to my introduction since Brueggemann wrote his response. Nonetheless, I consider Brueggemann's comments about methodology important.

25. There is, of course, a large body of literature on "meaning" in the phenomenological tradition and in the field of philosophy of language. The idea that meaning is tied strictly to the agency of the interpreter is contested in the analytic tradition by semantic externalists like Hilary Putnam, who famously claimed that "meaning just ain't in the head"; Putnam, "The Meaning of 'Meaning,'" in *Mind, Language and Reality* (Cambridge: Cambridge University Press, 1975), 225. There is a lively debate as to whether Husserlian phenomenology is internalist or externalist. I am inclined to agree with Dan Zahavi that Husserlian phenomenology has much in common with Putnam's natural realism, which rejects both metaphysical realism and skepticism; Zahavi, "Internalism, Externalism, and Transcendental Idealism," *Synthese* 160 (2008): 355–74. Martin seems to be worried that the rhetoric of givenness indicates a commitment to metaphysical realism. In fact, I would argue that phenomenology rejects *both* metaphysical realism *and* the skeptical position advocated by Martin.

26. On "counter-intentionality," see Marion, *Being Given*, book V.

27. See Robyn Horner, *Rethinking God as Gift: Marion, Derrida, and the Limits of Phenomenology* (New York: Fordham, 2001).

God's Word and Human Speech

ROBERT SOKOLOWSKI

The Problem

The Second Vatican Council, in the Dogmatic Constitution on Divine Revelation, declares, "Holy Mother Church, relying on the belief of the apostles, holds that the books of both the Old and New Testaments in their entirety . . . are sacred and canonical because, having been written under the inspiration of the Holy Spirit *they have God as their author* and have been handed on as such to the Church herself."[1] After this statement that the scriptures have God as their author, the Council refers to men who were chosen and employed by God and who "made use of their powers and abilities, so that with him acting in them and through them, *they, as true authors*, consigned to writing everything and only those things that he wanted." God is the author of the scriptures, and men are also true authors of the same scriptures. The statement needs clarification. In particular the two meanings—divine and human—of the word "author" need to be explained. Concomitantly, the meaning of the word "God" needs to be thought about and related to this context.

God and the human writer of a scriptural passage are not two authors in the sense in which two human beings can be the coauthors of a composition, with each contributing part of the whole. Nor do we have two authors in the sense in which one person serves as a stenographer for another. In scripture the divine and human authors are each fully authoritative in their own way. The God of Christian faith can be the author of the scriptures even while the human writers are also its authors. God must be so understood that this formulation is not contradictory. The issue is analogous to the mystery of the incarnation, where God must be understood as so transcendent to the world that the incarnate Word can be both God and man.[2] The Christian mystery of the incarnation would be an incoherence or a contradiction if understood within the confines of a non-Christian understanding of the divine or if it were to be understood as the union of an angelic substance and a human being. The persistent Christological heresies of both ancient and modern times continue to show that a god understood as part of the world could not become man in the way Christians believe that the Eternal Son became man. Analogously, a god who is part of the world could not be the author of the sacred writings in the way that the Council says they have God as their author.

Phenomenology can help address such issues concerning scripture. It deals with the manifestation of things. It traces the way things can be identified in speech and human experience. It discusses words and their meaning, clarifies how words present things, examines the difference between both speaking and writing and speaker and author, and shows how things spoken about can remain absent and mysterious while still being intended by us. Such phenomena occur in our ordinary use of language and our standard experience of things, but they also occur in a distinctive manner in scripture and revelation, where they need to be described in their own terms.

Beatific Seeing and Hearing

We in our present state cannot enjoy the beatific vision, but we do have something like a beatific hearing. Such hearing—as well as the listening associated with it (we need to listen if we are truly to hear)—provides the title of this essay, "God's Word and Human Speech." God, because he has chosen to do so, becomes present to us in the modality of being heard or at least being heard about, even while we cannot see him. According to our Christian faith, God becomes present to us through human words, which words are also spoken or written by him.

We ourselves, in our day and age, do not literally hear God himself, but we do read about him in the scriptures. The scriptures, furthermore, present God as actually speaking to men: to Adam and Eve, Noah, Abraham, Moses, the prophets, and the psalmist. According to the scriptures, God speaks *to* some human beings directly, not just through angelic intermediaries. Furthermore, he also speaks *with* some human beings, who answer and question him and even argue with him; think of Abraham and Jonah. Man uses his logos, his speech, and his reason, not only in regard to God's created world, but even in the presence of God himself, and while his usage of words and reason is reverent, it can on occasion also be audacious. Human reason and its verbal expressions are not extinguished but perfected in the presence of God.

More specifically, in the New Covenant, God—God the Father—speaks to us in a new and distinctive way, in and through Jesus Christ, his eternal Son and eternal Word. God speaks with men by using a particular human voice and making that voice his own. But we ourselves, in our day and age, do not bodily hear the voice of Christ as the New Testament figures did or as Saul did on the road to Damascus. We hear it through the mediation of words that are written and read, and so we believe even though we have not seen (John 20:29). What are words and what is writing, that they can bring God to our minds and hearts, if not to our eyes?

The Difference between Hearing and Seeing

To set a stage for the theological issue of God's word and human speech, consider the difference in the natural order between hearing words and seeing things. Hearing makes things present to us, but in a manner that is associated with a distinct kind of absence. If we just hear about something, about some event or entity in the world, we do *not* see it. We hear about it instead of seeing it. Hearsay is not vision. If the thing is there before us on its own, then words spoken by someone else might help us to see it better, but the words will not have brought the thing to us in the first place; and yet that is precisely what words spoken about something absent are able to do. They introduce the thing to us; they bring it to mind. Words can even allow us to reach something that has never been seen by us. They allow us to anticipate seeing something for the first time and to anticipate it thoughtfully, not just as a matter of sensory expectation. Words enable us to know what we are hoping for.

Speech introduces an intellectual sense of absence into our experience. It allows us to think explicitly about what is not here and to intend it in its absence. It also heightens the sense of presence of which we become capable. When we finally see something we have only heard about, we have a more distinct sense of its being present than we would enjoy if we merely came upon it without such an anticipation. Such presence is more intellectual precisely because of the verbal intervention that has taken place, precisely because the words have come between us and the thing in question. The same thing that we heard about and thought of explicitly as absent has now become present, and this presence is more forceful because of the acknowledged absence that preceded it; the thing is recognized explicitly as *not* absent any longer and as no longer intended in its absence. We distinctly experience the thing's identity and being.[3] We experience the specific kind of presence that this thing has.

Words and sights thus involve an interplay between presence and absence, between what is directly given to us and what we can think about but cannot see. This contrast between the present and the absent, as realized in natural vision and speech, occurs also in Christian life, where we deal with a new and eminently radical kind of absence and transcendence. In Christian faith we respond to the God who is not just very far away; he is more distant than that. We *could* not expect God to become presented as one of the things in this world, even though he grants these things their being and is intimately present to them through his causation. It would be an incoherence to expect him to appear as part of the world. God is not part of the world—not even a spiritual part of it or one of its powers. Rather, in the words of the book of Job, he is the one who laid the foundation of the earth and determined its measurements and so is there before and beyond it (Job 38:1–7). He is not measured within it. But although he cannot be present to us as part of the world, he does come to us through speech. He is presented to us not only as the one who made and sustains all these things in his wisdom and power, but also as the one who could be in undiminished goodness and greatness even if "all this"—the universe of things—did not exist. This is what it means to say that God is before and beyond the things that are. This is the kind of absence and distance between us and him.

This absence is different from all the varieties of absences that we normally deal with. We cannot overcome it by going somewhere or doing something—not even by going on a pilgrimage or a mission. It is not the absence of an entity whose presence we can achieve by our own management, either with incantations that might call him up or with the help of scientific devices. And yet the God who is beyond our vision can be given to us in words that we hear. Words can bring God to mind, and they can somehow let him be "in" our minds. St. Anselm bears witness to this when he writes in the *Proslogion* that the fool, "when he hears this very thing that I say (*cum audit hoc ipsum quod dico*), . . . understands what he hears (*intelligit quod audit*)," and, Anselm continues, "what he understands is in his understanding (*quod intelligit in intellectu eius est*)."[4] Words serve as the vehicle that allows this theological presence to arrive in our understanding through faith and so somehow to be in us. Anselm's argument needs the *dico* and the *audit*, the speaking and hearing, and the persons who speak and hear. What are words, that even in this theological domain they can somehow bring to mind what seeing cannot?

In summary, words introduce a sharp differentiation between presence and absence. They do so in regard to ordinary things in the world, but they also let the contrast between presence and absence take on a new meaning and reach into an absence and a hoped-for presence beyond the margins of the world.

Writing

Writing introduces an even more acute and comprehensive sense of absence than speech. Writing resembles speech because in both, the object being discussed can be absent, but writing differs from speech because in it the speaker can be absent, as well. When we read something, the page and the script are present to us but our minds are turned toward something other than the page we look at, and in addition we are deprived of the presence of the one who speaks to us in and through that page. The page is there instead of the object and instead of the speaker. The written word is detached from the voice that originally uttered it as well as the hand that wrote it. We may not even know who *is* the speaker behind the words that lie on the page. The unattached words, however, seem to have great authority precisely because they have been written down and because they say the very same thing every time they are read.[5] They are less fleeting than a voice, which vanishes immediately, and they do not waver in their conviction. The written words have greater authority because of their fixity and because someone thought them important enough to set down and to hand on.

Writing involves other absences besides those of the object and the speaker. There might have been a scribe, an editor, and a publisher, someone who selected these pieces of writing for preservation and replication. We can read the written words of the original speaker, but these other mediators also come into play, and they contribute to the reading. We might discover clues in the writing that tell us something about these people, but often enough we know practically nothing about them. It is one thing to trust the words of someone who is speaking directly with us, but how can we trust the words of an unknown speaker or writer that have come through so many unknown hands? The written words are present to us—everything hinges on them, and their presence is unquestionable—but their presence is surrounded by multiple kinds of absence.

This complexity of absences occurs in regard to the sacred scriptures, and once again the theological context introduces new forms of absence that surpass those found within this world, mysterious and perplexing as these may be. The God we read about in the scriptures is believed to be the first and ultimate speaker behind these texts. The God who achieved our salvation in the work of his Son is also the God who recorded this achievement in the scriptures and who now addresses us through them. But since the scriptures are writings, God as their author is also absent from them, as are the human authors and editors, each in their appropriate manner. The thing we do unquestionably have present to us is the written text, which, however, was brought to us by many different hands.

The Church as Speaker of the Scriptures

But we do have a tangible and immediate speaker of the scriptures. It is the church. Sacred scripture does not speak on its own; it exists through time as spoken by the church. The church, however, presents herself as the collector and transmitter of the written words, not as the author who could rewrite them (even though she can translate them). Once the scriptures had been composed and canonized—once remembrance had given way to writing—the church became the speaker who reads and quotes the scriptures but not the author who writes or rewrites them. Although she, like the apostles at Pentecost, can express the text in different languages, she leaves the text alone. The church repeats and interprets these words, but she also subjects herself to their authority and measures herself against them, and she must, consequently, accept them as they are given to her. As the Sacred Constitution on Divine Revelation says in the passage we cited earlier, the scriptures "have been handed on as such *to* the Church herself."

The church and the scriptures are reciprocally related as part and whole. Each is a whole to the other as part. The writings have been composed, collected, and kept alive within the church, and in this sense the church is the whole of which the scriptures are part. But what the writings narrate, the actors and actions that are contained in the writings in turn have established the church in her being and authority, and in this sense the content of the scriptures is the whole of which the church is a part. The scriptures present the substance and the origin of the church as well as the normative image to which she must conform.

The role of the church as the speaker of the scriptures is brought out when she presents the scriptures as the word of God, but this role is even more vividly performed when the church reads the biblical passages in her liturgy and when she incorporates parts of the scriptures in her teachings and prayers and makes it possible for us to think and to pray in the same manner.[6] We take fragments from the scriptures and compose our prayers and thoughts from them. Such usage is neither bricolage nor a shoring of fragments against our ruin. The church's use of scripture in her teaching and actions makes possible for us a way of life that is coherent because reconciled with God. It is in such situations of prayerful reading, whether in the church's liturgy and teaching or in the private prayer of believers, that the scriptures most fully come to life. It is there that they serve, not as an object of our curiosity, but as the words through which God speaks to us and we to God. At this point the primary author of the scriptures, God himself, comes to the fore and acts as author, as the one who authorizes and speaks. At this point the human authors, who have finished their work, recede into the background. As Benedict XVI says, "A voice greater than man's echoes in Scripture's human words: the individual writings (*Schrifte*) of the Bible point somehow to the living process that shapes the one Scripture (*Schrift*)."[7]

Taking the church as "the closest perceptible speaker" of the scriptures may be a good way to express the difference between scripture and tradition in the church. If the church is the one who speaks the scriptures, she is something distinct from them; she has her own life and memory and her own subsistence, as well as her own prudence. She does not disappear into the text or become simply its commentator. She presents and interprets the scriptures, and at critical moments she may need to judge as erroneous certain interpretations of them, but she is there as the speaker who does so, even as she subjects herself to the scriptures. A speaker who quotes a speech does not vanish into the quotation. The tradition of the church, what she hands on in her living faith, is not just the scriptures but also the church herself as the one who speaks and interprets them. Scripture and tradition could be expressed respectively as the word of God and the immediate, worldly speaker of this Word.

Tradition can also be described as remembrance. As Francis Slade puts it, "Scripture as the New Testament is the Church remembering her beginnings and earliest times. To make sense of these things, these beginnings, meant remembering what had preceded them, the Old Testament. These things were proclaimed, indeed are proclaimed, in the liturgy."[8] Slade's remarks call to mind a remark of St. Justin Martyr, who refers to the gospels that were read in the liturgy as the remembrances of the apostles, the things recounted from memory.[9] Slade continues, "The Church reminding herself of her first times is Tradition." He also comments more generally on the relationship between scripture and tradition: "The Protestants had it exactly backwards. The Church is not founded on Scripture as if Scripture came before the Church and the Church derives from it, so that Scripture trumps Tradition." Scripture is not a detached and isolated text but the written form of memory, and the reading of such writing activates this remembering. To believe the scriptures is also to believe the church, whose original witness is expressed and described in the scriptures.

But besides speaking the scriptures, the church also epitomizes them in her creed, the articles of her faith. The Nicene, Athanasian, and Apostles' creeds are particular formulations of this, but the creed of the church can be taken in a more general sense as the expression of the substance of her belief. The creed and the catechism of the church are inseparable from the scriptures: they need scripture, but scripture also needs them if it is to be heard. The church does not rewrite the scriptures, but she does formulate the creed, which orders the scriptures and clarifies what is to be taken from them. Doing so is part of her task as the speaker of scripture. The creed does not simply repeat the scriptures but specifies explicitly the new dimension of being that comes to light in biblical revelation. Such a highlighting of scripture is not an external addition to what scripture says; as St. Thomas Aquinas puts it, the creed or *symbolum fidei* "is not added to Sacred Scripture but rather is drawn from Sacred Scripture."[10] Such a recapitulation and ordering of scripture through the creed is a distinct activity that is not more repetition or citation. It accomplishes something that the scriptures could not do on their own. It is an essential part of the way in which the church speaks them and the way we as believers listen to and repeat them ourselves. In fact, for the Christian believer the catechesis and life of the church precede the scriptures phenomenologically. As Dom Anscar Vonier, OSB, puts it, "In most cases, love for Christ exists in the human soul long before the books of the New Testament have been taken up as a spiritual study" and "No one profits by the gospels unless he be first in love with Christ."[11]

The Magic of Words

In my remarks on sacred scripture I have emphasized the theme of absence, but I now wish to discuss the contrary theme of a direct presence. I wish to discuss the presence of words in their material being. All the absences we have talked about circle around and come to rest on the acoustic or visual presence of the very words that make up scripture. The words in the Bible, as well as the scriptural words used in teaching and prayer, enter essentially into the transactions between God and man. The palpable words of scripture are the pivot around which our devotional and theological activities occur. My immediate question is, how can we more fully appreciate the power that the words of scripture possess in their material and yet thoughtful being? This power was formulated by the prophet Jeremiah when he said, "Your words were found, and I devoured them; your word became my joy and the happiness of my heart, because your name was called down upon me, O Lord, God of hosts" (Jer. 15:16).[12] Jeremiah devours the words he has found; he carries out the two activities that human beings do with their mouth, teeth, and tongue, the two activities of eating and speaking, taking in and sending out. How can things like this happen through the simple and ordinary instruments that we call "words"?

Let us begin again with words in the natural order, and here I would like to introduce a corrective to the way we normally think about words. I wish to claim that it is misleading to think of words as expressing essentially what is in our minds—that is, our ideas or our concepts. We need to find a way to think of words as somehow more obviously containing the *things* that they signify, not simply our ideas of those things. We need to discover or recover what we could call a better "identity theory" of knowledge and signification. It is not enough to say that there is an identity between the thing known and the intellect or the soul of the knower. We also need to say that there is an identity between the thing known and the *word* by and in which it is known. We need to find a way to say that the thing we know does not just enjoy a cognitive existence in our minds, but that as a thing *named* it enjoys something like a cognitive existence *in its name*. I think that such an adjustment in our theory of knowledge will also help us to see that the thing known does also exist in our minds. It will help us clarify what cognitive existence is. It will, in addition, help us to appreciate the force of the words of scripture.

It seems to me that Thomistic and Scholastic theories of knowledge have underplayed the role of spoken words—the external words, *verba exteriora*—in their metaphysics of knowledge. They say that an object (and its form) can enjoy two kinds of existence: real existence in the "external" or "extramental" world and cognitive or logical existence in the minds of those who know it.[13] But I would like to show that the thing (and its form) can also enjoy an analogous existence in the name of the thing. In fact, I would say that the thing and its form cannot exist cognitively in human minds without the help of names as well as phantasms. A given name serves to specify a phantasm and to register the form that is present within it. The Scholastic and Aristotelian theories of knowledge recognize that we need phantasms if we are to think, but I would add that we also need words, whether such words are publicly declared or spoken silently in our hearts. Such spoken words or names are indispensable in human understanding, and our appreciation of sacred scripture can be enhanced by recognizing this fact. I would also say that paying more attention to spoken words would make the Scholastic theory of knowledge more concrete and more convincing.

Words Contrasted with Pictures

I will develop this desired analysis by comparing words with pictures. Pictures are more tangible and more philosophically approachable than words, so they serve as a good starting point for our study, and the interplay between pictures and words is an extremely rich philosophical game preserve. Consider a thoughtful painting of some person or theme, such as the portrait of Robert Kerr, the first Earl of Ancram, by the Dutch painter Jan Lievens. Kerr had been a friend of King Charles I. On the execution of the king he went into exile in Holland. Lievens depicted him as old and dignified but also wasted and impoverished. The painting "contains" Robert Kerr, but because it is so successful as a portrait, it also "contains" or captures his intelligibility,[14] that which made and makes Robert Kerr what he is: not only his individuality, but also his humanity, his mind, his aristocracy, and his adversity, along with other things that define him. It contains what can be called his "form" or "*eidos*," but I find it more helpful to use the word "intelligibility" instead.

But the portrait does more than contain the intelligibility of Robert Kerr (as well as the intelligibility of "human being," "man," "dignity," "poverty," and the like). It also pictorially embodies it. The portrait is like an instance of this intelligibility—a replica-instance, it is true, but still an instance. It is something like a copy of Robert Kerr: not another Robert Kerr or his son or his clone, but a picture of him. It is Robert Kerr again, pictured. It captures him the way pictures capture things, and it does so "outside the mind." It seems intuitively obvious that the imaged Robert Kerr and his intelligibility are there "in" the picture that is hanging there on the wall. We are not tempted to say that the pictorial presence is only in our minds or only in our concepts.[15]

We turn now from pictures to names. The word or the name "Robert Kerr" does not embody Robert Kerr, nor does it embody his humanity or dignity. It is not a copy or image of Robert Kerr as the picture is. It does not show how he looks. The word does, however, contain his intelligibility, and it contains *only* that. The word is more spiritual than the picture because it just contains the intelligibility; it does *not* embody it. The name positively subtracts the embodiment from the picture. But if the word is more spiritual, it is still material. It is a formulated sound or a set of marks. It has its existence in sound waves in the space between speakers or in scratches on paper. But there is in principle no similarity, no iconicity, between the word and the thing, and this very lack of imitation prevents the name from being another pictorial embodiment of the thing it signifies. The name as such does not resemble the thing. The more refined spirituality

Jan Lievens, *Portrait of Robert Kerr*, First Earl of Ancram (c. 1578–1654). Scottish National Portrait Gallery. Accepted by HM Government in lieu of Inheritance Tax and allocated to the Scottish National Portrait Gallery, 2010.

of words also permits words to be combined by grammar into explicit statements and thus allows speech to be more flexible, precise, and declarative than images.

Words are radically different from pictures, but both words and pictures capture and carry the intelligibility of the things they represent. Comparing words with pictures allows us to appreciate more fully the objectivity of words, the fact that they are "out there" and not just in the mind, and yet it allows us to see the difference between names and images. We can appreciate the greater spirituality of words and the absence of embodiment in them. We can also see how words can be used to explain the meaning of a particular picture. Even the title of a picture is a kind of explanation, and a caption defines an image (as a word specifies a phantasm). Our words capture the intelligibility more precisely and explicitly than pictures do, which by themselves suggest rather than declare what they mean. Pictures call for words for their explanation, and words call for pictures for their embodiment.[16]

This is the magic of words. They capture and carry the intelligibilities of things and weave them syntactically into statements, arguments, narratives, and conversations. Our use of words enables us to become datives of manifestation and agents of truth as we enter into our mother tongue, use our inherited language with greater or lesser proficiency, and thereby play our part in the distributed rationality that is the human conversation. We make things clear for one another and for ourselves.

My claim about the role of words does not contradict the Scholastic understanding of knowledge, but it does complement it. It does so by adding the verbal dimension to the activity of knowing. Scholastic philosophy insists on the role of phantasms. My approach adds words, words that can also be spoken silently and hence internalized.[17] The interplay of pictures and words as public phenomena is paralleled by the interplay of phantasms and speaking that goes on inside us in the conversation of the soul with itself. This conversation is, after all, where the *Confessions* of St. Augustine take place—that is, where Augustine speaks to God, in the manner proposed to us biblically by the psalms. Augustine uses words as well as phantasms to do so, and he takes these words from sacred scripture. We do have concepts in our intellects, but they are more inseparably associated with words than the Scholastics seem to have acknowledged.[18]

The Name of God

When we look at the portrait of Robert Kerr, we see him and his intelligibility, which his name registers and contains. What intelligibility do we grasp when we read the sacred scriptures? We can distinguish three dimensions in the things that are presented to us in the Bible. First, the words of scripture simply inform us about a lot of things and events, some of them rather anecdotal (such as St. Paul's shipwreck near Malta) and some of them monumental (such as Abraham's sacrifice of Isaac or the passage of the Jews through the Red Sea). Many words and many intelligibilities are used to describe such events and to convey various teachings to us. Many phenomena are recorded and stories told. Second, all of these things and teachings are not just worldly occurrences; they are presented as God's actions and teachings in the world, in Jewish history, and in the life of Jesus and the church. They are presented as the works of God. Third, the scriptures do not stop with such deeds and teachings. The events, actions, and discourses in their turn go so far as to reveal the one who acts in them: they reveal something about God himself. They do not just imply God, as nature does; they reveal him as the one acting in the events that are narrated and as the one teaching what we are taught. The scriptures even give us the name for God, and in giving us his name they also identify him and reveal his intelligibility to us, in a way and to a degree that is appropriate for our present time.[19]

But I need to correct the way I have put it; I have been saying that the *scriptures* reveal God's intelligibility to us, but I should say that *God* reveals himself to us. God is the authoritative speaker of the scriptures, and it is always God who manifests himself in the events and statements that the scriptures contain, in all their complexity and variety. He even tells Moses (and indirectly us) the name by which he should be identified.

In both the Old and New Testaments we learn the name of God to be able to say things about him and about what he has done, but that is not all; we learn his name in order to be able to address him. In the Old Covenant God reveals his name to Moses and the Jewish people, and in the New Covenant Jesus reveals the name of God—God the Father—to his disciples and to us. He does so not as a lawgiver or prophet but as the Eternal Son, not as the one chosen by God but as the one sent by him and from him. Christ speaks and acts with the authority and the status of the God of the Old Covenant. In doing so he reveals the name and the intelligibility of the Father to bring us into the life that comes from the Father; the paradigmatic revelation of the name of God occurs in the prayer that Jesus gives to his disciples when they ask him to teach them to pray. He does so by his words, but also essentially by his actions and his death and resurrection.

We do not discover nor do we invent the name for God. We do not find God's name by investigating nature or history, nor do we devise it by our wit. We are biblically given his name, by himself and by his Son. In this way, we "find the right word" to use when we enter into the presence of God or speak with others about him. But if the right word for something captures the intelligibility of that being, can we claim that God's intelligibility is present to our minds? Does God himself somehow cognitively exist in us, and do we understand what he is?

Such claims would be pretentious, not to say irreverent. The name of God is not like other names. It is not the word for one kind of being among others. It is the name for the source of things, which is beyond them all and before their beginning. It does not express the greatest or best thing we can conceive, but that than which nothing greater can be thought and that which is beyond our understanding. It does not point beyond intelligibility but to an intelligibility that we can only darkly apprehend; it gives a new sense to what we mean by "intelligibility."

This name is not an indefinite symbol. It is extremely specific and even indexical. The name of God is the most proper of all names; it cannot be shared by anyone else, even though it is shared in God's own life by the Father, Son, and Holy Spirit. It signifies the Creator of all the things that are and the Savior who has spoken to us and thereby raised our speech into a new dimension and made it possible for us to respond to him. God has entered into our discourse as he has entered our world, and he has done so through speech and writing. The fact that there is a biblical text enables and allows us to use the name of God. This biblical text, furthermore, does not merely give us the name by itself; it also tells us what the bearer of that name has done and so tells us something of what he is. It embeds this word into his actions and teachings in the Old Covenant, and it tells us about his actions and teachings as he became part of his creation in the person of his Son. The text informs us about things that happened in our world, and it presents them as the actions of God. In doing so it brings out something like the properties of God, and it also shows how people should—and how they should not—respond to him. The name is not a mere encryption but part of a narrative and a form of address. It thereby gives us a glimpse of an understanding and opens the possibilities of faith.

Our minds and our souls are changed by this word, and we exist differently because of it. If we receive this name in faith, we become capable of living in response to the One it signifies and addresses. Since an understanding can provide an opening for action, the life of the church and the lives of her saints can be seen as attempts to manifest the meaning of the name of God. Christian language is internal to a way of life, and to know the idiom of this language is to know the idiom of this way of life.[20] We are enabled to live with God and to anticipate seeing him in his kingdom, and these possibilities have been opened to us, rational animals that we are, through the words of scripture and the names that scripture gives us.

Allowing Words to Do Their Work

Words capture the intelligibility of things, and if they are proper names they also grasp particular things themselves in their intelligibility. If this is so, then the very words exercise a power on those who hear and use them.

Just having the words exist around us, just hearing them and speaking them, and even just bringing them to mind in silent speech and in the listening associated with internal discourse is to have the things they signify somehow present to us and in us. The words do the work. What we need to do is to let them sink into us and shape our minds. Even if we do not understand them fully, and even if we do not yet assent to them, they are there exercising their effect. Words can work on us even if what they signify is still only obscure to us. Even as vague and enigmatic, the things and their intelligibilities are fully there, in their entirety, to exercise their logical implication. They have their fields of force. In the case of the sacred scriptures, we need to let the words work on us and let them take possession of our minds, which is equivalent to letting the understood presence of God become more and more vivid to us. The words of the gospel, with God as their author, have their own way of doing what they do. They have their own insistence.[21] Unbelief can be seen not just as a denial of what these words say, but as a refusal to let them enter into us.

Of course, as the scriptures themselves repeatedly remind us, words alone are never enough. Because of what they express in the scriptures, they will not have been truly accepted if they have not flowed over into responsive action. Hearing must lead to faith, and faith must express itself in hope and in charity. Such responses, however, are themselves given their form through the words that have made them possible. There cannot be hope and charity without faith, nor can there be faith without receptive hearing. Perhaps we are so concerned about not falling into a merely verbal faith that we underestimate the effect that the words themselves can have.

The Critical Project

Since these words are human things, however, they can be examined by human sciences, and so before concluding I would like to say a word about critical methods in biblical studies. In the foreword to his book *Jesus of Nazareth*, Pope Benedict XVI says, "The historical-critical method—specifically because of the intrinsic nature of theology and faith—is and remains an indispensable dimension of exegetical work. For it is of the very essence of biblical faith to be about historical events." And he goes on to say, "Faith must expose itself to the historical method."[22] In the exegesis of the past century and a half, we have seen the development of historical criticism, source criticism, and form criticism. These scholarly efforts have helped us understand the scriptures, and they are legitimate because of the mystery of the incarnation. God became man in history, and so his human presence must be historically visible. His historical presence in the new dispensation is reflected in Old Testament, which anticipated the incarnation, as God chose a particular people and became present to them and to the nations as Savior in the world.

Furthermore, the human authors of the sacred scriptures were writers whose intentions we may be able to determine by appropriate methods. Authorial intent leaves clues in the text, and so does the work of scribes, editors, and publishers. If, for example, the stories of Jonah or of Esther were deliberately composed as stories and not as historical recordings, and if we had at first read them as historical narratives, it would be good for us to learn what their human authors wanted them to be. This sort of form criticism can help and not threaten us in our reading of the scriptures. The scriptural writers announce God's presence, and a clearer understanding of what they intended to say can only help us to better receive the word of God.

But there is one aspect of these scientific procedures that I would criticize, and it is the word "criticism." I would offer a critique of criticism. Why not just call these activities something like historical investigations (instead of historical criticism), source inquiries (instead of source criticism), and form studies (instead of form criticism)?[23] The term "criticism" has a Kantian overtone, and it recalls the *Critique of Judgment* or the *Critique of Pure Reason*. In the Kantian project, everything, even reason itself, has to be brought before the tribunal (the *Gerichtshof*) of reason. Philosophic reason sits there as judge, and it carries out its critical judgments "in accordance with its own eternal and unalterable laws."[24] Even religion must be evaluated within the bounds of reason alone. Religion has to present its credentials, its permits to be believed. Who or what is philosophic reason to judge things in this way? What kind of sovereignty does it claim? In this Kantian project, philosophy does not receive and contemplate things; it does not wonder at and clarify what is there; it does not merely distinguish things one from another, nor, in the case of Christian faith, does it simply contrast revelation with other forms of manifestation; instead, it claims that it can determine what really is there, and it claims it can do so on its own terms, the terms of pure reason, not on the terms of what is being presented for recognition, not in terms of the being of things. Critical reason claims that it is able to administer the acid test that will determine the truth of things.[25] The evidentiary role of prephilosophical reason is taken over by philosophy. In this project, philosophy governs and judges; this is the Enlightenment, not the perennial philosophy. We need to deconstruct the constructivist philosophy and let things be what they are and show up for what they are, including the things of revealed faith. We need to restore and save the phenomena, including the manifestations given in faith.

The New Testament declares to its readers that the God who created the world and who guides the people he has chosen has become present within the world and among that people as the man Jesus of Nazareth. This revelation occurs in what the New Testament says about Jesus, in what it says he said and did, and in the way it describes people's reactions to him. Some people, such as the apostles and disciples, are described as recognizing the man Jesus as somehow the presence of God himself; others are described as outraged by his claims of affiliation with the God he calls his Father and by the actions he performs with an authority that seems to be that of God himself. In the New Testament, God is presented as not only Creator and providential power, but as becoming part of his creation and his people as the Savior of men. This revelation does not just tell us about a particular divine accomplishment; it also deepens our understanding of what God is. It shows that God's transcendence is so intense that he could become part of his creation without diminishing his divinity.[26]

Or perhaps, instead of saying that it deepens our understanding of God, we should say that it makes more clear to us the unknowability of the God who is so revealed; we know in a new way how God exceeds our understanding. The God who creates the world is beyond our comprehension because of his power and eternity and his difference from things created, which give us only the faintest glimpse of his being. The God who becomes incarnate and redeems us through his suffering and death on the cross is beyond our comprehension because of his unimaginable mercy and love. We might come to an appreciation of God's power through the spectacle of his creation once we realize that the whole of things cannot account for itself, but who could have anticipated that God himself would save us and would set things right in this way? We might have expected that God might save us through a man, but not that he would redeem us *as* a man and by descending to this ultimate humility of service. Such redemptive action could not have been anticipated by us, but once it was accomplished its perfection and suitability become evident. What more glorious way could have been conceived for the victory of God over the death and disorder of sin? What more internal way of healing could have been devised? What implications does it have for the way we understand ourselves and conduct our lives? This action of God as an agent within the world deepens the Old Testament demand for a decisive response in faith, a response different from the dialectical inquisition to which religious myths and legends give rise. It calls for theology and not just philosophy.[27]

God's act of redemption discloses his love for us, and it also reveals the ingenious benevolence that has been at work from the beginning in the being of things. It reveals in addition the kind of generosity that exists between the Father, Son, and Spirit: it reveals something of the life within God himself.[28] When Christ says, "The Father and I are one" (John 10:30) and "The Father is in me and I am in the Father" (John 10:38), he speaks both as the eternal Son and as the man Jesus.

This action of God is presented in the scriptures and epitomized in the creed. Is this action somehow visible to historical method? It depends on what historical inquiry is supposed to discover. History does not just describe bodies in motion. It attempts to recover the intentions and understandings of the people who made the history. It also attempts to recover the understandings of those who recorded it (to the extent that the historian is investigating a text and not things just left behind by the people in question).[29] What did Jesus understand himself to be doing, what did his interlocutors take him to be doing and saying, and what did the authors of the New Testament believe him to have done? The historian is obliged to present such intentions and understandings, whether he agrees with them or not.[30] He may decide to work independently of the creed of the church, but he cannot define his project as an *alternative* to the creed without becoming something other than a historian himself and thereby composing a creed or recapitulation of his own.

Earlier we claimed that the church's reading of scripture involves remembrance and that all forms of reading engage memory. What sort of remembering is proper to the historian's attempt to recover the historical Jesus? The danger involved in a purely historical approach is that one may be inclined to think, first, that scripture trumps tradition and, second, that history trumps scripture.

Conclusion

The issue in the critical project is philosophical and theological, not just historical. The historical and linguistic investigation of the Bible need not neutralize the words of scripture and render them powerless. Our historical studies of the New Testament need not deconstruct the person of Christ and turn us into modern analogues of the people at Nazareth, who, when Jesus returned to them, took offense at him and said that he is just one of us, nothing more (Matt. 13:54–58; Mark 6:2–3). Because God became man, the words of scripture can be understood as both human speech and the word of God. In both human reason and Christian faith, words are the element in which we live. They are charged with intellectual energy and make possible the kind of life that defines us in our humanity. In the scriptures and the faith of the church words enable us, through the redemptive work of Jesus Christ, to become affiliated into the life of God himself.

The words of scripture are part of the mystery of the incarnation and not an afterthought. They are an analogue to the Eucharist, food for the intellect as the Eucharist is food for the soul, and both scripture and the Eucharist find their place in the corporate community that is the church. God became present in the world at a given time and place (there and then), and as a consequence he is present always here and now. The words of scripture activate this presence and make it possible for us to believe in the risen Jesus even though we have not seen him. They enable us to find life in the word that is his name (John 20:28–31, 1:12).[31]

Notes

1. "Dogmatic Constitution on Divine Revelation," in *The Documents of Vatican II*, ed. Walter M. Abbott and Joseph Gallagher (New York: Guild, 1966), 118–19; my italics in the text.

2. An analogous understanding is required in the mystery of grace, where the infused virtues and the actions that follow from them are truly our own while still being the work of God.

3. On the relation of names to the presence, absence, and identity of things, see Robert Sokolowski, *Presence and Absence: A Philosophical Investigation of Language and Being* (Bloomington: Indiana University Press, 1978), 23–32.

4. St. Anselm, *Proslogion*, in *Opera Omnia*, ed. F. S. Schmitt (Edinburgh: Thomas Nelson and Sons, 1946), 1:101; my translation.

5. On the reassuring sameness of written texts, see Sokolowski, *Presence and Absence*, 69.

6. Ideally the church would convey to her people a sense of the glory of God as a setting within which the word of God can be heard and received. The architecture, decoration, and music in churches should serve this purpose. Speaking about Balthasar's theology of "theophany" or "epiphany," Jeremy Holmes writes, "He notes that at decisive places in Scripture God's 'glory' manifests itself *before* his word is heard. Sinai, the burning bush, the calls of Isaiah and Ezekiel, Tabor, Damascus, the beginning of the Book of Revelation. . . . Man hears God's word not in his own power, but through the power of God's grace"; "Translator's Introduction" to Hans Urs von Balthasar, "Holy Scripture," *Nova et Vetera* 5 (2007): 711. The word of God also makes us more capable of recognizing God's wisdom and power in the cosmos and in natural phenomena. Such epiphanies, however, would remain underdetermined and merely bewildering without the words that followed and defined them.

7. Pope Benedict XVI, *Jesus of Nazareth*, trans. Adrian J. Walker (New York: Doubleday, 2007), xviii.

8. Personal communication; used with permission.

9. St. Justin Martyr calls the gospels the memoirs (τα απομνημονεύματα) of the apostles; see *The First Apology*, chaps. 66–67, in *The First and Second*

Apologies, trans. Leslie W. Barnard, Ancient Christian Writers 56 (New York: Paulist Press, 1997), 70–71.

10. St. Thomas Aquinas, *Summa theologiae* II-II, q. 1, a. 9, ad 1: "Quod quidem non est additum sacrae Scripturae, sed potius ex sacra Scriptura assumptum." This entire question in the *Summa* deals with the church's formulation of the articles of faith.

11. Anscar Vonier, *The Personality of Christ*, in *The Collected Works of Abbot Vonier* (Westminster, Md.: Newman, 1952), 1:100–101.

12. The Latin Vulgate version of Jeremiah 15:16 is particularly forceful: "Inventi sunt sermones tui et comedi eos et factum est mihi verbum tuum in gaudium et in laetitiam cordis mei, quoniam invocatum est nomen tuum super me Domine Deus exercituum." The role of words is mentioned at the beginning of the book of Jeremiah (1:9): "Then the Lord put forth his hand and touched my mouth, and the Lord said to me, 'Behold I have put my words in your mouth.'" God says this in response to Jeremiah's claim that he is only a youth and that "I do not know how to speak" (1:6).

13. See, for example, Joseph Owens, *An Elementary Christian Metaphysics* (Houston, Tex.: Center for Thomistic Studies, 1985), 29–42. As soon as Owens begins his study of being as being, he distinguishes between real and cognitional being: "The same things, quite apparently, can exist in two different ways. They can exist in reality, they can also exist in cognition; or they may have for the moment the one way of existing, while lacking the other. In contrast to the being that is conferred upon things by real existence, existence in the mind or imagination or sensation may be called 'cognitive being'" (31–32). The distinction between real and cognitional existence gives Owens the resources to distinguish in turn between a thing and its being. If a thing can enjoy cognitional being in the imagination, it seems plausible to me to say that it can also have a kind of cognitional being in a picture or in a name, even though such existence would depend on both the human subject and the pictorial or linguistic vehicle.

14. We might contrast a portrait with a mug shot, which contains scarcely any intelligibility. It does not really say anything about the person it identifies (a good picture is like a predication). The mug-shot photographer does not have to think about his target when he does his work, but Jan Lievens needs to think about his, and he thinks as a portraitist.

15. Thomas Hobbes puts a different accent on these relationships. He says that a picture or statue does not resemble an object but only the artist's phantasms: "These [statues and pictures] are also called images, not for the resemblance of any corporeal thing, but for the resemblance of some phantastical inhabitants of the brain of the maker"; Hobbes, *Leviathan*, ed. Richard Tuck (New York: Cambridge University Press, 1996), 448. See also 446, where images made by artists are said to be "representations of their own fancies."

16. We should also recall that words used to tell a story function something like pictures: a narrative remains verbal, but it engenders a pictorial embodiment in the reader's imagination.

17. There are two kinds of imagined words or imagined speech: (1) we might imagine ourselves speaking with someone else; and (2) we might speak with ourselves silently and imaginatively, when, for example, we are trying to resolve a problem. The second kind is a form of real speaking; see Sokolowski, *Phenomenology of the Human Person* (New York: Cambridge University Press, 2008), 143–47. The issues of the "internal word" and the "intelligible species" are treated on 286–303 of that book.

One might ask how Augustine in the *Confessions* uses these two kinds of internal speech as he addresses God. He does not simply imagine himself speaking with another person. Nor is he merely trying to figure out the solution to a problem, a procedure in which he would essentially be speaking with himself. Augustine is speaking to someone who, according to the faith of the church, can be understood as truly present to us within our internal life, someone who is more deeply present to us than we are to ourselves. Augustine speaks to someone who hears him. Each person has a singular sense of the presence of God or of the divine; it is analogous to and related to the unique sense we each have of the presence of "myself." See James G. Hart, *Who One Is*, vol. 2, *Existenz and Transcendental Phenomenology*, Phaenomenologica 190 (Berlin: Springer, 2009), 538: "God as You is, in contrast to Others, not singled out from among others known in the third-person, as is our use of 'you.' . . . When I faithfully think of God of necessity God does not remain a third-person but uniquely second-person. God's being You contrasts with all You's who are one among many." Such an internal sense of God is derived from the liturgy and public prayer in which God is addressed.

18. A few words about St. Anselm might serve as a complement to my remarks about Augustine. The phenomenon of pictures plays a strategic role in my argument. I use it as an analogy: the way things and their intelligibilities exist in pictures sheds light on the way they can exist in their names. I would like to draw a contrast between this argument and a step made by Anselm in chapter 2 of the *Proslogion*, where he makes use of pictures in his effort to show "that God truly exists." Anselm uses pictures to bring out the contrast between something's being in the mind and its being understood to exist: "For when a painter thinks beforehand (*praecogitat*) what he is going to make, he does have in his understanding (*habet quidem in intellectu*) what he has not yet made, but he does not yet understand it to be (*nondum intelligit esse*)." After he has done the painting, however, "he both has in his understanding what he has made and he understands it to be" (*Proslogion*, 101, my translation).

Anselm starts with the planned picture in the painter's intellect and moves to the actual picture, whereas my argument begins with the actual picture and with what the viewer—any viewer, not the painter only—recognizes in it. Also, Anselm deals with the difference between the *picture's* being in the mind and its being among things, but I deal with a thing and its intelligibility as being in the picture. My usage is more phenomenological, his more conceptual.

In chapter 10 of the *Monologion* Anselm uses the example of the craftsman (*faber*) to speak about the status of the form that exists prior to things that are to be created: "What else is it [this antecedent form] than a certain spoken expression (*locutio*) of things within reason itself, as when a craftsman who is going to make something by means of his craft first says (*dicit*) this work within himself by means of a conception of the mind (*mentis conceptione*)?" (24). Anselm does not say that the craftsman just imagines what he is going to make, but that he speaks it in his mind. The relation between speaking and conceiving—word and offspring—should be noted. Anselm also discusses externally spoken words and considers them far less important than "the natural words (*naturalia verba*)" of the mind: "Where these [the natural, internal words] exist, no other word is necessary for knowing the thing (*ad rem cognoscendam*); and where these cannot exist, no other one is useful (*utile*) for manifesting the thing (*ad rem ostendendam*)" (25). Anselm's thoughts are obviously influenced by St. Augustine.

19. There is no ordinary proper name—such as *Jupiter* or *Isis*—for God in the Bible. Such a proper name would connote an inappropriate familiarity, and it would also suggest that its bearer was one of many gods. The name revealed to Moses in response to his question (Exod. 3:13) is starkly singular and not one proper name among many. It transcends names and their meanings as its bearer transcends things and their definitions. It may signify the one who simply is, or the one that causes things to be, or the one that will be whatever he will, or the one who will be faithful. (All such meanings reflect and imply one another; God could not be truly faithful if he himself were subject to destiny.) The name revealed to Moses is more of an extreme description than a personal name; it may also be simply a refusal to give a name. As Pope Benedict XVI says, "God's answer to Moses is thus at once a refusal and a pledge. He says of himself simply, 'I am who I am'—he *is* without any qualification. This pledge is a name and a non-name at one and the same time"; *Jesus of Nazareth*, 143.

Other Old Testament names for God, such as *Adonai, Elohim*, and *El*, are words that designate divinities but that become proper to God as he becomes understood as the only one to whom they can truly apply. When this occurs they cease to be common nouns. God becomes revealed as not simply the greatest of the gods but as the only one, and the sense of divinity is changed. The others are seen to be not gods at all, not just as a matter of fact but even as a possibility. What people had taken as a common noun was discovered to be particular, but not as one name among many. (When a Christian loses his faith, the word "God" loses its particularity of meaning for him and becomes a common noun again. It is also no longer used as a name to address someone.)

In the New Testament the name "Father" becomes paramount because of the way that Jesus speaks of God. His way of using this word is self-involving in such a manner that it leads Thomas the apostle to address the risen Christ as "my Lord and my God." In the New Testament the name of Jesus acquires, in a derived way, the power and quality that had been proper to the name of God himself.

20. This sentence is an adaptation of one written by Donald W. Livingston in *Philosophical Melancholy and Delirium: Hume's Pathology of Philosophy* (Chicago: University of Chicago Press, 1998), 140: "Moral language is internal to a way of life, and to know the idiom of a moral language is to know the idiom of a way of life." In my text I state that understanding can provide an opening for action. It does so when the thing understood is the kind of thing that offers a possibility of acting. There are some understandings that reach beyond action. In the outermost reaches of theoretic philosophy, we can come to know things that cannot be affected by what we do; we cannot really do anything about the principle of noncontradiction, for example, or about the ultimate laws of nature, or about the principles of being. We can only contemplate such things; we cannot *do* anything in regard to them. Christian faith changes the way we are related to ultimates, because it says that our understanding of the primary principles of things (the truths about God), besides being a contemplative activity, also calls us to act in response to them. We can strive to obey the will of God, or we can turn away from it.

21. It is true that we might resist accepting the words of scripture; some people might go beyond denying them and may try to eradicate them as a bodily verbal presence. We might also try to resist the insistence of words in other domains, as in science or history or in regard to a story that someone else is telling us. There again we would enter into a curious kind of divided thinking: something is presented for our consideration, and we voluntarily turn away from the evidencing of the things in question. We don't want things to be that, and we don't want them to be said that way. The topic in question might deal simply with a minor issue, and our reluctance to face it may have little impact on us and other people. The issue at stake in the words of holy writ is more substantial, however, since these words present us with the name of God, and so both the insistence of the words and our acceptance or refusal of them would have a unique and definitive character.

22. Benedict XVI, *Jesus of Nazareth*, xv. Benedict emphasizes the importance of reading the Bible as a whole, which allows one part to shed light on another. The various parts of the scriptures are intricately interwoven. The injunction to read the Bible as a whole is not a scientific, historical principle. It is related to the understanding of God as author of the scriptures.

23. The term *"Formgeschichte"* is less offensive.

24. Immanuel Kant, *Critique of Pure Reason*, trans. Norman Kemp Smith (New York: Macmillan, 1929), 9, Preface to the First Edition, A:xii.

25. It is not the task of philosophy to determine "what really is there." That is the task of prephilosophical reason, the reason that brings things to light and verifies them in keeping with the manner of manifestation proper to those things. Philosophy can assist such prephilosophical intelligence by clarifying what is going on, but it does not replace it. In particular, religious thinking has its own manner of bringing things to light.

26. See N. T. Wright, *The Resurrection of the Son of God* (Minneapolis: Fortress, 2003), 712: "The challenge comes down to a much narrower point, not simply to do with worldviews in general, or with 'the supernatural' in particular, but with the direct question of death and life, of the world of space, time and matter and its relation to whatever being there may be for whom the word 'god,' or even 'God,' might be appropriate. Here there is, of course, no neutrality. Any who pretend to it are merely showing that they have not understood the question."

27. See Erik Peterson, "Was Ist Theologie?" in *Theologische Traktate* (Munich: Kösel Verlag, 1951), 14–27. Peterson says, "There is theology only in Christianity and only under the precondition that the incarnate Word has spoken about God" (27).

28. The primary exegesis of God's action in the world is given in the teachings and especially the parables of Jesus.

29. What is the difference between written texts (*scripta*) and things just left behind (whether *facta*, such as tools, pots, and shelters, or *relicta*, such as bones and wastes)?

30. Wright, discussing the resurrection in St. John's Gospel and the role of the historian, says, "John intends the narratives to be understood realistically and literally. Of course, he also intends that all kinds of echoes and resonances be heard within them; he always does; but these remain echoes and resonances *set off by a literal description of a concrete set of events.* This is not to say, of course, that we as historians can yet pronounce on the likelihood or otherwise of such events as having taken place. It is simply to insist that, precisely as historians, in this case readers of ancient texts, we are bound to conclude that this is how John intends us to understand them. . . . The multiple meanings the stories have are multiplications of the basic point, and as with all multiplication you cannot start with zero. The writer believes that these things happened. The indications are that any sources he may have used believed it too"; Wright, *Resurrection of the Son of God*, 675. Wright offers another comparison on 681: "You only get overtones when you strike a fundamental."

31. A version of this paper was given as the presidential address at the annual meeting of the Academy of Catholic Theology on May 25, 2010. Questions and comments after that lecture have helped me in the revision of the paper. I wish also to thank Kevin White and John C. McCarthy for their comments on earlier drafts. A version of this paper was also published in *Nova et Vetera* 11 (2013): 189–212.

Sketch of a Phenomenological Concept of Sacrifice

JEAN-LUC MARION

The Aporia of Sacrifice

Strictly speaking, we should not begin with sacrifice, at least in the sense of a noun, or of a substantive, because sacrifice (*sacrificium*) always results from the action of a verb, of the verb "to make" (*sacrum facere*): a sacrifice appears once an agent has rendered something sacred, has set it apart from the profane and thereby consecrated it.[1] Moreover, *sacrum facere* gave us *sacrifiement* in Old French, which states more clearly the process of rendering something sacred than the result of this process. The question of sacrifice concerns, then, first and above all the act of making something sacred and of wresting it from the profane (the act opposed to that of profanation), an act of which sacrifice is only a result in that it limits itself to recording, without explaining it. This clarification nevertheless raises a difficulty: how can we conceive the transition between two terms, the profane and the sacred, while their very distinction becomes, in the epoch of nihilism in which we live, indistinct and confused, if not completely obscured? It is as if the "death of God," and above all what has provoked it— the realization that the highest values consist only in the valuation that confirms them, and thus are only worth what our valuations are worth— have abolished any difference between the sacred and the profane and thereby any possibility of crossing over it by a *sacrifiement* (or on the contrary, by a profanation). Would not sacrifice disappear along with the sacred that is disappearing?

However, this is not the whole story. We still have a common, if not entirely vernacular, sense of sacrifice: sacrificing is equivalent to destroying; or, more precisely, to destroying what should not be destroyed, at least according to the normal practices of daily life—namely, the useful and the functional. In effect, beings understood as that which I make use of (*zuhanden* beings in Heidegger's distinction) are defined by the finality that links them not only to other ready-to-hand beings but ultimately to my own intention, which gathers the subordinated finalities of these beings into a network of finalities, all oriented toward myself as the center of a surrounding world. This being, not only useful but ready-to-hand (*usuel*, *zuhanden*), refers to me and, in so doing, becomes for me my own world: it is good insofar as it is mine; it is a good insofar as it is my good. As a result, doing away with it would amount to my doing away with myself; and if, taking a step further in the negation, I were to destroy it, then I would also destroy myself. Such destruction of property as such, and even as my property—thus this destruction of myself—has not disappeared in our own time and is still designated as "sacrifice." Even daily, we are subject to its paroxysm in the form of *terrorism*. Both common usage and the media rely on the semantics of sacrifice in order to qualify terrorist acts: the terrorist, it is said, *sacrifices himself* for his cause, or else, he *sacrifices* the lives of his random victims in order to draw attention to this very cause. Such terms, as approximate and thus misleading as they may be, nevertheless retain some relevance because pure violence, without any moral or even political justification, in its stupidity and its barbarism, in fact elicits a paralyzing dread before an act that in principle is alien to the world of living beings or the community of reasonable people and obeys the logic, absurd to us, of another world that moreover denies and annihilates our own. Terrorism abolishes property, innocent people, and the terrorist himself, because it accomplishes first and radically the destruction of all beings as useful and functional and the destruction for us of the organization of the world itself in terms of ends and accomplishment. Thus destroyed, the everyday thing (*l'usuel*) becomes the sacred insofar as it no longer belongs to the world in which we can live and in which it is our purpose or intention to live in the normality of the profane. Now, if we grant that terror under its polymorphous though faceless figures remains today our ultimate experience of the sacred and that this figure of the sacred, as debased as it proves to be, nevertheless allows us a common concept of sacrifice, then what makes a profane thing sacred, the *sacrifiement*, consists in its destruction. The terrorist produces the sacred (under the figure of absurd horror) by destroying life, including his own.[2] The process that makes the profane sacred entails the destruction of the thing thus sacrificed.[3] One access to sacrifice thus remains available to us to the extent that the experience of terrorism guarantees us the experience of the destruction of property as such and thus of the world as ours.

Nevertheless, this first result, by providing us an indisputable, because perfectly negative, access to the sacred and to the *sacrifiement*, only reinforces the aporia. For the point is not merely to deplore the fact that destruction is the only remaining figure of sacrifice today, but above all to ascertain the extent to which, even in this form, its intelligibility remains problematic. How, indeed, does destroying something contribute to making it sacred? What does sacrifice do if all it does is undo? What can it consecrate if it limits itself to annihilating? To what or to whom can it give, since it nullifies the content of any gift and nullifies itself as possible giver? The definition of sacrifice as the destruction of a good as such not only explains nothing of sacrifice but could actually explain its opposite—the self-appropriation of autarchy. Indeed, the wise and the strong want to rid themselves of a possession by destroying it and thereby becoming free of it; they alone can do this, and they prove it to themselves by surviving what they destroy in themselves: in making a sacrifice of other goods (by ascesis, renunciation, mutilation, and so forth), they demonstrate their autarchy to others; or rather they prove at least to themselves their autonomy and ataraxy. Sacrifice thus becomes the auto-celebration of the ascetic ideal, in which the ego attains a kind of *causa sui* by no longer owing anything to anyone, not even its own person to the world. Sacrifice, understood as the destruction of a good, can be inverted into a construction of the self, which sacrifices nothing of its own—only the world to itself.

Sacrifice according to Exchange

Thus we must give up on defining sacrifice only by the destruction of a possession. In fact, it becomes possible to speak of sacrifice only if one introduces a third term, beyond the destroyer and the good destroyed—precisely the third, the other. Even in the most banal understanding of sacrifice, for example, the sacrifice of a pawn or a piece in chess, the other already appears, even if only in the most basic guise of the mimetic rival, the alter ego, my opponent: even if, in making this supposed gift to my opponent, my purpose is simply to strengthen my position, it is my position vis-à-vis *him*, and I sacrifice this piece to *him*. In short, my sacrifice always assumes the other as its horizon of possibility. Thus it is the other that determines the destruction of a good, either because he benefits from it as its new recipient (I transfer it to him while mourning its loss), or because he shares its loss with me as my rival (I give it up in order to deprive him of it, in order to strengthen my position).

In this new sense, where it occurs within the horizon of the other, does sacrifice become more intelligible than in the previous case, where it is the pure and simple destruction of a good? Undoubtedly, because we notice immediately that it is in fact no longer simply a matter of destruction, but also of privation (with destruction, but also sometimes without). And this obtains on both sides of the alternative. On the one hand, I deprive myself of a good, because I can do without it, and in this way assure my autonomy (autarchy, ataraxy); in other words, I deprive myself of a good precisely in order to prove to myself that it has only a minor importance and that I remain myself even without it; hence by losing a possession that is other than me, I gain a more perfect possession of myself. On the other hand, I deprive myself of a good, not because I would simply destroy it, but because by destroying it or by making it unavailable to me, I want to divest myself of it to the point that, by this definitive loss, another might possibly appropriate it in my stead; in fact, I display this good I have renounced so that it may become available for the other to appropriate it. Nevertheless, these two situations clearly differ. In the first case, it is indeed enough for me to deprive myself of a good (to the extent that I myself survive), in order to prove its dispensable character and in this way demonstrate my autarchy: the sacrifice is accomplished perfectly by itself. The second case is rather different: admittedly, I manage to deprive myself of a good (I indeed sacrifice it) but this renunciation is not *as such* sufficient for some other to take possession of that of which I have nevertheless deprived myself; the sacrifice remains unfinished: my renunciation only allowed for the display of the good, which, though made available, still remains in escheat at this point in the process: less given than just given up. For even when I divest myself of a good, whether or not the other takes possession of it is not up to me; that depends only on the other. By my decision alone, the sacrifice can thus only be accomplished halfway; its realization does not derive from my simple act of dispossession, but awaits the other's acceptance, and thus depends upon another decision, on an *other* decision, come from elsewhere. I can at best act *as if* my dispossession were equivalent to a taking possession by the other, but I can neither assure that nor assume it. Dispossession cannot anticipate reception because the other's acceptance can come only from the other himself and thus by definition escapes me. Sacrifice involves my dispossession, but my dispossession is not enough for a sacrifice, which only acceptance by the other can ratify. If we assume that giving up is enough to begin the sacrifice, accomplishing it as a gift is contingent upon its acceptance by the other. There is nothing optional or secondary about this discrepancy that defines and marks the irreducible distance between me and the other, such that neither I nor the other can abolish it. Even when offered (or rather: precisely *because* offered), it is part of the definition of sacrifice that it can nevertheless be refused and disdained by the other—in this specifically lies the other's role. Thus, even if defined within the horizon of the other, the destruction or disappropriation of a good is not enough to account fully for the possibility of sacrifice.

Yet it happens that the most current explanation of sacrifice, produced by sociology and the sociology of religion in particular, presupposes exactly the opposite: that my dispossession of a good is enough for the effective accomplishment of a sacrifice. Sacrifice would consist in effecting the loss of a good (by destruction or by devolution) for the benefit of an other (divine or mortal, most often superior hierarchically), such that he accepts it and consequently renders a counter-gift to the one who initiated the sacrifice—with this reciprocity constituting the decisive presupposition. Obviously, the realization of the sacrifice by its initiator does not imply and does not at all guarantee the acceptance of the good that has been ceded and, still less, the reciprocity of a counter-gift. Nevertheless, this interpretation of sacrifice imposes itself, perpetuates itself, and prevails, even today. How does it manage to do so? By assuming what it cannot prove, to wit, that the acceptance and the counter-gift always (or at least in the majority of cases, as the standard situation) follow from the dispossession (with or without destruction). But, once again, how does this presupposition legitimate itself?—by implicitly basing the entire explanation of sacrifice on the model of exchange.[4] Moreover, in the majority of cases, we find the three terms "gift," "exchange," and "sacrifice" equated, or even substituted without distinction for one another. Just as the gift consists in giving up a possession in order to obligate the other to give back a counter-gift (*do ut des*), and just as exchange implies that every good that passes from the one to the other is compensated by a good (or a sum of money) passing from the other to the one, in like fashion, the sacrificer (the sacrificing agent) abandons a good (by dispossession, of exposure or destruction), so that the supposedly superior other (divine or mortal) will accept it and, in so doing, enter into a contractual relation and, by contract, return a good (real or symbolic). In the three cases, under the imprecise (and confused) names of "gift," "exchange," and "sacrifice," the same economy of contract obtains: I bind myself to you by abandoning a possession, *therefore* you bind yourself to me by accepting it, *therefore* you owe me an equivalent item in return. Henceforth, sacrifice does not destroy any more than the gift gives up, because both work to establish exchange; or rather, where sacrifice destroys and the gift cedes, both operate thereby to establish the economy of reciprocity.

We must conclude that destruction or dispossession and the horizon of the other still do not allow us to determine a concept of sacrifice, but only lead us to assimilate it with exchange in the same confusion that undermines the notion of the gift. In this context, at best, one would call sacrifice the imprudence of an incomplete exchange where a gift is given up without knowing whether an acceptance will ratify it, while at worst, sacrifice would be the illusion of a contractual arrangement that no one would ever have entered into with the one who is making the sacrifice—unless it were a matter of simple deception, of the other or of oneself, claiming to give up unconditionally, hoping all the while, secretly or unconsciously, to receive a hundredfold what one loses only once. It would be better instead to consider the very term "sacrifice" an impropriety, an empty or contradictory concept, and apply to sacrifice the contradiction that Derrida deplored in the gift: "The truth of the gift . . . suffices to annul the gift. The truth of the gift is equivalent to the non-gift or to the non-truth of the gift."[5] We can thus say that the truth of sacrifice culminates in exchange—that is to say, in the non-truth of sacrifice, since it should consist precisely of a relinquishing without return; it also ends in the truth of the non-gift par excellence—that is to say, the confirmation that whenever one believes he speaks of, and makes, a sacrifice, one still hopes for an exchange and a return that would be all the more profitable, since one claimed to have lost everything.

The Misunderstanding of the Gift

Nevertheless, a way could be opened through the aporia itself, and thanks to it. More precisely, the extension of the aporia of the gift to sacrifice might already indicate another path—by making us think sacrifice precisely in its relation to the gift. We would then no longer only think of it as the dispossession (yea, the destruction) of a good within the horizon of the other, but also as a moment of the more comprehensive phenomenon of the gift. For the phenomenon of the gift at the outset manifests much more than exchange: as we have attempted to demonstrate elsewhere, the gift can and thus must be separated from exchange by letting its natural meaning reduce to givenness. For, while the economy (of exchange) denatures the gift, if reduced to givenness, the gift excepts itself from the economy by freeing itself from the rules of exchange. The gift in effect proves able to accomplish itself, even and especially, by reducing each of the terms of exchange: without a giver (*donateur*), or indeed without a recipient (*donataire*)—thus freeing itself without reciprocity—and even without a thing given—thus freeing itself from a logic of equality.[6] As reduced to the givenness in it, the gift is accomplished in an unconditioned immanence, which not only owes nothing to exchange, but dissolves its conditions of possibility. The gift so reduced performs itself with an unconditioned freedom—it never lacks anything that would prohibit it from giving itself, because, even without invoking the terms of the exchange, it still shows itself, even all the more so. But if the gift proves unconditioned in this way, would it not offer sacrifice its most appropriate site, since sacrifice claims precisely (though without at this juncture justifying its claim) to give and to give up without condition? In this hypothesis, the solution to the aporia of sacrifice would come from the answer to the aporia of the gift—from the reduction of the gift to givenness. We will need then to proceed to a reduction of sacrifice to givenness in order to formulate sacrifice, as one of its moments, in terms of the phenomenon of the reduced gift.

Where, then, does the most evident aporia arise when the phenomenon of a gift unfolds? Precisely at the moment when the given gift appears. For when what the giver gives (a thing, a being, a piece of information [*une donnée*], a present) comes into full light, the gift as such inevitably starts to become obscured, and then to disappear. Indeed, the gift given, which takes on the consistency of the thing and of a being, occupies the center of the phenomenal stage, so as to conceal or even exclude everything else— that is to say, first of all the giver: for the giver disappears in his own gift. On the one hand, he must indeed give something, whatever may be the actual status of this something (a simple sign of good will or a real gift in itself, useful or useless, precious or trivial, inaugural or reciprocal); otherwise, he would not appear at all as a giver giving. But, precisely to the extent that he gives his gift truly and irrevocably, the giver allows his given gift to separate itself from him and assert itself as such, autonomous and thus available to the recipient, who appropriates it. The gift not only becomes a phenomenon independent of the phenomenon of the giver, but it excludes him, either by consigning him to the phenomenal background or by obscuring him completely. This disappearance of the giver does not result from any recalcitrance on the part of the recipient but from the very definition of the gift given; it is not ingratitude that causes the exclusion of the giver, yet this exclusion ultimately results by virtue of the very phenomenality of the gift given, in itself exclusive and appropriating. The giver must disappear (or at least his obviousness [*évidence*] must diminish and his presence withdraw) in order for the gift given to appear (or at least for its presence [*évidence*] to increase and for it to announce itself in the foreground). Otherwise, the gift given would not only not appear as such; it would not be truly given at all: its recipient would not dare to approach it or to extend his hand, or even to claim himself the recipient, because the tutelary and overhanging presence of the giver would still cast a shadow of possession over it. The recipient cannot take the gift given for his own, so long as he still sees in it the face and the power of its previous owner. The owner must withdraw from the giver, so that the gift can start to appear as given; but ultimately, the giver must disappear completely for the gift to appear as given definitively—that is to say, given up, abandoned.

And there is more. In effect, just as the gift appears only if the giver disappears, the gift thus abandoned ends by masking in itself not only the giver but the very process of the gift. If a gift appears as truly given only from the moment the giver yields it, the abandoning is reversed: the gift given appears because it, in turn, abandons its giver. But a gift without relation to any giver no longer bears the mark of any process of givenness, and thus appears as alien to what is given in it. Paradoxically, a gift truly given disappears as given, too. It appears henceforth only as a found object: a thing, a being or an object, which is found there, in front of me, by chance and without reason, such that I may wonder what status I should grant it: is it here in its own right (like a piece of fruit fallen from a tree), by the voluntary intention of an other (like an installation in a museum, a sign at the edge of the road), by involuntary accident (like a possession lost by its distracted owner, or stolen from him), or even possibly placed here by an anonymous giver, either for the benefit of some unspecified beneficiary (like the emergency phones on the side of a freeway), or for the benefit of an identified recipient, in which case it could be intended for an other, or for me? The gift-character of the found object is thus no longer self-evident; it is only one hypothesis among others, and not the least plausible. In the extreme, if my hermeneutic does not allow me (or does not wish) to recognize the gift as given, the gift as such disappears completely. What is specific to the gift—once we grant that it implies relinquishment in order to appear—thus consists in disappearing as given, and in allowing nothing more to appear than the neutral and anonymous presence, left without any origin, of a thing, of a being, or of an object, coming only from itself, never from elsewhere—nor originating from a giver or from a process of giving. The major aporia of the gift derives from this paradox: the gift given can appear only by erasing in its phenomenon its giver, the process of its gift, and, ultimately, its entire gift-character.

Two examples unambiguously confirm this paradox. First, the one in which St. Augustine analyses the case of "a fiancé who gives a ring to his betrothed; but she loves the ring thus received more than the fiancé who gave it to her. Wouldn't we consider her adulterous in the very gift made to her by her fiancé, even while she loves what her fiancé has given her? Certainly, she loved what her fiancé gave her, but if she were to say: 'This ring is enough for me, now I don't want to see his face again,' what would she be? Who would not detest this lunacy? Who would not accuse her of adultery? You love gold instead of your husband, you love the ring instead of your fiancé; if you truly have in mind to love the ring in place of your fiancé and have no intention of seeing him, the deposit that he gave you as the token of his love would become the sign of your loathing."[7] Of course, in the case of this caricatured ingratitude, the issue for the theologian is to condemn the sin in general, as the attitude that leads us to love the gifts of God while rejecting God himself, who gives them to us. But the phenomenological description of the gift remains no less pertinent here: the betrothed first sees the fiancé, the giver, then the gift, the ring; the fiancé intended of course that, by seeing the gift (the ring), the betrothed would not stop seeing his face, the face of the giver. He reckoned to benefit from a phenomenal structure of reference (Hinweis): the phenomenon of the ring offering its own visibility and, moreover, conferring it to the (absent) visibility of the giver, who, by this indication, would benefit from a second-degree visibility, by association. In this way, the giver, invisible as such, gives being to the visible gift, but in return the visible gift gives him a visibility by proxy. Yet this exchange (the gift of being for the given exchanged for the gift of appearing for the giver) is not phenomenally valid: in fact, the betrothed sees and wants to see only the ring, and not, by indication and reference, the facies sponsi, the face of the giver. The gift given, as such and at the outset (the ring), monopolizes all of the visibility and condemns the giver to disappear from the visible stage. Henceforth, not only does the fiancé/giver no longer enter the phenomenon of the gift, but the gift-character of the given is erased: the ring becomes the possession of the betrothed, who sees nothing more than herself in it, possessing it. Along with the giver, the gift itself disappears.

In an entirely different context, but along the same descriptive line, and in describing the es gibt, such that it determines the appearance of time and being (for neither one nor the other are, so that with respect to them it is necessary to say es gibt, it gives), Heidegger insists on the phenomenal characteristic of the gift, which gives (itself) in this it gives: "The latter [es gibt] withdraws in favor of the gift [zugünsten der Gabe] which It gives. . . . A giving [Geben] which gives only its gift [nur seine Gabe gibt], but in the giving holds itself back and withdraws [zurückhält und entzieht], such a giving we call sending [das Schicken]."[8] We understand that the giving can precisely not give itself, more exactly cannot give itself in person, precisely because it gives its gift (the gift given), makes it appear as such, and in order to arrive at this, must not only remain in the background but must withdraw itself from visibility. The *es gibt*, because it gives (and dispenses) being as much as time, neither can nor should give itself. The giving gives only the given; it never gives itself. The giving cannot return on itself in a *donum sui*, as *causa sui* in metaphysics claims to do. Can we advance in the understanding of this fundamental impossibility? Possibly, by considering difference as such—namely, the difference that Heidegger in this case no longer calls ontological (*ontologische Differenz*), but the different from the same, the differentiation (*der Unterschieden aus dem Selben, der Unter-Schied*). What differs here is called the unique *Austrag*, the accord, which unfolds at once as being and as a being, which are both given in the same gesture, but precisely not in a similar posture: "Being shows itself as the unconcealing coming-over [*zeigt sich als die entbergende Überkommnis*]. Beings as such appear in the manner of the arrival that keeps itself concealed in unconcealedness [*erscheint in der Weise der in die Unverborgenheit sich bergenden Ankunft*]. . . . The difference of being and beings, as the differentiation of coming-over and arrival [*Unter-schied von Überkommnis und Ankunft*], is the accord [*Austrag*] of the two in unconcealing keeping in concealment."[9] In fact, nothing is clearer than this phenomenological description of the *es gibt*: when it is given, or more precisely when it gives (understood in the trivial sense: when it functions, it works, it performs), the being arrives in visibility because it occupies and seizes visibility entirely (just as the arrival, *Ankunft*, of a train, precisely in the banal sense of the term, fills the station and focuses every gaze upon it). But beings can neither unleash nor prompt the visibility that they appropriate in this way: only being can open and uncover it, because it alone consists precisely in this display, because it alone comes from a coming-over (*Überkommnis*), opening the site that an arrival (*Ankunft*) will eventually occupy. This arrival receives its site, but by occupying it, it masks it and also renders invisible the coming-over that had opened it. By occupying the entire stage, beings make this very scene invisible. Being thus disappears in the visibility (*l'évidence*) of the being whose arrival covers up its nevertheless unconcealing coming-over. The being thus hides being from view by a phenomenological necessity that attests that being never shows itself without a being or, moreover, as a being, as *Sein und Zeit* has already repeated with decisive insistence. The process of the givenness of the giving thus reproduces, here ontologically, in the agreement of being and the being according to the *es gibt*, the aporia of the gift in general, which St. Augustine had described in a theological context.

It is characteristic of the gift given that it spontaneously conceals the givenness in it; thus a characteristic of the phenomenon of the gift is that it masks itself. Is it possible to locate the phenomenon of sacrifice within the essential aporia of the phenomenality of the gift? And, in being articulated there, might the phenomenon of sacrifice even allow us to solve the aporia of the gift?

The Lifting of the Given and the Relieving of the Gift

By virtue of its visibility, the given constitutes an obstacle to that which makes this very visibility possible. What then makes the visibility of the gift possible, if not the process of givenness, whereby the giver turns the gift over as given, by handing it over in its autonomous visibility?

We should here note carefully that the gift given does not mask only (or even first of all) the giver, as an effect is detached from its efficient cause, or as the beneficiary of a favor refuses out of ingratitude to recognize it. The gift given masks the very process of giving givenness, a process in which the giver participates without constituting it intrinsically (he can even recuse himself without the process of giving being suspended). For, as we noted previously, a gift (reduced) can remain perfectly possible and complete even with an anonymous or uncertain giver, or indeed without any confirmed giver. In fact, at issue here is one of the cardinal figures of the reduction of the gift to givenness. The question thus does not consist in reverting from the given to the giver, but in letting appear even in the gift ultimately given (in a being arrived in its arrival [*arrivage, Ankunft*] the advancing process of its coming-over, which delivers its visibility by giving it to the gift, or, more generally, the very coming-over that delivers the gift phenomenally (the *Überkommnis* that unconceals the visible). At issue would be the suspending of the gift given, so that it would allow the process of its givenness—namely, the given character of the gift (its given-ness [*donnéité*] to translate *Gegebenheit* literally)—to appear in its own mode instead of crushing it in the fall from the given into a pure and simple found object. So it is not a question of suppressing the gift given for the benefit of the giver, but of making this gift transparent anew in its own process of givenness by letting its giver eventually appear there and, first and always, by allowing to appear the coming-over that delivers the gift into the visible. At stake here is the phenomenality of this very return: to return to the gift given the phenomenality of its return, of the return that inscribes it through givenness in its visibility as gift coming from somewhere other than itself. The gift appears as such—in other words, as arriving from somewhere other than itself—only if it appears in such a way that it ceaselessly refers to this elsewhere that gives it and from which it finds itself given to view.

That the gift given allows the return from which it proceeds to appear: this defines the signification and the phenomenological function of sacrifice—such is, at least, our hypothesis. To sacrifice does not signify relinquishing a good (by destruction or dispossession), even if this relinquishing were possibly for the other's benefit; rather, it consists in making appear the referral from which it proceeds, by reversing it (by making it return) toward the elsewhere, whose intrinsic, irrevocable, and permanent mark it bears insofar as it is a gift given.[10] Henceforth, sacrifice presupposes a gift already given, the point of which is neither destruction, its undoing, nor even its transfer to another owner but, instead, its return to the givenness from which it proceeds, and whose mark it should always bear. Sacrifice gives the gift back to the givenness from which it proceeds by returning it to the very return that originally constitutes it. Sacrifice does not separate itself from the gift but dwells in it totally. It manifests this by returning to the gift its givenness because it repeats the gift on the basis of its origin. The formula that perfectly captures the conditions of possibility of the gift is found in a verse from the Septuagint, ὅτι σὰ τὰ πάντα καὶ ἐκ τῶν σῶν δεδώκαμέν σοι—"all things are yours and it is by taking from among what is yours that we have given you gifts" (1 Chron. 29:14). To make a gift by taking from among gifts already given in order to re-give it, to "second" a gift from the first gift itself, to make a gift by reversing the first gift toward the one who gives it, and thus to make it appear through and through as a given arising from elsewhere—this is what accurately defines sacrifice, which consists in making visible the gift as given according to the coming-over of givenness. At issue is absolutely not a counter-gift, as if the giver needed either to recover his due (in the manner of an exchange) or to receive a supplementary tribute (gratitude as a symbolic compensation); rather, the point is the recognition of the gift as such by repeating in reverse the process of givenness and by reintegrating the gift to it, wresting it from its factual fall back to the rank (without givenness) of found object, non-given, un-given, in the end, to make visible not only the given but the process of givenness itself (as coming-over, *Überkommnis*), which would otherwise be left unnoticed, as if excluded from all phenomenality.

Sacrifice does not return the given to the giver by depriving the recipient (*donataire*) of the gift: it renders givenness visible by re-giving the gift. Sacrifice effects the redounding (*la redondance*) of the gift. As a result, sacrifice loses nothing, above all not the gift that it re-gives; on the contrary, it wins—it wins the gift, which it keeps all the more that it makes it appear for the first time as such, as a gift given, finally safeguarded in its givenness (given-ness, *Gegebenheit*). Sacrifice wins, but without even having to play the game of "loser wins" (as in the so-called pure love of God), as if it were necessary to lose much in order to win still more by retribution. Sacrifice wins by re-giving (*redondance*): it conquers the true phenomenon of the gift by restoring to it, through the act of re-giving, the phenomenality of givenness. Sacrifice re-gives the gift starting with the recipient and makes the gift appear as such in the light of its givenness and, sometimes, for the glory of the giver. In this, it corresponds to forgiveness (*le pardon*): forgiveness re-gives the gift as well, but starting from the giver, who confirms it in the light of givenness for the salvation of the recipient. Forgiveness and sacrifice correspond to one another in this way so as to make the phenomenality of givenness appear by the double redounding of the gift, beginning either from the recipient or from the giver.

The Confirmation of Abraham

Thus we have determined sacrifice according to its phenomenality by inscribing it within the framework of a phenomenology of the gift: its function is to make appear what the gift, once given, never fails to cover over and hide—the process of givenness itself—such that on the basis of a review of this process, the giver eventually becomes visible again, as well. Can we confirm this determination of sacrifice by a significant example? Certainly, if we consider the episode of the sacrifice of Abraham, or rather of the sacrifice of Isaac by Abraham, related in Genesis 22:1–19. Without glossing over its radically theological status (indeed, how could one do so?), we shall sketch an interpretation of it first according to the principle of the phenomenality of sacrifice.

Certainly, there is a sacrifice involved, specified as such: "[O]ffer [your son Isaac . . .] as a burnt offering upon one of the mountains of which I shall tell you" (22:2)—but it is a sacrifice that precisely does not take place, at least if one confines oneself to the common determination of sacrifice (a destruction or dispossession allowing an exchange within the framework of a contract). Understanding this sacrifice presupposes, paradoxically, understanding why Isaac has not been sacrificed ("Abraham went and took the ram, and offered it up as a burnt offering instead of his son" [22:13]). Or more precisely, it involves understanding why, while there was no sacrifice following the common understanding (no destruction of Isaac), there was indeed, according to the biblical account, fulfilment of the obligation toward God, since God acknowledges, "[N]ow I know that you fear God" (22:12). Now this is possible only if we grant that this account does not follow the common determination of sacrifice, but instead follows its phenomenological concept—that of sacrifice conceived on the basis of the gift and of the gift reduced to givenness. It is here that we must therefore locate the concept. A first moment seems evident: God demands of Abraham a sacrifice and even a consuming sacrifice (where the victim is consumed in fire, leaving nothing to share among God, the priest, and the one offering, in contrast to other forms of sacrifices). This demand of sacrifice falls upon Isaac, the one and only son of Abraham. Do we have here a sacrifice according to the common concept? Precisely not, because God asks nothing out of the ordinary of Abraham, nor does he enter into any contractual agreement with him; he simply and justifiably takes back Isaac, who already belongs to him, and even doubly so. First, quite obviously, because all first-borns belong to God by right: "The first-born of your sons you shall give to me. You shall do likewise with your oxen and with your sheep; seven days it shall be with its dam; on the eighth day you shall give it to me" (Exod. 22:29–30). Or again: "Consecrate to me all the first-born; whatever is the first to open the womb among the people of Israel, both of man and of beast, is mine" (Exod. 13:2). The question consists only in knowing what this belonging and this consecration really imply. The answer varies, from actual putting to death (in the case of the plague on the firstborn of Egypt, Exod. 12:29–30), to the ritual sacrifice of animals in the Temple, right up to the redemption of the firstborn of Israel, prescribed explicitly by God (Exod. 13:11–15, 34:19; Num. 18:14), who forbids human sacrifices.[11] In this sense, Isaac belongs first to God, before belonging to his father (Abraham), in the same way as any other firstborn, of Israel or of any other people.

God has nevertheless another right of possession over Isaac, radical in another way: Isaac in effect does not belong to Abraham, who could not, neither he, nor his wife, on their own, engender him ("Now Abraham and Sarah were old, advanced in age; and it had ceased to be with Sarah after the manner of women" [Gen. 18:11]). Thus, Isaac belongs from the beginning and as a miracle to God alone: "Nothing, neither word nor deed, remains impossible for God. At the same season next year, I will return to your home and Sarah will have a son."[12] And in fact, "The Lord visited Sarah as he had said, and the Lord did to Sarah as he had promised. And Sarah conceived, and bore Abraham a son in his old age at the time of which God had spoken to him" (21:1–2). Thus, by right, Isaac, child of the promise through divine omnipotence, comes to Abraham only as a pure gift, unexpected because beyond every hope, incommensurate with what Abraham would have possessed or engendered himself. But this gift nevertheless disappears as soon as Isaac appears as such—that is to say, as the son of Abraham, or more precisely, as the one whom Abraham claims as his son: "Abraham called the name of his son who was born to him, whom

Sarah bore to him, Isaac. . . . And the child grew, and was weaned; and Abraham made a great feast on the day that Isaac was weaned" (21:3, 8). And for her part, Sarah, too, appropriates Isaac as her son ("I have borne him a son in his old age!" 21:7), since she drives out as a competitor the other son, natural born, whom Abraham had had with Hagar (21:9–14). And the call that God addresses to Abraham aims only to denounce explicitly this improper appropriation: "Take your son, your only son Isaac, whom you cherish"—because Isaac precisely is not the possession of Abraham, who therefore must not cherish him as such. The demand for a sacrifice opposes this illegitimate appropriation, which cancels the gift given in a possession, the most original right of the giver to have his gift acknowledged as a gift given, which is to say, simply acknowledged as an always provisional, transferable, and alienable usufruct: "Go to the land of Moriah, and offer him there as a burnt offering" (22:2). Abraham hears himself asked not so much to kill his son, to lose him and return possession of him to God (according to the common concept of the gift), as, first and foremost, to give back to him his status as gift, precisely to return him to his status as gift given by reducing him (leading him back) to givenness.

And Abraham accomplishes this reduction in the most explicit and clear manner imaginable. Isaac, who reasons according to the common concept of the gift, of course notices that his father does not have (that is to say, does not possess) any possession available to sacrifice (to destroy and to exchange in the framework of a contract): "[W]here is the lamb for a burnt offering?" (22:7). Abraham, who already reasons according to the phenomenological concept of sacrifice, as gift given reduced to givenness, answers that "God will provide himself the lamb for a burnt offering" (22:8)—which means that God decides everything, including what one will offer him, and thus that neither Abraham, nor even Isaac, will be able to give anything to God, except what God, himself and in the first place, has already given to them; in a word, this means that every gift made to God comes first from God as a gift given to us. The place of sacrifice is thus called "God provides" (22:14). It should be pointed out here that the Hebrew says יִרְאֶה yir'eh (from the root רָאָה r'h, to see, to foresee, to provide), but that the Septuagint first understands, for the name Abraham attaches to the mountain, God saw (εἶδεν, second aorist of ὁράω), and then, for the name that it later retains, ὤφθη, God appears (passive aorist of ὁράω). Thus, it is as if the fact that God sees and provides and therefore quite clearly gives the offering of the sacrifice, or put another way, gives the gift to give—that is, makes the gift appear as such, given by the giver—were equivalent to the appearing of the giver, to the fact that God gives himself to seeing. So God gives himself to be seen as he gives originally, as he shows that every gift comes from him. He appears as the giver that the gifts manifest by referring to him as their origin and provenance.

Abraham, and he alone (not Isaac), sees in this way that God alone gives the gift of the burnt offering, such that God subsequently appears to him. But he had already recognized God as the giver of gifts from the moment that he had finally agreed to recognize Isaac as for him the principal among the gifts given by God, and thus due to God. So it is no longer important that Abraham kill, eliminate, and exchange his son for God's benefit in order to accomplish the sacrifice demanded (according to the common concept of sacrifice); rather, it matters exclusively (according to the phenomenological concept of the gift) that he acknowledge his son as a gift, that he accomplish this recognition of the gift by giving it back to its giver, and, thus, that he let God appear through his gift rightly recognized as a gift given. God clearly understands it as such, since he spares Isaac. It is important to note that to the extent that he restrains Abraham from killing Isaac, God specifically does not refuse his sacrifice, but nullifies only the putting to death, because the putting to death does not belong to the essence of sacrifice: the actual death of Isaac would have ratified only sacrifice in its common concept (destruction, dispossession, exchange, and contract). In fact, God lets Abraham go right to the end of sacrifice, but understood in the sense of its phenomenological concept: the recognition of Isaac as a gift received from God and due to God. And in order to recognize it, one need only acknowledge Abraham's loss of Isaac, a recognition accomplished perfectly without his being put to death, and from the moment he is accepted as a boundless gift: "The angel said, 'Do not lay your hand on the lad or do anything to him; for now I know that you fear God, seeing you have not withheld your son, your only son, from me'" (22:12). By refusing to let Isaac be put to death, God does not thereby refuse to acknowledge the gift offered by Abraham; he accepts the sacrifice all the more, understood this time in the strict phenomenological sense. By sparing Isaac, henceforth recognized (by Abraham) as a gift (from God), God re-gives Isaac to him, gives him a second time, presenting a gift by a redounding (*don par une redondance*), which consecrates it definitively as a gift henceforth held in common and, ultimately, transparently between the giver and the recipient. The sacrifice redoubles the gift and confirms it as such for the first time.[13]

Sacrifice in Truth

Thus sacrifice requires neither destruction nor restitution, nor even exchange, much less a contract, because its basis is not the economy (which dispenses with the gift), but the gift itself, whose aporia it endeavors to work through. For the function of sacrifice is only to allow the recognition of the giver and, through him, the entire process of givenness, by reducing the given. In this sense, sacrifice can be understood as a destruction, but a destruction taken in the sense of *Abbau*, of the deconstruction that frees by putting into the light of day what accumulation had covered up. Sacrifice destroys the given by clearing it away in order to uncover that which had made it visible and possible—the advance of givenness itself. This deconstructive and uncovering destruction can thus be better named a reduction: the bracketing of the gift given allows the giver's gesture to rise again to the visible, makes the recipient recover the posture of reception, and above all gives movement back to the coming-over of givenness in each of the three terms involved (giver, recipient, and gift given). Sacrifice is a redounding of the gift originating with the recipient (just as forgiveness [*le pardon*] consists of the redounding of the gift from the giver). In this way one succeeds in raising the epistemological obstacle of an economic conception of sacrifice by recognizing that "to sacrifice is not to kill, but to abandon and to give" (Bataille),[14] to the point that it becomes possible to conceive, as Levinas puts it, an "approach of the Infinite through sacrifice."[15] It constitutes an approach to the infinite because the reduction of the ever-finite given opens the only royal way toward the illumination of a possible infinite—not a being, even one that is given, and even less a necessarily determined and possessable object, but the process of an arrival (*une advenue*)—always comes from elsewhere and, for that very reason, is inalienable and unavailable. Unless the very access to being depends on sacrifice, if, like Patočka (and doubtless in opposition to Heidegger), one decides to think the es gibt resolutely, on the basis of givenness, such that givenness requires sacrifice, but also alone renders sacrifice intelligible: "In sacrifice, *es gibt* being: here Being already 'gives' itself to us, not in a refusal but explicitly. To be sure, only a man capable of experiencing, in something so apparently negative, the coming of Being, only as he begins to sense that this lack opens access to what is richest, to that which bestows everything and presents all as gift to all, only then can he begin to experience this favor"[16]—which can finally be transposed into theological terms, for it may be that St. Augustine says nothing different when he defines sacrifices as "*opera . . . misericordiae, sive in nos ipsos, sive in proximos, quae referuntur ad Deum* [works of mercy shown to ourselves or to our neighbours, and done with reference to God]."[17]

Translated by Stephen E. Lewis

Notes

1. Editor's note: Jean-Luc Marion gave this essay as part of the Richards Lectures at the University of Virginia (2008), which were subsequently published as *The Reason of the Gift*, trans. Stephen E. Lewis (Charlottesville and London: University of Virginia Press, 2011), 69–90.

2. The same goes for anyone who puts his life in danger, ultimately for nothing, or almost nothing (the "adventurer" or the so-called extreme athlete). The question arises: at what point does such a figure, mundane as it appears, correspond—as its modern heir—to the figure of the master in the dialectic of recognition (the slave remaining within the domain of the profane, where he does not destroy himself)?

3. This was moreover the classical argument (forged by the Reformation, then taken up by the Enlightenment) against a peaceful but also radical figure of sacrifice—monastic vows: to renounce power, riches, and reproduction amounts to destroying goods, which allow the world to live and to increase, and this renunciation even makes one enter into the field of the sacred, in this case into a life that, if it is not outside the world, is at least oriented eschatologically toward the alteration of this world.

4. The attempts to define sacrifice made by Henri Hubert and Marcel Mauss in the famous *Essai sur la nature et la fonction du sacrifice* (published first in the *Année sociologique* in 1898, then in Marcel Mauss, *Oeuvres*, ed. Victor Karady, vol. 1, *Les fonctions sociales du sacré* [Paris: Minuit, 1968]; *Sacrifice: Its Nature and Function*, trans. W. D. Halls [Chicago: University of Chicago Press, 1964]) are characterized by their poverty and their silence on the central (in fact the only) problem of the function and the intrinsic logic of sacrifice (its signification, its intention, its mechanism of compensation), contrasting all the more with the wealth of details on the actual practice of sacrifice. So if we suppose that "[s]acrifice . . . was originally a gift made by the primitive [*sic*] to supernatural forces to which he must bind himself" (193; trans. Halls, 2, modified), it remains to be understood whether and how these "forces" tolerate being thus "bound." The same abstraction and the same insufficiency obtain in the definition that is ultimately adopted: "Thus we finally arrive at the following definition: *Sacrifice is a religious act which, through the consecration of a victim, modifies the condition of the moral person who accomplishes it or that of certain objects with which he is concerned*" (205; trans. Halls, 13): what does "consecration" here signify? How is the person in question "modified"? When is it a matter of "objects" more than of him, and which objects? And, indeed, in what sense can or must this act be called "religious"? Who or what allows the "modification" in question? No response is given, because the questions are not even raised. These extraordinary approximations lead back inevitably to the features, themselves already highly imprecise, of the Maussian concept of the gift: (a) Sacrifice becomes a reciprocal gift that won't acknowledge itself as such: "If on the other hand, one seeks to bind the divinity by a contract, the sacrifice has rather the form of an attribution: *do ut des* is the principle" (272; trans. Halls, 65–66,

modified); but what does it mean to bind "contractually" a "divinity" that has precisely the characteristic of being able to recuse itself from any contract and any reciprocity? (b) The destruction is assumed to be effective by itself, and, without further consideration, it is assimilated to the accomplished sacrifice without recognizing that at best it fulfils only one of its conditions, but not the principle one (acceptance of the gift by the divinity): "*This procedure* [the sacrifice!] *consists in establishing a line of communication between the sacred and the profane worlds through the mediation of a victim, that is, of a thing that in the course of the ceremony is destroyed*" (302; trans. Halls, 97); but who cannot see that the difficulty of such a "line of communication" consists precisely in the fact that the "sacred world" has no reason to accept it unless one can explain how the contrary could be the case? (c) Thus one ends by granting that the sacrifice, in the end, isn't one: "The sacrifier gives up something of himself but he does not give himself. Prudently, he sets himself aside. This is because if he gives, it is partly in order to receive" (304; trans. Halls, 100). One can hardly avoid reading this conclusion as an admission of failure to supply a rigorous definition of sacrifice.

5. Jacques Derrida, *Donner le temps*, vol. 1, *La fausse monnaie* (Paris: Galilée, 1991), 42; *Given Time*, vol. 1, *Counterfeit Money*, trans. Peggy Kamuf (Chicago: University of Chicago Press, 1992), 27.

6. See Jean-Luc Marion, *Étant donné: Essai d'une phénoménologie de la donation*, §§9–11 (Paris: PUF, 1997, 1998), 124–61; Marion, *Being Given: Toward a Phenomenology of Givenness*, trans. Jeffrey L. Kosky (Stanford, Calif.: Stanford University Press, 2002), 85–113; and, to begin, Marion, "Esquisse d'un concept phénoménologique du don" (cited at the beginning of this notes section, in an unnumbered note).

7. "Quemadmodum, fratres, si sponsus faceret sponsae suae annulum, et illa acceptum annulum plus diligeret quam sponsum qui illi fecit annulum, none in ipso dono sponsi adultera anima deprehenderetur, quamvis hoc amaret quod dedit sponsus? Certe hoc amaret quod dedit sponsus; tamen si diceret: Sufficit mihi annulus iste, iam illius faciem nolo videre, qualis esset? Quis non detestaretur hanc amentiam? Quis non adulterinum animum convinceret? Amas aurum pro viro, amas annulum pro sponso; si hoc est in te, ut ames annulum pro sponso tuo, et nolis videre sponsum tuum, ad hoc tibi arrham dedit, ut non te oppigneraret, sed averteret"; St. Augustine, *In Epistulam Primam Iohannis Tractatus* 2.11; English translation available in *The Fathers of the Church: St. Augustine, Tractates on the Gospel of John 112–24, Tractates on the First Epistle of John*, trans. John W. Rettig (Washington, D.C.: The Catholic University of America Press, 1995), 154.

8. Martin Heidegger, *Zeit und Sein*, in *Zur Sache des Denkens*, in *GA* 14 (Frankfurt: Klostermann, 2007), 12; *On Time and Being*, trans. Joan Stambaugh (New York: Harper and Row, 1972), 8.

9. Heidegger, *Die onto-theo-logische Verfassung der Metaphysik*, in *Identität und Differenz*, in *GA* 11 (Frankfurt: Klostermann, 2006), 71; *The Onto-*

theological Constitution of Metaphysics, in *Identity and Difference*, trans. Joan Stambaugh (Chicago: University of Chicago Press, 2002), 64–65 (trans. modified).

10. Let us recall that we are dealing here with the three marks of the phenomenon as given; see Marion, *Étant donné*, §13, 170–71; *Being Given*, 119–20.

11. See the analysis of Roland de Vaux, *Les sacrifices de l'Ancien Testament* (Paris: J. Gabalda, 1964). In another sense, if one grants Ishmael the status of true firstborn, though born of a slave, he too is found rendered unto God by the sending into the desert (Gen. 21:9 ff.).

12. I translate Genesis 18:14 following the version of the Septuagint (μὴ ἀδυνατεῖ παρὰ τῷ θεῷ ῥῆμα), in conformity with Luke 1:37, which quotes it: οὐκ ἀδυνατήσει παρὰ τῷ θεῷ πᾶν ῥῆμα.

13. The death of the Christ accomplishes a sacrifice in *this* sense (more than in the common sense): by returning his spirit to the Father, who gives it to him, Jesus prompts the veil of the Temple (which separates God from men and makes him invisible to them) to be torn, and at once appears himself as "truly the son of God" (Matt. 27:51, 54), thus making appear not himself, but the invisible Father. The gift given thus allows both the giver and the process (here trinitarian) of givenness to be seen; see my sketch in Marion, "La reconnaissance du don," *Revue Catholique International Communio* 33/1, no. 195 (January–February 2008).

14. Georges Bataille, *Théorie de la religion*, in *Oeuvres complètes* (Paris: Gallimard, 1976), 7:310; *Theory of Religion*, trans. Robert Hurley (New York: Zone, 1989), 48–49 (trans. modified). More explicitly, Josef Ratzinger writes, "Christian sacrifice does not consist in a giving of what God would not have without us but in our becoming totally receptive and letting ourselves be completely taken over by him. Letting God act on us—that is Christian sacrifice. . . . In this form of worship human achievements are not placed before God; on the contrary, it consists in man's letting himself be endowed with gifts"; Ratzinger, *Introduction to Christianity*, trans. J. R. Foster (1990; San Francisco: Ignatius, 2004), 283.

15. Emmanuel Levinas, "Enigme et phénomène," in *En découvrant l'existence avec Husserl et Heidegger* (Paris: Vrin, 1949, 1974), 215; "Enigma and Phenomenon," trans. Alphonso Lingis, in *Emmanuel Levinas: Basic Philosophical Writings*, ed. Adriaan T. Peperzak, Simon Critchley, and Robert Bernasconi (Bloomington: Indiana University Press, 1996), 77.

16. Jan Patočka, "The Dangers of Technicization in Science According to E. Husserl and the Essence of Technology as Danger According to M. Heidegger" (1973), in *Jan Patočka: Philosophy and Selected Writings*, ed. Erazim V. Kohák (Chicago: University of Chicago Press, 1989), 332 (trans. modified in light of the French translation: Patočka, *Liberté et sacrifice: Écrits politiques*, trans. Erika Abrams [Grenoble: Jérôme Millon, 1990], 266). On this question, see the work of Emilie Tardivel, "Transcendance et liberté: Lévinas, Patočka et la question du mal," *Cahiers d'Études Lévinassiennes*, no. 7 (March 2008): 155–75.

17. St. Augustine, *De civitate dei* 10.6, *Bibliothèque Augustinienne*, vol. 34, 446; *The City of God against the Pagans*, trans. R. W. Dyson (Cambridge: Cambridge University Press, 1998), 400; see also St. Thomas Aquinas: "omne opus virtutis dicitur esse sacrificium, inquantum ordinatur ad Dei reverentiam" (*Summa theologiae* Iia-IIae, q.81, a.4, *ad*).

To Exist without Enemies

JEAN-YVES LACOSTE

You have heard that it was said, "An eye for an eye and a tooth for a tooth." But I say to you, Do not resist one who is evil. But if any one strikes you on the right cheek, turn to him the other also; and if any one would sue you and take your coat, let him have your cloak as well; and if any one forces you to go one mile, go with him two miles. Give to him who begs from you, and do not refuse him who would borrow from you. You have heard that it was said, "You shall love your neighbor and hate your enemy." But I say to you, Love your enemies and pray for those who persecute you, so that you may be sons of your Father who is in heaven; for he makes his sun rise on the evil and on the good, and sends rain on the just and on the unjust. For if you love those who love you, what reward have you? Do not even the tax collectors do the same? And if you salute only your brethren, what more are you doing than others? Do not even the Gentiles do the same? You, therefore, must be perfect, as your heavenly Father is perfect. (Matt. 5:38–48)

These verses from Matthew's Gospel belong to the discourse or sermon said "on the mountain," on a mountain that apparently was a hill. In this Sermon on the Mount, a number of antitheses are front and center. "You have heard that it was said . . . but I say to you. . . ." Jesus positions himself as a critic of the law (Matt. 5:21) or as a critic of popular Jewish wisdom (hate for enemies appears neither in the Tanakh nor in the classical rabbinic texts). In the gospel account, Jesus not only speaks [*parle*] (in the strong sense of [*parole*] "speech" in which someone's "word" is given),[1] but, as recounted, his speech-act, truly a word-event, quite easily passes for the gift of a new law: thus the hill readily appears as a new Sinai where the new law is offered—let us say, the *Torah messianica*. Therefore the first word that the commentator is compelled to use is that of authority. The "I" who speaks here is not anonymous. To state brutally that it is the Messiah of Israel would be risky: criticism of traditions, in terms of the "it was said, but," is common in Judaism's Second Temple Period. Nevertheless, this "I" is not that of any rabbi or doctor. "An eye for an eye, a tooth for a tooth" was written in the law. The law concedes a right to vengeance. And if we are familiar today with the radical teaching "you will not avenge yourself," to utter it despite the letter of the law is anything but banal. None could make such an assertion without claiming a certain authority. To pronounce this prohibition from the outside, as a non-Jew, would have been insignificant: Socrates would have had every right to do so, because he could have judged a law that was not his own, whose logos was not his own. Jesus's words, however, were the words of a Jew. Moreover, they are the words of a Jew who does not take up the task of casuistic reasoning, which is always tolerable in the rabbinic world (no "case" appears in the discourse), but of one who takes his distance vis-à-vis the law.

Jesus's place in Judaism is thus put in question from the beginning of his teaching. Most importantly, it is not put in question by the Jews (although later it certainly will be) but by Jesus himself: "But I say to you. . . ." Who is the I that can give himself authority over the law? This question is meant to embarrass and most of all to embarrass listeners and readers— whether his contemporaries or ourselves—for whom, before all else, Jesus's Jewishness is taken for granted. Recent New Testament exegesis has familiarized us with "Jesus the Jew," and one ought not turn back from these gains. Amid the plurality of Judaisms of the period, certainly, criticism of the law—at least criticism of its literal application—was not necessarily intolerable. Rabbinic Judaism had the means to face the uneven and rough edges of the Mosaic legislation with flexibility. The rabbi, however, played the role of the interpreter, as audacious as his interpretations could be. Jesus, in contrast, did not interpret. He opposes his word to that of Moses. It is true that he opposes Moses by presenting himself first as the one who "fulfills" and proffers the strictest literal respect for the law (Matt. 5:17). But what is the meaning of "fulfill"? Is asserting the expiration of a precept to fulfill the law? Moreover, may an anonymous Jew set himself up as the one who fulfills the law—*plèrōsai*, who carries it out to its fullness? The Jew must observe the law. Whoever refuses to participate in the system of legally permitted vengeance is certainly not explicitly repudiating the law. Yet there is more. Jesus is not speaking as a rabbi when he criticizes the *jus talionis*, but neither is he refusing to act upon this legal right as a private individual. Jesus's words are public. "But as for myself, I tell you" is followed by commandments. These commandments were not in the Torah, whether in the written Torah or even in the oral Torah. These are thus "new" commandments, solemnly given. But who among the Jews can give orders in this manner?

The word upon which we stumble here is thus a word of an uncertain origin. How is Jesus speaking as a Jew when he claims "to fulfill" the law? As a Jew critical of Judaism? In the name of a higher authority than Judaism? No conclusive evidence proves that the redactor of the Gospel of Matthew was familiar with the Pauline corpus and Paul's critique of the *nomos*. Moreover, it is evident that this New Testament author is the one most concerned with the continuity of "Christianity" and "Judaism." "To fulfill," in his perspective, cannot mean "to criticize," in the ordinary sense of that verb. Yet the antitheses, on Jesus's lips, remain his "taking his distance." A distance taken undoubtedly within Judaism—after all, outside Judaism, pagan nations alone are to be found. . . . Within Judaism, however, his speech could absolutely not pass for a peaceable word. The Judaism contemporary to Jesus is partially fragmented, to the point of having generated sectarian movements. Nevertheless, no sect ever questioned the law itself. The radicalism of the Qumran community fed upon a violent polemical relation with the Temple and the Jerusalem priesthood without these polemics ever becoming criticism of the law. For example, we are aware of the respect that the Qumran sectarians bore toward the scriptures on account of the faithful copies of biblical books found on carefully preserved manuscripts. Early Christianity did not hand down manuscripts of the law, either in Hebrew or Greek. Rather, as the so-called Essene communities, it passed on its own texts and endowed them with the highest authority. Yet the ever-averred continuity between the ancient and new "disposition"—a conviction that was sealed clearly over against Marcion, with the assertion that the Old and New Testaments form a diptych where each leaf calls upon the other—forbids, in any case, interpreting Jesus's words in terms of a rupture. But there is more. The antitheses of the Sermon on the Mount are, in fact without any doubt, speech-acts [*actes de paroles*] that seek to impose [*surplomber*] their perspective on the law and Israel's traditions.[2] Israel's prophets had spoken out against the people, the priesthood, the kings, but they had never raised their voices against the law and the theological traditions. They had spoken out against the false use of the law, which is altogether different from Jesus's words. In addition, they were active in what should be called pre-rabbinical periods. In contrast, Jesus began his public speaking at the time of the major rabbinic teachers. Elsewhere in the gospels, he directly confronts the world of the synagogues and the Second Temple. In this passage, however, the scope and bearing of "but as for myself, I tell you" is more expansive. Nothing in the text indicates that which would obviously be false—that is, that the impersonal voice ("it was said") that said "an eye for an eye, a tooth for a tooth" definitely brings into play the authority of YHWH. Yet "it was said," and this "said" is inscribed in the law. Where then can be found an authority capable of criticizing the law and even declaring it null and void? The rabbinic tradition had the means to hedge the law to the point of avoiding all literal application of the *jus talionis*. The rabbis circumvented the law in the name of the law and of its intelligent application. But nothing of the sort can be adduced in our case. Matthew displays no antinomianism: his inclination is radically other. Thus he speaks here against his own inclination, or rather he lets Jesus speak and adapts himself to what Jesus wants to impart. Regardless of his individual identity, the redactor of the First Gospel tells us most likely what he is constrained to say: Jesus's words cannot be inscribed in a tradition, most evidently not in the rabbinical tradition, since the speaker is not speaking as a witness to the law, and thus he possesses both a more-than-prophetic and more-than-rabbinic authority—an authority that we are tempted to naively call messianic.

The term "Messiah," "Christos," never appears on Jesus's lips. The Sermon on the Mount should not be made into a scene in someone else's scenario; neither should the one who utters the discourse be made to wear the clothing of a new Moses. Moses and Eli will appear later, but to render homage not to the Christ, but to the Son of God. In the strictest sense, Jesus never receives a messianic mantle in the gospels. It is true that some have suggested that in the time leading up to Easter, Jesus could have been known, here and there, as "Jesus the Christ."[3] Yet if the hypothesis cannot be disproved, certainly Jesus's teaching offers no substantive confirmation. His teachings are one thing; the rumors surrounding him are another. The content of Israel's messianic expectation remains enigmatic. Some took Jesus for the awaited messiah. He was condemned to death like a zealot, but denounced by the Sanhedrin who perceived him as a false messiah. Still, was he actually anointed "messiah"? We are tempted (naively) to assert that his speech [*parole*] is messianic. Probably it is so, on account of its self-proclaimed authority. Nevertheless, his speaking is both messianic and other than messianic. "But I say to you"—these words are of an extreme banality. To contradict [*contre-dire*: contra-dict, counter-say] is common currency. Moreover, to contradict the law is something any pagan could have done. How does this contradiction thus become of interest here when it is spoken by a candidate to messianic dignity? The answer quickly follows: it interests us inasmuch as it forces us to define with a little more precision the meaning of the formula "fulfillment of the law." *First*, in his rejection of the *jus talionis*, Jesus does not present himself as one who removes the force of a commandment, of a *mitzvah*. He had only finished stating that the commandments, *entolai* in Greek, possess an eternal validity—which cannot but embarrass the Christian reader, but which also guarantees Matthew's fidelity to the "historical Jesus," thus enrolled among the lovers of the law. "An eye for an eye . . .": the law is present here in its most impoverished form, as a penal code. It does not set forth what is required of each Israelite to prove his faithfulness to the Covenant, but what the Jewish community can or must do in order to resolve its legal cases—which explains why the rabbinical tradition easily spared itself the task of preaching the literal application of precepts. To contradict the code, therefore, cannot appear as a contradiction of the law. Jesus is only dealing with the margins of the law. Still, *second*, Jesus definitely presents himself as one who is commanding and not as one who is offering a benevolent interpretation. He makes demands in his name. He also makes demands, as we will see, by invoking the name of YHWH. "What must I do?" The law asserts itself in full—we are expected to respect 613 prescriptions or prohibitions—and we have nothing to object to this oversight by the law of all aspects of Jewish life. Certainly we can adduce additions among the tradition and commandments originating with the rabbis, but the innumerable *mitzvot de-rabbanan* need to be carefully distinguished from the biblical commands. Jesus, however, in contradistinction to the rabbis, does not command alongside the law, but against the law. He forbids that which was at once permitted and potentially legally due, at least in theory. Thus his commandment must be grasped as a "counter-command." He does not violate the law. But he speaks out against the letter of the law and its everyday use, of which the rabbis solely struggled to provide a mitigating reading. Finally, *third*, Jesus presents himself as the one who requires more than the law itself commands. Not an *iota* will be removed from the law (Matt. 5:18). Accounting even for every iota, the law does not exhaust the field of its requirements. Jesus's counter-command is thus in fact a "sur-commandment." Therefore, if the Messiah may be welcomed as the one who respects the law only to exceed it, then Jesus could well pass for a possible messiah.

How must the possibly messianic character of Jesus's speech [*parole*] be understood? As part and parcel of Moses' legislative utterances [*parole*]? Or of YHWH's utterance through Moses? In both cases as an increase, an extra added to the law? Yet the nearly impractical character of Jesus's "sur-commandments" prohibits such beliefs. Rabbinic *mitzvot* can be added to biblical *mitzvot*, but the former will be as realistic as the latter. The law is realistic. It commands that which the Jew can do. As soon as that is stated, it would be better not to speak of a "messianic Torah" in regard to Jesus's preaching on the hill. Indeed, the prescription here is of a supererogatory character. Such an expression is obviously paradoxical. Supererogation is defined as the excess done in relation to the law—to all law. To speak of a "messianic law" must be understood, then, as the duty to do more than the law demands. But does this duty constitute another law? If Jesus were enriching the catalog of commandments, as any rabbi could do on his own authority and with his own scriptural exegesis, then the result would be no more than a surplus of law. Yet Jesus is not entrusting a new code of law to his disciples. Judeo-Christian communities, insofar as we know them (which is very little), observed the law without superimposing a "messianic law," whose concept is quite recent. They observed the law while seeking to respond faithfully to a speech given [*parole*] by the Messiah, a discourse that did not appear as additional legislation but as a definite (and often paradoxical) interpretation of the law. "But I say to you"—and yet "not an iota will be removed from the law." There lies the difficulty of a Christian reception of Mosaic law. Its reception can only take place within the hori-zon of that which the law, in its essence, cannot command. To offer one-self to another person's violence cannot be required of just any other human being. To not respond to violence with violence may be required (although Christianity quickly developed a theory of legitimate defense). But when it is asked of the disciples (and the Sermon on the Mount is a teaching ad-dressed, not to a crowd of children of Israel, but to a small number of sons of Israel, companions of a possible messiah), the requirement to refuse altogether the play of violence is over and beyond all possible command-ment. A Christian tradition distinguished precepts and counsels. Jesus, how-ever, is not giving counsels but orders. The Sermon on the Mount contains no wishes, but strictly imperatives. How do we accommodate them?

In addition to the commandment's increase, an evident feature of these imperatives, which permits us to perceive how to comprehend them, is that we lack the situations in which to apply them. When are we requisitioned, in the military sense of the term, to walk a mile with someone only to find ourselves "obligated" to actually walk two miles? No known legislation might tell us. Moreover, the example speaks of no concrete situations. We could invent examples—for instance, an irritating individual asks for my company along the way, and I would be advised to accompany him even further than he had asked. Unfortunately, such an example is without significance. Every morality, at least of those we know, demands a generosity of the kind exhibited by the one who, at times, must give more than is asked of him. To lend to whoever asks—here again there is nothing to note, apart from its obviously unrealistic character: in this case, no morality would ever prescribe such an act. The content of the "messianic commandments," however, is less important than their rationality—that is, the rationality of the excess that cannot be demanded, expecting satisfaction. The "but I say to you" does not propose a set of new *mitzvot*. Any pious (observant) Jew can carry out the commandments. The capacity for their achievement in daily life, without significant difficulty, is inscribed in their very nature. Yet can Jesus's sayings be carried out to the letter? Evidently not. Purely and simply we lack the requisite situations. Whoever demands my coat asks uniquely for my coat. The exaggeration "give him your tunic too" is not lacking in signification: it indicates the excessive character that clothes the gift in relation to the demand. The gift gives more than is demanded. My tunic—the clothing beneath which I am naked—is precisely that which none can ask of me. I could never give my tunic, in its literal sense—thus the classic example of the gift in Christian hagiography is a sharing [*partage*], where Martin de Tours cuts his coat in half in order to clothe a beggar pierced by the cold. Martin does not give his coat, but half of his coat. He will certainly miss that half. In any case, he has given, and "well" ["*bien*": note the play on "good" and an owned good, a possession] given. Thus, none will demand my tunic. The idea of giving it is also somewhat absurd. But exactly what absurdity is at issue here? The answer follows: it consists in the absurdity of a gift that gives beyond everything that can possibly be given in all earnestness—that which can be expected of none and by none. The very logic of the gift is overturned. Should the gift be thought starting with its overturning [*bouleversement*]?

We can make the attempt. The juridical commandment is necessarily such that we have the capacity to fulfill it, whether its justness is mediocre or can barely be discerned. The same is true for cultic or ceremonial commandments, as for moral commandments. I have the duty and the capacity, for example, to contribute to the functioning of the state—for instance, paying taxes. I have the duty and capacity to offer, in the Temple, a sacrifice corresponding to my social position. Finally, I have the duty and capacity to give that which morality expects me to give—for the very good reason that it cannot expect more, although it may at times expect much from me. But when it is demanded (demanded, not suggested) that I give even more, one must admit that the gift, in this situation, in its apparent absurdity, gives foolishly.[4] It is foolish to give my tunic and my coat when it is reasonable and charitable to share my coat with a stroke of the sword.

Giving, then, as giving more than is demanded or can be demanded, such would be the logic of the gift. This logic is of course an "illogic." The example of Martin of Tours, noted previously, confirms this assertion. Martin in the traditional hagiography is the giver par excellence. He is the one who knows how to give. Nevertheless, the problem that arises with such an example is that Martin gives reasonably. He gives half and keeps half. He meets the demands of morality, and this morality need not be qualified "Christian." He bears no reproach, either from the (abstract) part of the moral law or concretely from the one to whom he gives. Thus, this anecdote inscribed in the memory of every Christian is deceptive. It speaks to us of the gift, but of the gift that is due, whereas the gift cited in the Sermon on the Mount is a gift that cannot be expected, that properly speaking is "not due" [indu: unjustifiable, not owed]. If someone asks me to walk a mile with him, I have no reason (apart from distress) to refuse to give him a little of my time, thus a little of who I am. If he forces me to walk with him, he may have very good reasons for so doing. Still, at least one thing is certain: no law is asking me to walk with him more than one mile; and if I give more, I am obeying, in fact, a principle of generosity that has no foundation in either an ethical logos or in a *mitzvah*. The gift, therefore, is at one and the same time more than legal and more than moral. We must will the good. In the examples that we encounter on the lips of the one who preaches on the hill, however, the definition of "the good" is jostled. Whoever gives his tunic and his coat, despite the lack of reasons for the request, whoever walks a mile and then another mile, does not give abundantly but over-abundantly. He exceeds all that can be required of him by exceeding everything that is concretely required of him. And if any can be found to accept a principle of benevolence that requires overabundance, he must be numbered a fool.

This affirmation does not rise to criticize reason. It comes into play to remind us that the ethical is reasonable—a discourse addressed to a reasonable animal who is capable of receiving it. The reasonable expectations of morality, moreover, are quite frequently very high. The virtues, in the Aristotelian sense, are certainly questions of moderation, of a middle term. Still, virtue is not undemanding. None acquires magnanimity without effort or, we may say, without practice or *askesis*. And if we move from the Aristotelian concept of virtues, in the plural, back up to the Platonic concept of the unity of virtue (to possess one is ipso facto to possess them all), we confront an equally difficult task. The overabundance of the gift cannot pass for a devaluation of the abundance of the gift, as we encounter it in classical thought, and for that matter, in the experience of Israel. In giving half of his coat, Martin seems irreproachable, and justly so. But one element is missing here, which may fit within the Catholic definition of the "hero-ics of the virtues," as defined by Benedict XIV. Martin is in part a legendary character, after all. The anecdote that we recounted is well known, but Martin's generosity truly cannot be considered heroic. He gives reasonably. In other words, he does not give foolishly [*follement*]—and for this very reason, the anecdote is inscribed in everyone's memory as the example of the successful fulfillment of one's moral duty.

Thus: to give foolishly [*follement*]. The adjective "foolish" leads us in-evitably to mention an experience that remains poorly explored, "folly in Christ." Whether in the Byzantine or the Russian tradition, the "fool in Christ" appears as a stranger to all virtue ethics. His comportment—we know nothing of him but his behavior—is visibly not virtuous. It often appears immoral. It is true that this immorality is simulated: the fool in Christ is the one who seeks to pass for a sinner in order to remind us that we are all sinners. But if eccentricity is tolerated in a number of cultures, beginning with biblical culture (more than one prophetic experience is that of a fool in YHWH), we encounter much more than a simple eccentricity when a believer dresses himself as a holy clown. The fool in Christ is a fool *in Christ*. The role that he plays is a role recognized by the ecclesial tradi-tion. In any case, we are confronted with an incarnation of the unreasonable [*déraison*], or at least of a certain sort of unreasonableness [*déraison*]. Strictly speaking, such actions cannot be demanded and expected of him. In no way does he present himself as someone who is fulfilling one or many com-mandments. Within the church, his aberrant behavior appears as a protest against all "reasonable" Christianity. The referent of his folly, if we seek its comprehension, is thus nothing but the primordial folly of the cross. The fool in Christ is not another crucified. Rather, he is the one who crucifies the common rationality at work not only in any civilized community, but also in the community of those who claim to partake of a crucified messiah without correctly taking stock of the logos of the cross. To correctly assess the rationality of this logos, however, is inevitably to take one's distance from any other logos. Folly in Christ is not the sole "logically" Christian experience. Nevertheless, such folly tells us how far Christian experience can take us: to the point of annulling the border between that which must be described here prudently as the rational and the irrational.

Thus we are led to the foolish commandment par excellence: love of enemies. To give to the one who wishes to borrow, why not? (even if we are in the vicinity of the unreasonableness of the gift—that is, of the gift made to someone who does not deserve it and may even make bad use of it—in short, in the vicinity of the unjust gift). But in what realm of pos-sibility can the prescription to love the enemy be founded? Matthew, the

Greek Matthew, uses the verb *agapan* and Delitzsch's Hebrew translation uses *ahav*. Yet these words are not subject to debate. Regardless of the love in question, by which the enemy must be loved, this love will always be folly. The enemy—my private enemy, the *inimicus* and not the *hostis*—is defined as whoever I do not love. I do not love him because his enmity compels me. I can certainly love the enemy of my city, the *hostis*, because he may not manifest any enmity toward me personally and because his enmity is dictated by his city and its possible military decisions. We can be at war and respect each other, even love each other. Hostilities are not aimed at me, at my personal and private self, but at my public self, my belonging to a city with which the other's city is at war. Indeed, most often neither he nor I participated in the deliberations that led to the declaration of war. In contrast, can I love the one who leads a private war against me, one in which he wars uniquely against me? Such possible love is most improbable, insofar as a logic of the probable is satisfactory. "It was said: you shall love your neighbor": Jesus ratifies that biblical command. "And you will hate your enemy": neither the scriptures nor the rabbinic traditions have ever uttered this command. Still, this "was said," and it belongs to a popular wisdom without divine warrant.[5] Thus, according to a proverb that is posed audaciously as a complement to the law, to enmity we can only respond with enmity. *Agape* is indiscernible, biblically speaking, from *philia*; the enemy is then the non-friend: to his enmity we can but respond with our enmity. How is it possible to become the friend of the non-friend? The following lines provide an answer. "Pray for those who persecute you." The command has become concrete. At first glance, the logic of love consists of an uncontrollable affectivity. The logic of prayer, in contrast, is characterized by its being willed [*voulue*]. We can certainly pray involuntarily: a brief cry of admiration or distress that bursts forth as an unpremeditated invocation. But we can just as well pray deliberately. Moreover, we can pray-*for*—for our friends, for example. If we can pray for a friend—for instance, if we decide to pray regularly for X or Y (indeed all spiritual life partakes of regularity)—it follows that we can also pray for the enemy. In this case, the enemy is the persecutor (whoever he may be and whether or not the allusion is to the persecutions undergone by early Christianity). Indubitably we are capable of praying *for* him. The verb used, *proseukhestai*, can also designate a prayer uttered for our own advantage. We could thus pray to the enemy that he spare us. Yet clearly this is not the situation described here. We are asked to pray *for* the enemy. In addition, the command is utterly succinct to the point of being pithy. What content should we give to our prayer? Shall we pray that his heart be warmed toward us? Shall we pray for his happiness, independently of the hostility that he bears toward us? The commandment turns on two words: pray for. We are told one and only one thing: facing an enemy, as undifferentiated as he often is, the only duty is to pray for him. Then, we need only understand from the following verse that whoever acts in this way acts as the son of a Father who, insofar as he makes rain fall on the just as well as on the unjust, loves both the one and the other. God certainly does not pray for his enemies. But he wills the good of his enemies. Therefore he loves them.

Consequently, love of enemy and prayer for the persecutors are perhaps but one and the same. What more could I give to my enemy than my prayer? We pray spontaneously for those we love. What happens when we no longer define love in terms of affections but in terms of doings? With respect to the enemy, what I feel—of which I am not the master—matters little. He is my enemy not so much on account of some "hate" that he bears toward me (I do not plumb the depths of the "kidneys and the hearts"—Jer. 17:10) but on account of his hostile comportment toward me. To love him would be to respond to his hostility with gestures of peace. What gesture would be more peaceful than prayer? I can pray begrudgingly for my persecutor. But even if I begrudge the task, I will actually have fulfilled the commandment to love. "You shall love" inevitably comes across as an empty, senseless injunction as long as we understand love [*l'amour*] as no more than an involuntary phenomenon, as a content of, and only of, affective consciousness. The injunction becomes, however, pregnant with meaning as soon as we understand "to love" ["*aimer*"] as "to will to love" ["*vouloir aimer*"], translated into behaviors that are not necessarily governed by our feelings in the sphere of immediacy. Thus, I do not pray for my enemy: I decide to pray for him, and this prayer is an act of love. Therefore, suddenly, we are proceeding to redefine love, and moreover to a redefinition to which attention has never, or at least rarely, been given. Love is defined ordinarily on its own terms, as the description of what the person who says that he loves feels. The love in question, when directed toward the enemy, in contrast, is defined outside of all feeling. It is a commanded love, which seems contradictory. Ordinarily love cannot be commanded. Enemy-love can only be commanded (even if, with regard to the enemy, it is not forbidden [by whom?] to feel compassion). Indeed, the commandment here has the character of a *mitzvah*. The law that imposes this *mitzvah* is certainly not a "messianic Torah" but a law that is more than messianic, exorbitant in relation to all known messianisms. "You shall love the Lord your God." In this case, the order is rational. The love in question in the law is always a love in acts: the treatise on love in Maimonides's *Mishneh Torah* speaks of little besides behaviors to adopt and never of religious feelings of love. Nevertheless, love of enemy, realized in prayer for the persecutor's well-being, differs from love of God insofar as the persecutor does not deserve our prayer. He certainly needs it: we must pray for the evil rather than the good. In any case, to pray, even in its most negligible form (to make a little time to address a few words to whoever asks us to pray), is a noteworthy sacrifice; and the act of sacrifice (a little of one's time, thus a little of oneself) must pass for an act of loving. As the believer loves the Lord his God, he loves his persecutor. Love appears then as an acting before being an affection [*patir*]. It may even be nothing but an acting in the absence of all corresponding feelings. This acting may not respect the entire commandment. It bears in itself, in any case, an authentic initiative of reconciliation and thus of the law's fulfillment [*accomplissement*].

Paradoxically, everything may appear easy as soon as we pass from the commandment to love without limit to the injunction that concludes the passage: "Be perfect therefore, as your Heavenly Father is perfect." Perfect, *teleios*, is an unremarkable, commonplace word. But the text echoes another challenging summation that says, in words placed in God's mouth, "be holy, for I, YHWH your God, am holy" (Lev. 19:1). This ancient text also contains an interdict against vengeance. Most of all, concluding a Jewish code of good behavior, it contains the injunction—that humanity could not possibly have invented—upon which the complete ethic of Israel stands or falls: "You shall love your neighbor as yourself" (understood all too often leniently, as if only Israelites were the neighbors of each Israelite). "Perfect," in Matthew's Greek text, need not be the translation of the Hebrew *kadosh*. Delitzsch uses *shalem*, to all appearances with good reason. Nevertheless "perfect," in a discourse addressed to Jews, certainly bears the connotations of holiness. The incredible has thus been stated (in Leviticus) and restated (in Matthew); in one case, the son of Israel, in the other the disciple of Jesus, are called not to just any kind of holiness (all cultures apprehend some type of holiness commensurate with their experience of the human and the sacred), but to divine holiness. We know—and we owe it to Schelling's powerful exposition in his time—that "holy" also means "separated." "Holy be your name": whoever makes this demand prays ipso facto that the name of God be elevated "above all names"—that is, that it be separated from all orders of nomination. Between the creator and the creature, at first there is nothing but rupture. Yet a point of contact also exists. Although the biblical text never provides an interpretation, it is said that from the beginning, a relation of "image" and of "resemblance" is established between the human and God. The church fathers will seek its interpretation. One key idea in their interpretation, a negation, is pertinent for us: the image and the resemblance are never rooted in a holiness proper to God that humanity would have shared from the beginning. The command given in Leviticus 19:1 thus exceeds that which was given at the origin. The speech given on the hill must be understood, thus, from this first excess [*débordement*]. Therefore that which the speech declares is not unprecedented [*inouï*]. The centuries that separated the two texts, in any case, do not take the edge off Jesus's words. Moreover, these words claim no predecessors; this should surprise us. The speech enters neither into a logic of anti-theses, in terms of an impossibility, nor into a logic of fulfillment. It states that which has already been stated, but does not confess its origins. There is more. The commandment passed on by Moses in Leviticus—an ancient commandment in relation to its reprise by Jesus—intervenes as an introduction to other commandments. In the same way, in Matthew, Jesus's restatement does not have the last word: chapters 6 and 7 follow, and are anything but appendices. Furthermore, Jesus will never return to this command (the gospel accounts, however, are but short summaries) and will reserve the name of the "greatest" and the "first" commandment for love of God and love of neighbor, considered together as a single injunction (Matt. 22:38–39). It is a New Testament *hapax legomenon* that does not acknowledge its origin in the Old Testament. Taking up Leviticus 19:1 again, in its own manner, the text proceeds to nothing but a revelation of the highest possibility offered to the human—to a revelation of man to himself.

The Second Epistle of Peter, a text that is likely more recent, can shed light on this revelation. The author assigns an exorbitant destiny to the community that is to receive his letter: the Christian is called, no more, no less, to partake of the divine nature. *Theias koinōnoi phuseōs* : the language is obviously different. We learn of a nature, *phusis*—a term that is absent in the gospels. Yet in saying that humanity can partake of divine *phusis*, it rejoins, without adopting the form of the commandment, that which is said by Moses and by Jesus. It is nearly incorrect to say that YHWH is holy. He is the Holy, frequently named the Holy One of Israel, the one that Israel is privileged to proclaim and know as holy. But to use another term from the Old Testament, the biblical passages of interest here speak of a God who is not "jealous" of his holiness or of his "nature." Second Peter 1:4 is at the origin of a concept of "divinization" or *theosis*. Eastern, Greek theology will use it abundantly, and Western Latin theology will not ignore it. To commune with the divine nature, to be holy as God is holy, thus to be perfect as he is perfect: the biblical text exceeds everything that Greece and Rome, which had a concept of human perfection, were ever able to think. With this argument, every possible parallel between pagan holiness and Jewish or Christian holiness loses its validity. Marcilio Ficino prayed to "saint Socrates": Christian humanism christianized paganism. Still, Socrates, if he was saintly, was not holy as God is. Paganism, on the other hand, in its popular practice, recognized that a man could accede to the status of God by the simple decision of a monarch. Origen, in his *Contra Celsus*, builds up a heap of sarcastic responses to the apotheosis by the Emperor Hadrian of his lover Antinous. Caesar could decree that after having been a young man, henceforth Antinous was a god. He could order the building of a temple and appoint a priesthood ("clergy") to look after his cult. But regardless of the powers of the "civil religion," the divinity recognized by the state was clearly not the divinity of the God of the philosophers. Moreover, as regards the god of the philosophers, whether Aristotle's or the god of Cleanthes's "Hymn to Zeus," no pagan thinker would have dared to say that man could partake of its nature. In his discourse on the Areopagus, Paul is capable of finding a pagan citation stating that gods and humans are "of the same race" (Acts 17:28). The quote from Aratos, however, speaks of that which humans are, and not of that which they are commanded or have the vocation to become. If Leviticus and then Matthew speak of a sanctification, which *Secunda Petri* designates without innovation as divinization, the matter at hand is not that of a fact. The son of Israel or the disciple of Jesus receives the order to be holy or perfect—to speak of holiness is to speak of perfection. The end of Christian life is the Christian's communion with the divine nature. Furthermore, this nature is that of the one who receives rather belatedly the name of the All Other and incontestably is Very Other. The provocation of our texts is therefore clear: in relation to his present humanity, let us say his factual humanity, the human being, has the vocation to become Very Other. Very Other: in sum, very other than oneself. Thus, there is more than an encouragement to convert, which would always run the risk of being understood in terms of a *way* of being. The brutal terms are those of being itself. Holiness, perfection, are divine names: as God is the Very Other—Augustine will call him *aliud valde*[6]—God is the Holy and the Perfect. Because he is Very Other, he appears to us as utterly imparticipable. The biblical texts contest this very claim: the human being can partake of the divine nature and therefore of the divinity of God.

Theological minds will resent the abrupt and nearly unbelievable character of this commandment. From Denys the Pseudo-Areopagite to Gregory Palamas and beyond, the following tactic will be adopted: asserting that God is "participable," but *amethktôs*, "imparticipably." This formula, owed to Denys, is a paradox that names a problem without resolving it. Still, some problems cannot be solved within history. . . . Palamas, in contrast, resolved the problem with the proposal of a distinction between "essence" (*ousia*) and "energies" or "activities" (*energeiai*). Humans, according to Palamas, can partake of the divine energies which are participable, and "divinization" consists in that participation. Of the divine essence, however, humans cannot partake—if they participated therein, it would be no longer divinization but apotheosis. This is a veritable solution and an elegant one. Objections nevertheless arise. The first comes from Latin theology, which reproaches Palamism for undermining divine simplicity—the most beautiful of the divine attributes, according to Thomas Aquinas. The second bears upon Palamas's theory's paternity in elaboration of Denys's *ametekhtos metekhetai*. Palamas, in fact, theorizes, whereas the Pseudo-Areopagite does nothing but indicate the limits of all theorizing. In theorizing, Palamas gives himself a perspective on God (and on divine incomprehensibility) whose legitimacy can be contested. He seeks to defend apophasis—but perhaps he says too much. Finally, the third objection will lead us back to the biblical text: it is neither the divine *ousia* nor an extra-essential divine aspect in which the author of the *Secunda Petri* gives us the mission to participate, but a *phusis* in which no distinction is established. Holiness and perfection: the texts from Leviticus and Matthew imply a duty to resemble God as God and not God in part. To be holy because YHWH is holy, beyond all Hellenistic conceptuality, to be perfect as the heavenly father is perfect, entails that there is no divine thing that this "because" and "as," taken literally as they require, set aside. Therefore, if we see in these commandments an over-determination, on the order of the precept, of the image and of the resemblance in question in Genesis, then we must conclude that "perfection" and "holiness," in their proper nomological order, are the ultimate content of a relation of resemblance given in the beginning. The Greek fathers traditionally distinguished between the image and the resemblance: the image would have been given at the beginning, and the resemblance would be an eschatological gift. The human is in the image of God, either as bearer of the logos, as the one who is also endowed with an incomprehensibility, or also, in recent theology, as a being of relation [*être de relation*]. Would "resemblance," then, not have to be thought also in terms of participation in divine holiness or, in a concept late to appear in the Bible, in the "divine nature"? Factually speaking, we are not holy. A prescription is not a description. The nomological is not the factual. The commandment of perfection is addressed to imperfect creatures (to whom else could it be addressed?). We are not divinized in the present of our experience. But we—children of Israel or disciples of Jesus, and not utterly other [*tout autre*] than God, but molded in God's image—have the vocation to be gods by "participation."

But now, we must take a necessary step back. What is man? And what does he do if called to the same holiness that defines the being of God? He is, in fact, he is *only* the one who carries out commandments that may appear excessive—at least in relation to the law or the moral laws—and whose ability to render us divine really may look unfathomable. To lend to whoever asks is a good maxim, even if it carries a certain risk. Giving of one's time is an excellent thing. To override that which reason demands of us possesses its own rationality, that of the supererogatory. But upon engaging in the logic of the supererogatory, are we thereby close to a perfection equal to God's? Such a proposition seems derisory. The Sermon on the Mount puts forth more than wisdom. As such, it could dispense with the communication of a commandment of divine perfection that we perceive as incommensurate with the previously imparted commandments. Can the call to be perfect as God is perfect consist in no more than giving one's tunic in addition to one's coat? Does doing more than the pagans do put on the way of a holiness partaking of God's holiness? The comparison of the codes—that of Leviticus and that of the Sermon on the Mount—and of their central precept leads to an intellectual scandal. Incontestably, the code demands much. To carry out the precepts of the law of Moses or of the law of Christ makes it possible, if we can believe Origen, for us to lead an authentically "philosophical" life. Yet from the philosophical life to holiness, understood as participation in divine holiness, there is more than one step to take; there is an abyss. Can this abyss be crossed? These texts leave us without a response or rather do not offer a response and charge us with offering one. Holiness is that which separates God from the non-God. Divine perfection is incommensurate with human perfection—and when we attempt a definition of human holiness (which began when the Roman Church, in the tenth century under Pope John XV, started regulating the appointment of the title "saint"), we are not often speaking truly of perfection. The Roman Church, in its canonical documents, never states that the saint has communion with the divine nature. It says that he carried out the commandments, that he understood the counsels and followed them, that he led a heroically virtuous life, and so on. But it never asserts that he has been perfect as God himself is perfect or that from now on he is perfect as God himself is perfect. Caution (perhaps involuntary) is understood easily. The believer is righteous "and a sinner," and sin has no place in a life led in the image of divine holiness. Certainly we have heard that "man infinitely surpasses man."[7] But when we question the short texts that we are reading and ask how man surpasses man, we are sent back to a more-than-wisdom, assuredly, to a folly, but to nothing that clearly and distinctly reflects divine holiness: every resemblance necessarily sends us back to an even greater dissimilarity.

One matter that we already explored remains for reconsideration: this love of enemies, which we too quickly (albeit deliberately) reduced to a nearly facile practice of prayer for the enemy. We must *will* to love our enemies, with a willing as great as their enmity, because spontaneously we do not allow ourselves such love: only an *askesis* would render it possible. Must we, however, simply content ourselves with willing and acting—in this case, to enact the gestures of prayer? Love of enemies, insofar as they have been enemies, is proved by a gesture—by the crucified Jesus's prayer for his executioners. The duty to forgive is inscribed in a modest form (the remission of debts) in the prayer entrusted to the disciples in the next chapter of the Sermon on the Mount. Nevertheless, is forgiving in this way precisely to love? Also, does the experience of the one who loves find its unique paradigm in the performance, in the "doing"? At this point, we can contest this sort of claim in light of the double prescription of divine holiness and perfection. We could say that God is "pure act of being," but that consists in saying at most that in God nothing is in the modality of possibility. We certainly could go further if we pushed to its final conclusion the equation of divine love and being (in which case God would be said to be "pure act of loving" and even "love itself subsisting") by including in divine *agape* that which the scriptures of Israel command us to include—that is, the divine "bowels." Divine love is merciful. God is logos, he is spirit; yet it must also be said that he has a "heart." When Nicolas Cabasilas speaks of God's "foolish love" [*amour fou*] for man, *manikos erōs*,[8] he is not speaking first of God's behavior (even if, upon consideration of the events of Good Friday, it is incontestably foolish), but definitively of that which we must (and we will dare to utter the word) name: divine affectivity. God acts and does not suffer. But insofar as God loves, or better, insofar as he *is* the lover [*l'amant*], since there is only place for his love, God affects himself in the love that he bears toward his creatures. To speak of divine autoaffection will permit us at least not to attack divine impassibility. On this basis, we can assert calmly that the holiness and perfection of God cannot be disassociated from his love and that love of enemies—the test of the Christian life according to Silouan the Athonite— implies not only our doing but also our feeling [*notre sentir*]. How do we love our enemies? Now we can respond that the precept would lack meaning if it were not possible to carry it out. In addition, we would not know exactly what loving would mean if we loved none but our friends—that is, if we did that which the tax collectors themselves know how to do

(Matt. 5:46), following the wisdom of the world. Matthew says nothing of a communion with the divine *phusis*, but more modestly, of the filial rank that the disciple will receive by observing the commandment. In any case, he clearly states that God's love makes no exceptions (as in Matt. 22:16ff), and that if his rain falls on the unjust as well as the just, the former as well as the latter are recipients of one and the same love. To be holy as God is holy, to love as God loves: this incredible commandment certainly is not more achievable after probing its logic. Yet have we come to full knowledge of its logic?

A word was missing in Matthew's text that we find in Luke's parallel text, the "Sermon on the Plain." Luke may have abridged Matthew's text, or he may have used another source. As in Matthew's sermon, love of enemies is the first calling. Yet another calling accompanies it: "Be merciful as your Father is merciful" (Luke 6:36). As mercy enters the scene, with the duty of *oiktirmōn*, the shift from doing to affection is executed without nuance. The Father is merciful. As he is the Holy One, so he is the Merciful One. The Greek term, contrary to the Latin term that we use (*miseri-cordia*), does not name the heart. But clearly it connotes the heart. There are "works of mercy": clothe the naked, visit the sick or the prisoner. We can understand them, however, uniquely by inscribing them within the logic of a heart filled with pity [*apitoyé*]. The merciful individual has pity on his brother. From pity to love, no step must be taken: pity is to act lovingly. Here, action and compassion overlap to the point of agreeing completely the one with the other. Mercy first goes out to the enemy. It performs the good and does so in love—*agape*. And if it "does" as much as it feels, our task is to understand that the order of doing (*agathopoieite*, Luke 6:35) is inseparable from that of feeling. Matthew compares the behavior of the disciple to that of the tax collector; Luke compares it to the behavior of the sinner in general. The disciple must do more than the sinner (his vocation to holiness, in negative terms, is the vocation to be a non-sinner). That which the sinners concede to other sinners is not annulled (my friend is also a neighbor among all neighbors), but it is certainly exceeded. The prescribed conduct, to show mercy, will make of the one who adopts it a "son of the Most High"—less than a saint in the image of the Saint, if we stick to the letter, but a merciful son in the image of the merciful Father, which thus takes us far enough into Matthew and Leviticus. To do more is thus identical to loving. Love of enemies is concrete. I have things to forgive, and cannot do so if gestures of reconciliation—for example, an outstretched hand—do not take place. These gestures, however, put the affections into play as much as the actions. Therefore, to assert that I must love my enemy as I love my brother is not unreasonable [*interdit*]. In addition, the enemy is near, as close to me as my brother—any notion of a proximity limited to the community of the children of Israel explodes into a myriad of pieces.

We have nearly come full circle. The commandment to love my enemy required, in a first reading, to be concretized: to love is first to pray for the enemy (and without a doubt it may come to pass that that is the best one can do). Nevertheless, the experience of loving only and truly unfolds within an apparently illogical logic—illogical because it is non-Greek—wherein divine holiness and divine mercy are given to us to share as a vocation. The enemy, in the Greek and Roman world, might run up against my impassibility—for example, in Stoicism, where nothing from the exterior can affect the philosopher. In contrast, the enemy in the Judeo-Christian world incontestably affects us: his enmity is a source of pathos. Yet, faced with this affection, the recourse to a commandment that in Greece would appear in all ways as immoderate [*démesuré*], as *hubris*, does not offer us just any solution to our existential and theoretical pain, but is the only possible solution. Here and now—before the formulation of the commandment—I do not love my enemy who presents himself to me with the unique quality of being "odious." But once the commandment to be merciful has been formulated, then the pity to which the enemy must inspire us is the only possibility. Since Socrates, we have known that he who commits an unjust act is to be pitied more than he who suffers it. We learn more, however, when love of enemy is bound to divine perfection, mercy, and holiness. Then the enemy appears as the one whom God loves. In other words, as the object of God's mercy, he is God's friend. Nothing indicates that by loving him, I will compel him to love me, for love relations are not necessarily reciprocal. Still, that is without much significance. When Luke tells us, "Give and it will be given unto you," he does not say that it will be given to us by those to whom we have given. The gift of which he speaks, the one that I will receive, is on the contrary, a gift incommensurable with mine. Indeed, the "overflowing" measure will be poured out upon us all the more certainly by God. It will be poured out, in any case, because we will have given, if not with "all our heart," at least through a gift born in our heart as much and even more than in our will. And the dissymmetry between the gift I give and the gift I receive indicates that whoever hears the command to show mercy (as we are told to do) as—*kathōs*—our Father, cannot consider himself prescribed to act with a properly divine omnipotence. The human individual's mission is to be holy, but not to be the Holy One, to be merciful, but not to be the Merciful One. Every vocation, certainly historical and probably eschatological, encounters its limit here: I am called to communion with the divine nature, but God alone is God, and

God alone will remain God. Our gift will be always imperfect or partial. The fact remains that, insofar as we remain faithful to the commandments, it is our very selves that we will give when we love the enemy. After all, forgiveness effaces the identity of the enemy. Already the simple words "I forgive you" have the value of performatives. When they have been uttered, the enemy has ceased to be an enemy. But what then does he become? He does not become a friend. In the logic of the gospel, he becomes again a "neighbor" equal to a "brother." His quality of neighborliness was but only that of the one who was manifesting his ill will toward me. Now it is that of the one to whom I have manifested good will (in forgiving) and to whom I am required to manifest my good will again and again—since he is no longer anyone but my brother. Love resides in forgiveness; it is proved also after forgiveness. If the text is mute on this matter, an observation deserves to be made: whoever hears the command to be merciful has already been the object of divine mercy. We must forgive because we have been forgiven—not by an enemy but by a divine friend.

The one who forgives does what he can. We do not dispose of complete authority over the life of our hearts. Yet God is not first God and only afterward merciful: mercy is what God is, on equal footing with love. "Be holy," "be merciful"—the absolute future in terms of *theōsis*, of course, can only be heard by and is only possible for a believer. Moreover, the horizon opened by the commandments of the Sermon on the Mount and the Sermon on the Plain are perceptible only by the one who sees those commandments fulfilled in the person of the man who comes from God—the Son—and probably in him alone. To speak of holiness, of perfection, of divinization, is to speak, at one and the same time, of the condition of the disciple as *imitator morum Dei in Christo*. Love of enemies is achievable [*realiser*], or nearly achievable, in the earthly city: after all, many have lived it out. In fact, it can only be achieved in this city where everyone is not a friend or a fortiori a brother. Attending to the commandment is thus not to be put off until tomorrow and has no eschatological future: it is pertinent only in history, in the place where we have enemies. On the other hand, the command was fulfilled [*realisé*] by Jesus during the period that led to his death. Let us admit, then, that it takes place in an interval, in an "in-between" [*entre-deux*]. The deified man has no enemies to love, since he loves all people equally. The sinner or the tax collector, stereotypical figures, greets none but his friends and believes he is authorized by popular wisdom to hate his enemies (the law does not authorize this behavior, but neither does it explicitly forbid it). Jesus's words, therefore, rejoin the disciple in his present condition. This condition is an interim in which there remains a place for commandments, thus for an ethos (appropriate at once for the contemporary disciple and for believers in following generations), a condition that is not eschatological. Further along in the discourse (Matt. 6:9–10), Jesus formulates three demands, generally called "eschatological." The disciple must pray for the sanctification of God's name, for the coming of the reign, and for God's will to be done. If these commandments are called eschatological, the reason is simple, although every commentator does not clearly state it: the disciple lives in a world where God's name is not sanctified, where his reign has not yet come, and where his will is not done. God's reign is near when Jesus speaks, but it is not yet realized. When this reign is realized, however, prescriptions will be unnecessary and useless, since all citizens of the kingdom will be holy. Jesus's words are addressed to sinners for whom they open a pathway—only and strictly in this sense can we say that Jesus, who is not a rabbi, participates in his way in the play of *halakha*. The command to forgive thus tells us: first, where we are (in a world where friends and enemies live side by side); second, how we can love in this world, in light of whom we are to become, by seeking reconciliation of all with all; and finally, where we are going, toward a city where legislating will be unnecessary, since the law, more than being inscribed on the hearts of the children of Israel, will be fulfilled and will have purely and simply disappeared.

Love of enemies, excess of the gift—these ways of conducting oneself belong neither to the kingdom, where there will no longer be enemies, nor to the world, where the *hostis* will always be present at the borders of the city and where the *inimicus* also will never be absent. Nevertheless, these behaviors affirm the desire for the eschatological peace of which the world can shelter no more than pale sketches. Still, those who hear these demands are the disciples—they are even the church, *ekklesia*, which Matthew alone among the gospel writers names (Matt. 16:18, 18:17). Might this church count as an eschatological anticipation? The discourses clearly affirm it, but do so by assigning concrete tasks to be carried out in the world. God's reign is near, *eggus*, but it is not in any way more than near. The world is not transfigured when Jesus, candidate messiah and more than messiah, speaks. Enemies exist. We can turn them into brothers (though the passage does not say so) if we approach them with the force of forgiveness, but we know that resentment is as present in the world as forgiveness. The economy is not abolished in these messianic or pre-messianic times: some seek loans, and the disciple is invited to give according to their requests. Thus, the life that is put forward for the disciple as a task—of course, the term is absent—is the Christian life. As such, it can but proceed to the critique of all life led within the strict limits of the world, even if it were led wisely. Our incapacity to forgive from the "depths of the heart" will remind us always that belief alone is insufficient in order to be holy in the image of the Holy. Our difficulty in giving will remind us all the more. The last word, however, belongs to the spoken words of blessing that open the Sermon on the Mount. Certainly these words, as those pronounced in the synagogue at Capernaum, are "hard"—*sklera* (John 6:60)—to hear and understand, as the audience indeed asked, "who can understand them?" The response is simple: only those who are not content to seek happiness (*eudaimonia*, a term missing in the New Testament) and accept the difficult logic that makes men "blessed," *makarios*, can hear and understand them. Love of enemy is to be heard as a word of beatitude and as a way of beatitude or blessedness. This speech may be the royal road that leads through the Sermon on the Mount and beyond. And it reveals humanity by starting from its future—we would not need it if we were satisfied to know who we are in the limits of our present.

Translated by Reuben Glick-Shank

Notes

1. The French "*parole*" has no exact equivalent in English. It can denote the notion of a speech—whether actually qua spoken discourse or essentially qua verbal-ness of a discourse, written or spoken, as a speaking—as well as the notion of words or a word given—whether as locutionary and illocutionary content or yet as perlocutionary, performative effect. In light of the "speech" character of the Sermon on the Mount, I will generally translate "*parole*" as speech but will indicate where it appears and will sometimes translate it as "word" when the context in English demands it.

2. Translator's note: *surplomber* means "to overhang," as in being on the edge of a cliff or a rocky outcropping but in a secure place, looking down over a valley—that is, to overshadow, loom over, dominate.

3. See Anthony E. Harvey, *Jesus and the Constraints of History* (Philadelphia: Westminister John Knox, 1982).

4. Translator's note: In the following paragraphs, I will consistently translate "*follement*" and "*fou*" as foolishly, foolish, or fool, as they lead to the English term "fool in Christ." But in French, "*fou*" does not distinguish between the English notions of foolish, mad, and crazy.

5. Hermann Leberecht Strack and Paul Billerbeck, *Kommentar zum neuen Testament aus Talmud und Midrasch* VI, Part 1 (Munich: C. H. Beck, 1922), 353, are in fact incapable of finding any parallel and speak of a "popular maxim according to which the average Jew at Jesus' time ordered his behavior toward his friend and his enemi."

6. We should add that Augustine implicitly refuses to create a concept of God as "wholly other" in this passage (*Confessions* 11:9:1), even if Rudolf Otto, *Das Heilige* (Munich: Beck, 1963), 32, makes much of it. Augustine feels the

fear aroused in the man who senses his non-resemblance to God. But he also "burns" to feel and know himself as resembling God. God is not an *aliud valde*; and whoever says *aliud valde* does not mean "all other."

7. Blaise Pascal, *Pensées*, in *Oeuvres complètes*, ed. Jacques Chevalier (Paris: Gallimard, 1954), 1206 (no. 438).

8. Nicolas Cabasilas, *La vie en Christ*, ed. Marie-Hélène Congourdeau (Paris: Cerf, 1990), 6:16.

The Manifestation of the Father
On Luke 15:11–32

KEVIN HART

I

It is the most prominent of Jesus's parables: Christianity itself, one might almost say. So familiar is it that it is known almost before it is read. There have been innumerable glosses on it, from Tertullian and Clement of Alexandria to Elizabeth Bishop's retelling of the story in her two sonnets, "The Prodigal."[1] Augustine's *Confessions* is a spectacular elaboration of it, as is a part of the fourth volume of Karl Barth's *Church Dogmatics*.[2] There have been endless sermons and commentaries on it, both popular and scholarly;[3] and we think too of paintings of the prodigal among the pigs (Dürer) and the scene of reconciliation with the father (Guercino and Rembrandt), along with George Balanchine's ballet *The Prodigal Son* (1934), based on Prokofiev's music, itself inspired by the parable, and Benjamin Britten's opera *The Prodigal Son* (1968), along with other literary works that respond to it.[4] Some of these, like Gide's and Rilke's, inhabit the story so fully and so powerfully as to make it change direction.[5] Literature aside, it seems that after so much exegesis the hard work of reading has already been done for us and that all we have to do is receive the truths that come from the story. So the parable appears to stand completely in a light that illumines its every detail and to revolve of its own accord for our inspection, leaving no facet unseen. We read the parable in church, in a seminar, or at home, and say almost automatically "Forgiveness," "Atonement," "Conversion," "Compassion," or "Sinners and Pharisees," even "*Exitus-Reditus*," among many other expressions, all of which have been made available to us by millennia of allegorizing or theologizing that translate the parable into moral or soteriological terms, by centuries of psychological speculation on the relations of the father and his two sons, on parental indulgence and sibling rivalry, and by decades of withering historical-critical analysis.

Could it be, though, that this of all the parables of Jesus has not yet been made fully manifest, that parts of it remain hidden in a darkness to which we are so habituated that we cannot even make it out, and that the parable needs to be nudged a little to reveal itself? It seems unlikely, but then again this is a parable that for all its centrality to Christianity has been slanted to misinterpretation for generation upon generation, being called the parable of the "prodigal son," which is only one aspect of the story. The tradition begins in the early church, though it is heavily marked in the Reformation. Textually, the two words are found in sixteenth-century editions of the Vulgate and may be found also in editions of the Breeches Bible later in the same century. The side-note in scripture reads, *De filio prodigo ad patrem reverso*. The French speak of *le fils prodigue*, while the Germans talk of *der verlorene Sohn*, which fits in with the Lukan parables of the lost sheep and the lost coin. It should be noted, though, that the tradition has also stressed another aspect by way of allegory: the duality of the two sons, taking them mostly to represent Gentiles and Jews. That tradition begins with Tertullian, although the exegeses of Jerome, Ambrose, and Augustine are more authoritative, as the *Glossa ordinaria* confirms. Jerome and Ambrose also allow for another reading—the so called "penitential reading"—in which the younger son is the repentant sinner and the elder son the self-righteous Christian, and Chrysostom joins them in this interpretation.[6] Other dualities emerge later: Spirit and Body (Gottfried of Admont) and the Active Life and the Contemplative Life (Hugh of St. Cher), among other doublets.[7] For some exegetes, the younger son is prized over the elder, while for others—Bonaventure, for example—both brothers have significant flaws that make stark moral and spiritual discriminations between them hard to substantiate.[8]

Yet more recent, closer readings have shown what now seems very clear: that while the story turns on two sons, the father is the central character.[9] So perhaps we now know what is being told to us in this story; and yet perhaps we still do not feel the pressure and the texture of the "how" behind the "what": not the formal poetics of the narrative so much as how the phenomena give themselves and how they are received. How does the father manifest himself? How do his sons receive what he gives them? How do the two sons seek to live their lives? How does each son let death into his life in his own way? In order to pass from the "what" to the "how" we must pass beyond the historical-critical method and read the parable as though for the first time. What is silent must be heard (or its silence brought forward); what is hidden must be seen. And so we open up the Gospel of Luke and begin to read:

And he said, "There was a man who had two sons; and the younger of them said to his father, 'Father, give me the share of property that falls to me.' And he divided his living between them. Not many days later, the younger son gathered all he had and took his journey into a far country, and there he squandered his property in loose living. And when he had spent everything, a great famine arose in that country, and he began to be in want. So he went and joined himself to one of the citizens of that country, who sent him into his fields to feed swine. And he would gladly have fed on the pods that the swine ate; and no one gave him anything. But when he came to himself he said, 'How many of my father's hired servants have bread enough and to spare, but I perish here with hunger! I will arise and go to my father, and I will say to him, "Father, I have sinned against heaven and before you; I am no longer worthy to be called your son; treat me as one of your hired servants."' And he arose and came to his father. But while he was yet at a distance, his father saw him and had compassion, and ran and embraced him and kissed him. And the son said to him, 'Father, I have sinned against heaven and before you; I am no longer worthy to be called your son.' But the father said to his servants, 'Bring quickly the best robe, and put it on him; and put a ring on his hand, and shoes on his feet; and bring the fatted calf and kill it, and let us eat and make merry; for this my son was dead, and is alive again; he was lost, and is found.' And they began to make merry. Now his elder son was in the field; and as he came and drew near to the house, he heard music and dancing. And he called one of the servants and asked what this meant. And he said to him, 'Your brother has come, and your father has killed the fatted calf, because he has received him safe and sound.' But he was angry and refused to go in. His father came out and entreated him, but he answered his father, 'Lo, these many years I have served you, and I never disobeyed your command; yet you never gave me a kid, that I might make merry with my friends. But when this son of yours came, who has devoured your living with harlots, you killed for him the fatted calf!' And he said to him, 'Son, you are always with me, and all that is mine is yours. It was fitting to make merry and be glad, for this your brother was dead, and is alive; he was lost, and is found.'"

While still in the aura of this astonishing text, I recall some points about it in order to have them acknowledged before I put them to one side. The parable is told just the once in the New Testament, in the Gospel of Luke, and before it begins we see publicans and sinners approaching Jesus, with the Pharisees murmuring that this strange rabbi from Galilee consorts with sinners. Since the parable is told in only the one version, it does not embroil us in the anxieties of transmission analysis, though it makes us wonder if it comes from a source outside Luke, in the hypothetical document that scholars call "L," or if it comes entirely from the author we call Luke or from another follower of Jesus rather than from Jesus himself.[10] How the parable came to be in Luke and only there cannot now be answered, unless someone discovers other versions of the parable in papyri long hidden in desert caves. Similarly, how the parable intersects with the group of parables in Luke 15, or with narratives in other religious texts, such as other rabbinic parables, or a story in the *Saddharmapundarika Sutra*, better known as the *Lotus Sutra*, cannot be our concern here.[11] Nor can how Islamic thinkers have used the parable to criticize Christianity as falling away from its authentic vision of God's mercy into messianic confusion and idolatry.[12] Perhaps the parable opens paths from Christianity to other religions, Judaism and Buddhism in particular, and so offers us ways of seeing that the outside of Christianity is not entirely separate from it. Perhaps it allows us to see how we deviate from our own faith. My concern is rather with a "how" at the heart of the parable itself, a double "how," in fact—how God is and how we relate to him—which we find by reading this parable about the manifestation of fatherhood to two apparently quite different sons.

II

"There was a man" [Ἄνθρωπός τις], Luke's Jesus begins, and with those words the world of work and commercial exchange is bracketed for a while. Those who first heard the story belonged to a culture of storytelling in which oral narrative is a vehicle of wisdom as well as pleasure. On agreeing to listen to or read the parable, one is led from one's own situation in life, whatever it may be, to an essential meditation on being human that will encompass the lives of any audience members, each in a singular manner. One is not led outside all circuits of exchange, though, for something can be given back to Luke's Jesus: attention, of course, but also acceptance or rejection of what he has to say, which implies a shift of perspective on how to live from now on.

At first we know very little about the man in the parable: only that he has property, οὐσία, and two sons. We hear of one son right away and anticipate hearing of the other. When we first see the man, he is passive; his younger son has asked something of him, and we hear nothing of their conversation or what precedes it. Pauses in conversation are sometimes called "accountable silence," but here, in this exemplary story, there are unaccountable silences: what the father presumably says to the son would be important, yet is passed over, and we hear nothing of what the mother says.[13] So familiar is the story and so quickly does it move that we can miss the fact that the narrator neither lets us see nor lets us hear the mother. Not that one would expect to see or hear a woman in the story. In a first-century Semitic family the father is predominant by virtue of being the legal and spiritual head of the household, with the eldest son being next in the line of authority; and yet one needs to stress that we see no mother because the parable is about fatherhood—finally about God as father—and among the parents the focus must be exclusively on the figure of the father for the story to work as parable. Could it be otherwise? Only if the parable came from another culture and another time: as it stands, it is a story that exhibits a wholly male world, except, of course, for the allusion to harlots.[14] But not an entirely symmetrical world, for here, as everywhere, the relation between father and son is asymmetrical. The father gives life to his sons, and the sons cannot return the gift of life. They can give love, respect, annoyance, sorrow, even death to the father, but never life.

What we hear from the younger son is disconcerting. He says, "Father, give me [δός μοι] the share of property [οὐσία] that falls to me." The son is not eliciting a gift, strictly speaking, so much as implying that he wishes no longer to participate in the free circulation of life on the farm as gift. He requests both his share of the property and the right of disposal. It has been argued that the son's request is perfectly reasonable and that he has done nothing blameworthy in making it. In Jesus's day, a time of great hardship, people migrated in order to do better elsewhere.[15] Torah is clear that property usually must be distributed to sons at the death of the father (Num. 27:8–11, 36:7–9; Deut. 21:15–17), although it may be settled beforehand by deed of gift. Yet Sirach 33:20–24 suggests that it is not prudent to do so, and even a gift is not usually to be realized until the death of the donor. That the son asks both for his portion and for it to be realized now amounts to a silent allusion to the death of the father. It is as though the father silently hears, "You might as well be dead as far as I am concerned." The son wants the money immediately in order to go to the "far country," presumably a Gentile land where he will be well away from his father's watchful eyes and where (as he may not fully grasp) it will be almost impossible to remain ritually pure. Were the son's request of the father morally neutral, the dramatic structure of the narrative would fall apart. It would be hard to see why the father is not completely surprised by the boy's admission on his return of having done anything so very wrong. Of course, the father would see when running to the child that he was in a bad way but may well think that he had been robbed and beaten on the way home. All the boy would have done, so far as the father knew for sure when running to him, is to have left in order to have a better chance in life: a regrettable but understandable decision. Instead, the father accepts that the returned boy has indeed "sinned against heaven" and against his parent, against Father and father, without knowing anything about him squandering his portion, and guessing from his condition that he must be impure. He may have boils, he may have had contact with corpses (and, as we know, pigs), and he would not have been able to keep kosher.[16]

We might take the elder son when he vents to his father to imply that his brother has "disobeyed" the father's command, which would presumably be not to leave home, diminish the value of the family property, and risk impurity. The status of the story of the younger son wasting his portion is unclear: *we* know that it has happened, but what exactly does the family know of it? Has the father heard of it before the return of the son? Has the brother? And how reliable is the information they would have heard from the "far country"? It could be that the father simply sees the son, now destitute, and puts two and two together on the spot. The son has not been robbed and beaten but has returned penniless. His sin has been the impetuous request that insults the father and breaks the law, doubtless compounded (as the father would instantly recognize on seeing him) by grievous mistakes made in the far country. The brother may earlier have heard gossip from people who traveled to the far country; far more likely, he may have been told only now by the servant boy what all the servants and locals instantly recognized—the younger son is back and indigent—and in his anger at the father's throwing of a party put two and two together and got five. I shall return to this. The main point I wish to make now, however, is that in venturing his request the younger son anticipates two things that are materially distinct though bound together by the one event of death, the realization of his inheritance and the father's demise. Actually, he does not ask for his "inheritance" [κληρονομία], a word the evangelist uses elsewhere in the gospel (Luke 12:13, for example), which would imply a responsibility for it, but only for what falls to him, his share [μέρος] of the οὐσία, as so many possessions the value of which can be realized. He already shares in the property he desires because he is a member of the family, enjoying his father's "living" [βίος]. In asking for what will be his, the younger son refuses to see the property as an invisible gift that he already receives but solely as so much visible material that can be cashed in and possessed individually.[17]

Does the younger son wish to migrate for economic reasons, or does he wish to leave because he cannot bear working the farm at home, now and forever? We do not know. We might say without too much speculation, though, that he wants freely to try life himself now, to have his future begin now, whether because for him life must lived to the limit in the present or because (it is the same point but seen from behind), young as he is, he anticipates his own death and wishes to live fully before dying. To block *his* death by living to the hilt now, the younger son must first mark his *father's* death. Certainly we see the father as injured. We expect him to beat this ungrateful child and hear him say harsh things to him. Because we neither see nor hear anything of the sort, do we also regard him as foolish, not maintaining his rightful preeminence in the family? Sirach 33:20–22 would incline us to do so. For us moderns, it is hard not to let the image of King Lear or Père Goriot pass through the mind, though in doing so we risk making a hasty induction.[18] The narrative is so sparing of details that we have little traction for any speculation as to character or motive. We are reading a first-century parable, not a Renaissance tragedy or nineteenth-century novel. Besides, the father may permit the younger son to have what he asks for while not countenancing it to the slightest degree. And that may be a sign of wisdom and love.

In acceding to the request of the younger son, the father must also distribute property to the elder son but without right of disposal. He too no longer receives the οὐσία fully as gift. The property would be divided unequally, as Torah requires, the elder son receiving two-thirds of the whole (Deut. 21:17). No mention is made of the elder son's response to this, and no mention is made of any conversation about the impending request between the two sons. There should have been a conversation; it would have been the elder son's duty to protect the father from insult from the younger son, and—once the insult had been given—to reconcile the son to the father. Perhaps the elder son has coolly anticipated coming into his share of the farm sooner rather than later through the action of his brother. Equally, he may feel that responsibility has settled on his shoulders too quickly, thanks to his brother: his life has run toward him, taking away his youth. There may have been a rift between the two sons; it would be an impetus for the younger son to act as he does and for the elder son to be silent. At any rate, the younger son gathers up his goods in only a few days: his animals and coats, some shekels, no doubt, and—given his destination—Greek and Roman coins. So quick he is to leave the family, the community, and the land of Israel, that he does not take enough time to get the full value of his inheritance. His father and brother are left with less of the farm than the family had before, certainly with less disposable property, and with the gnawing sense that it has been sold off cheaply. This boy is impossible! He passes more than one limit before finally going into "a far country," a Gentile land, and so seeks unknown possibilities. He believes that life is elsewhere and that it is now to be given to him in abundance. He does not see that he is not only breaking his link with the family but also shattering the normal rhythm of family life: he keeps nothing for the future, for looking after his father, for the family he will have in years to come, and for himself as head of that family. Rather, being young and thoughtless, he "squandered his property in loose living" [διεσκόρπισεν τὴν οὐσίαν αὐτοῦ ζῶν ἀσώτως]. Meanwhile, the elder son, economist *par excellence*, stays home, living out tried possibilities, having been thrown into the midst of life with all its cares by the younger son's thoughtless death wish for the father.

Jesus's narrative is relentless; it is a machine that has been wound up very tightly and uncoils rapidly. Two bad things happen, one right after the other: "And when he had spent everything, a great famine arose in that country, and he began to be in want." Death, which has appeared until now only as a qualitative limit, something linked to property rights, begins to appear as a quantitative limit for him here and now. Without resources, and especially without family, community, and the protection of the Lord God, the young man is in grave trouble. Still, he does not go home. In a great famine it would be impossible for him to avoid contact with corpses. He receives the possibility of death but differently from before; he now seeks work, for he has no choice in the matter, and certainly the Gentile to whom he has attached himself does all he can to shake off this clinging Jewish boy. The job assigned to him is offensive, as the master would have known full well: the lad must look after pigs and—so dire is his condition—he even wishes to eat the carob pods that comprise their food in this bad time. According to Talmud, he is cursed because he has become impure.[19] According to everyday knowledge of farm life, were he to venture to take the pigs' food, the swine would maul him. His boon companions have abandoned him, and he is cut off from family and community by his own decision. Marking his father's death has led, before very long at all, to the bringing closer of his own death: "I perish here with hunger!" [ἐγὼ δὲ λιμῷ ἀπόλλυμαι]. It is just then, when death presses hard, that we are told that he "came to himself" [εἰς ἑαυτὸν δὲ ἐλθὼν], or, as we would say, he came to his senses or woke up to himself. He must get close to death before he acknowledges his mistake and returns home. This is hardly a scene of ideal repentance. When he says to himself, "I will arise and go to my father," for how long has he realized that he had done wrong, not merely gotten into a bad way? His decision seems more pragmatic than moral. Now, though, he wants to live, not just to recover his health but also to live in the right way. This does not mean, as he readily accepts, that he can live in relative comfort as he once did, but it does mean that he can live within the circle of his family and community, even if considerably further from the center than before.

How the son comes to himself is given to us in overhearing his interior voice. (He comes fully to himself by dividing himself into speaker and hearer.) He rehearses to himself what he will say when he shakes off this uncaring master to whom he has no real connection and returns home: "Father, I have sinned against heaven and before you; I am no longer worthy to be called your son; treat me as one of your hired servants." There is acknowledgment of sin, but no clear statement of repentance. He may be decrying his own stupidity as much as expressing remorse. Yet the son sees the father in anticipation, and the imagined speech to him begins appropriately; it acknowledges his fault before God as well as before his father. He is, after all, enjoined by Torah to honor his mother and his father (Exod. 20:12) and to look after his father in his old age (Sir. 3:12), things he had forgotten or pushed aside, and we remember the rest of the verse from Exodus: "that your days may be long in the land which the Lord your God gives you." Yet the lad has so far only come to *his* senses, not to his *father's* senses. Having started by thinking primarily about property and money, he still sees the world in terms of value that can be nicely calibrated: "I am no longer worthy" [οὐκέτι εἰμὶ ἄξιος], as though being a son is only a matter of corresponding to a particular value in a culture carefully indexed to honor and shame. On the long trip home from the "far country," the lad still thinks of himself as impure and unworthy, as having devalued himself, especially in the eyes of God and his father.[20] (No mention is made of the brother. It is still the *father's* farm, the boy knows full well.) The new, lower relation should be of himself as servant and his father as master. All this time the son is absent from the father, or rather, as we learn from the story, the son is still cared for, present to the father in the mode of hope, of anticipation of a final homecoming. The son anticipates the father as a master; the father anticipates the son as son. "But while he was yet at a distance [δὲ αὐτοῦ μακρὰν ἀπέχοντος], his father saw him." This could be a chance observation, a momentary glance at the dusty plain, although the parable is an exemplary narrative, not a realist story, and the stronger reading is of the father always having an eye on the horizon since the son left because he is, after all, a father. His love is invisible and silent for most of the parable.

The parable reaches its first climax with the scene of how the father's invisible, silent love becomes visible and vocal, how the younger son is received: the father runs to him, breaking all expectations of proper, dignified behavior. Why does he do this? Because he "had compassion" [ἐσπλαγχνίσθη]: a rare thing for human beings, according to the New Testament, and one commended by the evangelist (see Luke 1:78, 10:33). In the unforeseen embrace of his father, the son cannot reach the end of his rehearsed speech, which he has otherwise got nearly word-perfect. He cannot get to say, "treat me as one of your hired servants," and thereby renegotiate a different relationship with the father. As soon as the father hears the words "no longer worthy to be called your son," he interrupts the boy. Once again, there is no conversation, not because nothing is reported but because the father is too overcome by emotion to speak directly to his son. He turns from the son and speaks to those who *are* servants. Once the father was passive and the younger son active; now the roles are reversed. The scene of forgiveness is outside all economy; there is no reason for the father to act as he does in embracing the disgraced son, calling for "the best robe"—his own, without a doubt—, "a ring" (so that the younger son has authority with the servants), and "shoes" (to indicate he is not a servant), in short reinstating him as an honored member of the family and, with the slaughter of the fatted calf and the ensuing party, reintegrating him into the entire community. The feast is a startling contrast to the boy desiring to eat the pigs' food and not being able to do so and a contrast too with the servants' usual fare, bread. By rights, the son should have been received, if at all, in the house and should have had to fulfill rites of purification (Parah Adumah, for one) and been required to abase himself before the father. Yet this son who has been impossible, who has gone beyond the limit of the possible, is treated with a love that is equally, or more than equally, impossible, outside any and all expectations and limits. What manifests itself in the father is not parental authority or the primacy of religious ritual but the phenomenality of fatherhood; not just biological life or the legal right to respect, but compassion and forgiveness. The father is prodigal, like the son; unlike the son, though, he is prodigal in love, not money.

The father does not have a legal, social, or cultural reason to act as he does in forgiving the son. And yet he does not simply act "without why" but gives a cogent reason for his deeds: "for this my son was dead [ὅτι οὗτος ὁ υἱός μου νεκρὸς ἦν], and is alive again [καὶ ἀνέζησεν]; he was lost, and is found."[21] The father whose death had been cruelly anticipated, brutally brought forward by the son, and whose relationship with his younger son has been assigned a discounted cash value turns out to have seen his son choose death rather than life: he was dead to the father for his thoughtless behavior, dead to the family, dead to the community, and dead to the Lord God. Only in returning to the father does the son return to life. The return of the son in a state of utter destitution and saying the first words of penitence are sufficient atonement as far as the father is concerned. The father is the giver of life in all its modes, including family, communal, and spiritual life. Life here is seen not to be the fulfilling of one's highest possibilities (however misidentified and misunderstood they may have been by the son) but being in relations of love and fidelity, being reunited with the family, the community, in observing Torah, and in being before the Lord God. The younger son asked to be given something, and he received it. His true gift came only on returning home, however, and was unasked for, totally unexpected, and never able to be presumed.

Yet the parable has a second climax, one that is more troubling, in part because it is not resolved. The elder son, the one who remained within the realm of the possible, objects to the father's compassion for his wayward younger brother. On the way back from the field, where he would have been paying the workers their daily wage, he hears music and dancing and is told by one of the local boys [παῖς] what has happened. "But he was angry and refused to go in," we are told; and the sudden anger suggests the freshness of the news heard by the elder brother. Once again, the father comes out, risking losing face once more, and once again the father hears a speech from a son. The father must come out, since the elder son is breaking all convention in not greeting the guests. A family humiliation is about to brew. Now the elder son's speech is not as blunt as the younger son's wish for his inheritance and the right to realize it, but it is just as bad in another way. It flings salt in the father's face. He has *served* the father for many years ['Ιδού, τοσαῦτα ἔτη δουλεύω σοι] and not abandoned the family farm, as his brother once did. He has lived more as a servant than as a son, he feels, has borne responsibility for the farm, and directly accuses the father of withholding a gift that was his by rights: "you never gave me a kid [ἐμοὶ οὐδέποτε ἔδωκας ἔριφον], that I might make merry with my friends." The accusation is clear: you have not been a father, only a master. By the terms of settlement, the elder son would have been assigned the remaining property, including the fatted calf and the kids, although the father would maintain possession of everything until his death and have rights of use and enjoyment. Hence the father's right to reinstate the younger son in the family, "this son of yours," as the elder boy bitterly says, denying all relationship with him, this "son" who has—the elder boy grasps for an image sure to wound the father, one drawn from his sudden anger, vivid imagination, and likely local gossip—"devoured your living with harlots" [καταφαγών σου τὸν βίον μετὰ πορνῶν], Gentile harlots no less. It is the father's living, no doubt, but the elder son knows full well that it is *his* living, as well. Since the younger son left, he has had to carry more burdens in order to keep the farm going.

The father shows tenderness for the elder son, too ("Son [τέκνον: 'My child'], you are always with me") and full awareness of the legal situation ("all that is mine is yours"). Note that the father does not deny what the elder son has said; no attempt is made to make the lyrical moment of return the whole family story, one that occludes issues of fairness, only to stress the significance of the moment. The father's silence about justice and the anger that he sees in his elder son is not to be interpreted as a denial of the importance of being fair. Instead, the father quietly reaffirms the proper relationship that should be observed: the younger son is "your brother," he says. The elder son has conspired in affirming the father's death by not preventing his brother from injuring him; he has been physically alive but dead to the deep love that is shown by the father. For the father, it is clear that the younger son "was dead, and is alive," biologically and in every other way, as well. The father repeats his main statement, as the younger son does, though the father speaks publicly both times. The younger son is *alive*— what an impossible possibility! It is less clear that the elder son, who has always been with the father, is alive and not flirting with death by way of endangering his relationships. Will the elder son choose life (and come to the party) or death (and stay outside)? The younger son has seen his father first as dead, then as a master, and then as a true father. The elder son has seen him as a master but not yet as a true father. He still sees life as fulfilling possibilities, albeit more local and socially acceptable ones than his brother, possibilities limited by accepting the responsibilities of running a large farm in a hard time. He does not yet see life as being embedded in relations of love. Will he have that last perception of the man standing before him, or will he remain in his own "far country"? We do not know.

What we do know on reading the parable closely is that it is not a parable of choice, as it is often thought, largely due to the influences of reformers like Luther, along with Calvin and Counter-Reformation exegetes and preachers: we should be more like the younger son than the older son, seeking forgiveness for our faults rather than being obedient yet brooding all the while on some hurt, real or imagined.[22] Both sons refuse the gift of the father—unconditional love—the younger son at the start and the older son at the end, each because he is fixated on another good, freedom or fairness. And each son is the subject of an unfinished narrative: we think we know what has happened with the younger son, but we surely do not know the end of his story, for we have no idea how the older son will act. Nor is the parable simply a story of reversal: the father comes out to both sons.[23] Rather, we have been reading a parable of decision, one that offers eidetic possibilities that, structured according to a narrative, indicate that we should decide to be more like the father than like either son. The parable gives us all that we need to make the decision, and in making it the kingdom—the kingdom of the *Father*—breaks into our lives here and now.[24] We should be more like the father than we are now because the father gives continually without stinting, even when he is hurt, even when there are rituals that really should be observed. At no point does he choose death in any of its modalities (leave-taking or grudge-holding, for instance), only life. He allows his death to be marked and accepts the wound. The father manifests himself variously, not just at the miraculous moment of reconciliation but in accepting the leave-taking, in anxiously watching for the younger son, and in coming out to speak to the elder son and deflecting his anger. Each son is close to him even when, as we know, each is dead to him. The younger son's return to life is in fact a return to more life, to love understood as something freely given, not something to be measured or held in suspense until conventions have been observed and purity rites have been fulfilled.

III

Two questions have been surfacing and then hiding as I have been reading this parable. The first one is, "who speaks here?" And the second is, "what exactly does Jesus do here?" They are closely related.

I have called the narrator "Luke's Jesus" out of prudence, keeping one eye on the "L" hypothesis and the possibility that the parable is Luke's, not Jesus's, and another possibility that the parable may have originated with Jesus but been styled by Luke. Most likely received without a context, the parable is given one by Luke, one that fits his theology quite nicely. Some readers will adopt a minimal answer to the question "who speaks here?" while others will seek a maximal answer. A minimal answer will satisfy those whose interest in the text is oriented by the historical-critical method: it is "L" or Luke who speaks through a character called Jesus. If there is a link between the parable and the historical Jesus, it is not one that can be recovered or relied upon. On this understanding, the parable may be a piece of wisdom literature; it may point to something essential to Christianity, as experienced by the early church, but it has no more authority than that. A maximal answer may entertain the hypothesis of "L" or Luke's Jesus, though it may also allow both "L" and Luke to embody a story spoken by the historical Jesus. What makes it maximal, however, is the judgment that the parable has two authors, one human and one divine. For Catholics, whether the story comes from the historical Jesus, "L," or Luke is beside the point in terms of ecclesial authority (though not with respect to the conjunction of history and revelation), for the parable is canonical by dint of being in the Vulgate and the magisterium teaches that the Holy Spirit inspired what is included in the canon.[25] Protestants who hold to a doctrine of plenary inspiration will find common cause with Catholics, while those who do not will find the historical-critical method forever threatening to erode the authority of scripture. If Luke 15:11–32 is really the work of "L" or Luke and not Jesus, then it speaks with only one voice, or at most a first-century human voice and the voice of tradition, whether deemed hallowed or hollow.

We are used to thinking of scripture speaking with different voices. The allegorical hermeneutic of Origen enables us to see how that is possible, as does the literal exegesis of Theodore of Mopsuestia.[26] Doubtless both styles of reading have lost their power to recruit defenders with passion. Yet it is not difficult even today to grasp the thesis that a text speaks with two voices. Maurice Blanchot, for one, argues that we can hear or overhear a "narrative voice" beneath the "narrator's voice," the former being the endless sifting of words as they pass from being to image and back again.[27] More straightforwardly, one might say that certain texts—the 2010 State of the Union address, for instance—are at once the words of a particular person and of a structure, the president and the executive branch of government. One may hear the personal speech rhythm of Barack Obama while also hearing the impersonal voice of political authority. In many translated texts one may hear both the author and the translator, especially if one knows the work in its original language. (In reading *Odes* 4:7 ["Diffugere nives"] as translated by A. E. Housman I can hear both Horace and Housman.) In the case of Luke 15:11–32 one might wish to say that the text is authoritative with respect to salvation because it was uttered by Jesus (understood as God incarnate) or because it has been deemed canonical by the church. These disjunctions may be taken to converge or to diverge—that is, the parable may be regarded as canonical because Jesus spoke it or some version of it or because it is held that the Holy Spirit inspired scripture. In the latter case, "L" or Luke may have been thinking while writing that he was composing the story when in fact it was the Holy Spirit who was working through him. Also one may rightly say when one reads Luke 15:11–32 in English that one can hear the translator as well as the author. This is particularly so when reading the King James translation of the Bible with its distinctive cadences. There may be multiple voices in any text, then. I doubt that anyone can properly say that one *hears* an Aramaic original behind the Greek text, though a scholar of Semitic languages could construct an Aramaic text for the parable.

For the nonbeliever, Luke 15:11–32 is spoken by "L" or Luke; it is a historical text of profound importance to Christianity but one that has no revelatory claim upon us. For the believer, the Holy Spirit speaks the same text, regardless of whether or not Jesus, "L," or Luke also spoke it or wrote it. If we ask how one could pass from nonbelief to belief in reading the parable we approach a central question, both with respect to biblical hermeneutics and with the poetics of parable. There is nothing in the historical-critical method that allows anything miraculous—whether an event depicted *in* the text such as radical forgiveness or an event brought about *by* the text such as seeking such forgiveness—to have the status of evidence. Just because an evangelist testifies to the forgiveness of sins does not mean that there is such a thing as either sin or divine forgiveness, the historian will say; and just because a few or many millions of people became believers on reading a passage of scripture does not mean that God is the author or coauthor of the passage. Only the principle of sufficient reason, sufficient *historical* reason, governs the reading of the text, and by definition miraculous events fall outside the scope of that principle. Now, a phenomenological reading of the parable is not confined to sufficient historical reason, although it may learn a good deal from what historians say about the text; it is beholden to the principle of principles and so makes no prejudgment about the status of evidence.[28] In phenomenology, evidence is *Evidenz*, the making evident of something, and no rules are set in place to limit what makes itself evident. The otherness of the other person, the disclosure of distance in the icon, and the pathos of life that manifests itself in self-affect: all these are invisible, and all are evident for recent phenomenologists.[29] Toward the end of his life Heidegger spoke of the "phenomenology of the inapparent," and others have heard him and acted upon his words.[30]

No judgment is made in phenomenology about the rights and wrongs of belief or nonbelief with regard to what scripture tells us. Phenomenology merely allows the full range of *Evidenz* to be received. Each reader is given eidetic possibilities in the parable; no reader is asked in phenomenology to realize them or not to realize them in his or her own life. Now in Luke 15:11–32 one may see the father in the story as manifesting human fatherhood in compassion in his running to the son, and one may also see God as forgiving sins and brushing aside human (and religious) rules and regulations. The phenomenality of sin consists in allowing death to come forward (through the son's insolent request that breaks the law), and the phenomenality of God is registered in love impulsively coming forward, freely manifesting itself by way of overwhelming compassion for both sorts of people, the younger and the elder sons. One may receive this phenomenality in diverse ways, most usually as artistic pathos or as divine truth. Phenomenology as such is neutral with respect to the choice; it merely allows the choice to be made. So Luke 15:11–32 is open to a phenomenological reading. Also, though, it is *itself* an example of phenomenology, a narrative that nudges the phenomenon of the kingdom so that it comes forward and makes itself evident. How so?

Phenomenology is usually taken to be a style of philosophizing that began with Husserl and was revised variously by Heidegger, Merleau-Ponty, Levinas, and many others, right up to Henry, Marion, and Lacoste. In this tradition there is debate about the number and order of reductions, whether reduction is needed in the first place or even if reduction is faithful to phenomenological method.[31] One may speak of the "first reduction" (Husserl's), the "second reduction" (Heidegger's), and the "third reduction" (Marion's). This sequence is a narrative of the proper aim of phenomenology from securing an object to manifesting being to disclosing givenness: one that begins with "consciousness," passes to *Dasein*, and ends with *l'adonné*. In each case, the issue is a relation between phenomenon and subject or whoever comes after the subject.[32] Of particular interest, since it evokes not only the leading back to transcendental consciousness but also the motivation for this movement, is Eugen Fink's revision of Husserl's reduction, which unhumanizes the one who performs reduction and leads him or her to the very margin of the world.[33] Along the same lines, although perhaps sensing a Gnostic element in Fink's reduction, Lacoste advocates a "liturgical reduction" that leads the one who prays to the border of the world.[34] Rather than refine reduction endlessly in the wake of Husserl, one might, thanks to Husserl, see phenomenology being performed long before him, long before even Descartes or Hume, philosophers he credited with occasional phenomenological insight. Husserl clarifies phenomenology and purifies it in a particular way; he does not inaugurate its distinctive gestures but allows us to discern them in the past, even when they are at an angle to the ones that suit his post-Kantian agenda. I want to suggest that Jesus performs a reduction in his telling of parables and that we see more deeply into what a parable does when we recognize this.

In telling a story Jesus brackets everyday life and its worldly logic in order to lead those who hear him to a deeper place. *Epochē* and reduction, then: but not a reduction from transcendence to the immanence of transcendental consciousness, as Husserl taught, or a reduction from beings to being, as Heidegger proposed, or even a reduction from both to givenness, as Marion commends. Instead, Jesus leads us from using a worldly logic—one involving exchange, honor, law, and convention—to using a divine logic, one based on compassion and forgiveness. We pass from "world" to βασιλεία, from every inflection of "world" (αἰών, κόσμος, *mundum, orbis terrarum, imperium mundi*) to "kingdom." The parable is the means by which we shift our perspective on life to see how we are to live so as to be pleasing to the God we can now know (and not know). We are not asked to see how we constitute the meaning of phenomena but rather invited to see how we can be constituted as properly human by participating in the kingdom. If we examine this movement closely, we can see that it has two moments. The first is κένωσις: the one who learns from the parable empties himself or herself of the worldly logic that has controlled his or her life. One is stripped of worldly humanness, led to the very border of the world, as Fink and Lacoste stress in their versions of the reduction. The second is ἐπέκτασις: the listener stretches himself or herself into the kingdom of God—that is, into the embedded relations of unconditional love that are already available, with all the risk of being repeatedly humiliated and hurt by entering into those relations. One sees that it is not one's fellow human beings who provide models of how to live but only the Father who is Life itself.

IV

Several things follow from figuring parable as the reduction from "world" to "kingdom." The first is that the vehicle of the reduction is not philosophy or anything of central importance to philosophy in its modern formation. No *concept* of βασιλεία is given to us; the βασιλεία is not a utopia, church, or social group but a way of being with others that comports with how God is. Parable is an interlacing of metaphor and narrative, and we learn how to live as God wishes us to by being attentive to narrative (here: the story of the two sons) and metaphor (here: God is our father). Philosophical and theological concerns certainly follow from the reduction—in working out a doctrine of God, for instance—but they are not essential to it, except, of course, for clarifying the very notion of reduction in the first place.

The second thing that follows from thinking of parable as reduction is that the means of reduction, the parable, itself tells us something of God. He is *like* a human father and yet, at the same time, quite *unlike* any human father we know. God is like a human father in the ancient Semitic world in that he has sovereignty and that his child is always his child, yet few human fathers, if any, would completely throw aside all decorum, honor, convention, ritual, and sense of grievance, even if committed to the principle of unconditional love. God is unlike any human father, at the very limit of fatherhood as we know it, and manifests that fatherhood fully because he is wholly compassionate, and his relations with us are entirely and always relations of love, not obligation or utility. Luke is clear in his gospel that only God, Father and King, is truly compassionate. The phenomenality of God is given both in his running toward the sinner in love and mercy and in coming out to the righteous elder son with tenderness toward him. Humans, even pious ones, usually act differently. So parable gives us a structure of doubled revelation: how we are to know God (as Father) and how God transcends our knowledge of him (we cannot tell the depths and heights of what it means to call him "Father"). We are also told how we can become more like the Father by showing mercy rather than by clinging to a culturally and socially determined status. God comes to us *modus sine modo*, in a way without a way, without being bound by categories or even by religion, and we come to God *modus sine modo*, as well, though in another scansion of the Latin, at the very limit of our love for others. We love God as we love our fathers (and mothers, wives, husbands, children) but without any measure or bound, without any *quid pro quo*; yet God who is pure love, ἀγάπη, loves us outside all categories and all rules. We freshen the *imago dei* when we love without measure, which includes radical forgiveness.

The odd logic of "like but unlike" that governs the parable means that we can and should forgive as God does but that we never quite forgive as God does. Justice sticks in our throats, not because it is wrong but because we want it immediately. We might say that the father in the parable shows us lyrical forgiveness: it is immediate, pure, symbolic, a gift given without any thought of exchange, and one that in effect completely neutralizes the effects of the past. Perhaps there is more in God's reception of the sinner than pure forgiveness, but if there is we are not told what it may be. This scene of lyrical forgiveness is of two persons and two only; no consideration is taken of others—the elder son, the rest of the family, and the community—who are also wounded in one way or another by the past act. The father throws a party, but a party does not cure all ills, as the parable quietly points out in the passage about the elder son. The past has been neutralized in its effects, not erased in all its being. What will happen on the morrow? Will the father speak to the younger son about justice now that forgiveness has taken place? What would that justice be? I want to suggest that Luke 15:11–32 does not promote forgiveness over justice but rather concerns itself with the necessity of forgiveness before justice takes place. Forgiveness occurs and is always lyrical—without calculation, pure gift, a doubled act of κένωσις and ἐπέκτασις—but it takes place in order to open a narrative space in which justice may properly appear. The father forgives the son, and in doing so he summons an indefinite future in which the son, and indeed the entire family, can thrive once again. The narrative of forgiveness has a clear structure: the fault is in the past, forgiveness is in the present, and justice is in the future.[35]

Without forgiveness there can be no future in which broken relationships are healed; and yet without justice those relationships will not be healed. Forgiveness neutralizes the past and opens an alternate future for being in relation with others. The elder brother shows us a man concerned with the past and the future, not with the value of the living present; and the father points out to him the rightness of celebrating the moment of return, of accepting the brother back, of forgiving past faults. He says nothing against the elder brother's angry concern for fairness. It is not wrong; it is just inappropriate at the time. Tomorrow is the day for justice to begin, to work out the ways in which the younger son can start to restore damaged relationships. Fallen humanity seeks justice before offering forgiveness; the kingdom breaks in to show us that forgiveness must come before the difficult work of justice. Forgiveness, then, is always the mid-point of a narrative in which it appears: it responds to a past event or events, and it opens a new future in which all parties may flourish. Will the younger son act for justice? Perhaps he will need to be forgiven again (and again and again). The present can move into the future, but the future is not thereby eliminated or drained of moral significance. Without the mid-point, an irrevocable past will erase in advance all possible futures except the darkest ones of broken and stunted relationships.

When forgiveness is placed in terms of an overarching narrative, one that is not offered to us in Luke 15:11–32, one expects a clear change on the part of the one forgiven. Opened by an act of radical forgiveness, the future is nonetheless fragile: it depends on relationships being healed and trust restored among all parties. The future will be robust, workable, only if all parties take part in gift-giving, though not as simple exchange. For what they give to one another—help, kindness, patience, understanding, all in varying ways and in different circumstances—is unable to be measured or given at the one time and is incommensurable in any case. Mostly, it is invisible and silent, discreetly hidden in words about other things and in the performance of ordinary tasks. Without the younger son's gift-giving, all those hurt by the past deed or deeds will remain unhealed, and the same is true if it is only the younger son who gives. The future of the family remains invisible, unsaid, in the parable; yet what the younger son will do in the future is as important as what the elder son will do. What the parable makes perfectly visible is that the younger son can begin to live again now that he has been forgiven, while the elder son may destroy himself as well as others in not being able to forgive. Sin breaks communities; lack of forgiveness also breaks them, and the demand for justice can break them too if it comes out of sequence. Luke 15:11–32 is not an exemplary story about forgiveness; it is a story about the proper relation of forgiveness and justice.

That Jesus uses the metaphor of the father is clearly culturally determined, as already indicated. For us, who experience a quite different familial structure in twenty-first-century America, there is no theological reason whatsoever not to think of God also by way of the metaphor of mother. Not that we have come to this realization so recently, even with respect to this passage of Luke. In his great work "The Return of the Prodigal Son" (c. 1662) Rembrandt paints the young son, returned, with the father's hands on his back: the left hand is masculine and the right hand is feminine in appearance.[36] God, who transcends gender, has male and female traits in his dealings with us. Theologically, the parable helps to clarify what we mean by the *imago dei*. We have lost the image of God by a fall from the divine to the worldly, one that can always be repeated— we are fall*ing* creatures more than fall*en* creatures, falling because fallen and still alive, making difficult decisions in multiple, incommensurable relations—and that we can regain the image by exercising compassion in ordinary human relations. The Christian life is a perpetual movement of κένωσις and ἐπέκτασις, a recognition that the one leads to the other and that ἐπέκτασις itself involves κένωσις, for when we truly stretch ourselves in the kingdom we are continually emptying ourselves of what keeps us grounded in the natural and political world regarded as self-sufficient. Our center is in God, not ourselves (consciousness, intellect, feeling, the unconscious, the will), and without κένωσις and ἐπέκτασις we cannot find ourselves, let alone God.

Third, when we think of the parable as reduction from "world" to "kingdom" we recognize two things: that the parable is revelatory and that what is revealed is divine phenomenality, not an object or being but the invisible coming forward of love itself. This calls for reflection. For it is by no means clear that phenomenology is able to treat revelation. A phenomenon can be made to manifest itself fully, to come out from partial darkness into the light. We learn phenomenology explicitly (through philosophy) or implicitly (through art) in order to know how to do this the better. Yet no human, not even the subtlest of all phenomenologists, can make God manifest himself. The Father is hidden. We must wait for revelation. So we have no a priori right to assimilate "revelation" and "manifestation." When God reveals himself, he may also re-veil himself in order to preserve his holiness and to safeguard us against its blinding presence. We cannot figure God as phenomenon. Yet we may say that once God has revealed himself, this revelation may be made more fully manifest; such is the presumption of following the modes of revelation: scripture and ecclesial tradition. Now the kingdom of God *is* a phenomenon, one that we are enjoined in the synoptic gospels to help the Father make more manifest. True, only the Father can realize the kingdom; yet it is in our acts of compassion, forgiveness, and sacrifice—the very meaning of ἀγάπη—that parts of its outline are discerned on earth. Theologically, the pressing question is by what right we can say that the kingdom, which must be revealed to us, is a phenomenon and therefore able to be disclosed to us. The answer must begin with the evident: only Jesus can tell us a parable of the kingdom, such as Luke 15:11–32, which is held to have revelatory authority, and this situation obtains because only Jesus is one with the Father. All other parables are, as Barth says, *secular* parables of the kingdom; they may generally point us to it but only Jesus can reveal it to us.[37]

Since Jesus, and only Jesus, is the revelation of the Father and can preach the nature of God as Father, only he can authoritatively teach us what the kingdom of God is like. Yet since Jesus is also fully human, a dative for manifestation, he can present this revealed truth as a phenomenon. Now Jesus's concern is not the revelation of God in all its fullness (including, for example, the triune nature of God) but instead the revelation of the kingdom of God that is revealed in and through his earthly life, his teaching, and his acts. Where the historical-critical method forbids any passage from scripture to creed, phenomenology allows us to recognize that one vital element of the creed, the incarnation of God, is transcendentally supposed by Jesus's relating of a parable of the kingdom. What is the kingdom? Neither a concept nor a law but living in such a way that one is like God in being compassionate and forgiving to one's fellow creatures, living in such a way that God, and only God, is the true king, and understanding that this king is not like a hard master but like a father to us. It is living not so that love may cancel justice but so as to open a future in which justice may take place. Only Jesus can nudge this phenomenon so that it manifests itself to us, and he does so by means of parable. Of course, no one parable, not even Luke 15:11–32 or Luke 10:25–37, can provide all the aspects and profiles of the phenomenon, and so others must be told. Yet not even an infinite number of parables can exhaust the reality of the kingdom—participation in the divine life. When Islamic scholars criticize Christians for not being satisfied with Jesus's teaching in Luke 15:11–32 and imposing incarnation, cross, and resurrection upon the parable, thereby generating the idea of a God-Man, they miss the essential dialectical structure of Christianity that is latent in the parable we have been reading: the preaching of the kingdom by the one person who can do so brings about the cross, and the resurrection is a vindication of the kingdom as the true teaching of God and how to live here and now so as to enter the eschatological kingdom of heaven, eternal life with God. And when we look to the *Lotus Sutra* for a parallel with Luke 15:11–32 we surely find one, though it is drained entirely of the very dialectic that I have named.

When Jesus preaches the kingdom, saying that the true king is God and that his sovereignty is manifest in fatherhood and not mastery, he is responding to an urgent situation. The order of creation as we know it on earth has been compromised by the imposition of worldly logic as the only logic to follow: what was created in a proper relation with the Father has fallen from that proper relation. We must change our perspective and once again recognize that the true ruler of the created order is the Creator whom we may know as our *Father*. To preach that the authentic ruler of the earth is God, not Caesar or anyone else, is always to risk punishment of one sort or another. It will be said that no one has ever been executed for telling parables, and indeed there are reasons in addition to preaching the βασιλεία that the cross was built; yet Jesus was tortured and executed because his parables made people see that we are to live in a way that places God in contradiction to the world in all its modes, even the quest for justice. To preach the kingdom and to try to live there, in God's power, is to risk the cross: it is the most derelict κένωσις and the most painful ἐπέκτασις, the stretching out into the blank absence of God. The cross is the antitype of the parable of the prodigal son; it is the Father retreating from the son. The resurrection of Jesus is the overcoming of death, but it is more than that: it is also the vindication that his preaching of the kingdom is not one philosophy among others—that is, *philosophy*—but is the truth. The parable is changed retrospectively from being a story, a piece of wisdom literature one with the θεῖος ἀνήρ tradition to being sacred truth by dint of the resurrection of Jesus, the revelation that this strange rabbi was and is the Christ. The kingdom is the truth of creation, the truth that can be glimpsed again in a fallen world, and the truth of the world to come.

Aspects of the kingdom, as shown by Luke 15:11–32, include the unlimited compassion of the Father, to be sure, but cross and resurrection are also involved. They are immanent in the story when seen with hindsight: the destitution of the son in the "far country" is cross, and his reception by the Father is resurrection. Nonetheless, these immanent truths presume the transcendent truths, strictly outside the parable, of Jesus's death and resurrection. Only then do we see that Jesus's reduction from "world" to "kingdom" is not one more species of reduction, or one more literary story, but divine truth: truth as faithfulness and power.

Notes

An earlier version of this essay was given as a plenary paper at the Society for Mormon Philosophy and Theology, Utah Valley University, in March 2010. Part was given at the May 2010 meeting of the Academy of Catholic Theology in Washington, D.C. Later versions were given in the Divinity School of Duke University and as the 2011 Yves Simon Memorial Lecture at the Lumen Christi Institute at the University of Chicago. I wish to thank all those who participated in the discussions.

1. See Tertullian, *On Purity*, in *Treatises on Penance*, trans. William P. Le Saint (New York: Newman, 1959), 72–79; Clement of Alexandria, "Parable of the Prodigal Son," in *Ante-Nicene Fathers*, ed. Alexander Roberts and James Donaldson (1885; repr. Peabody, Mass.: Hendrickson, 1999), 2:581–84; and Elizabeth Bishop, *Poems, Prose, and Letters*, ed. Robert Giroux and Lloyd Schwartz (New York: Library of America, 2008), 54.

2. See Karl Barth, *Church Dogmatics*, vol. 4, part 2, ed. G. W. Bromiley and T. F. Torrance, trans. G. W. Bromiley (Edinburgh: T. and T. Clark, 1958), §64.

3. See Marsha G. Witten, *All Is Forgiven: The Secular Message in American Protestantism* (Princeton: Princeton University Press, 1993).

4. See the first volume of Dean Koontz's *Frankenstein* series, *Prodigal Son* (New York: Del Ray/Ballantine, 2008); Sammo Hung's film *The Prodigal Son* (1982); and Peter Wessel Zapffe's play *Den fortapte sønn: En dramatisk gjenfortaelling* (Oslo: Glydendal, 1951); also see Wendell Berry, "Making It Home," in his *What Are People For?* (San Francisco: North Point, 1990).

5. See André Gide, *The Return of the Prodigal Son: English Translation and Genesis*, ed. Aldyth Thain (Logan: Utah State University Press, 1960), and Rainer Maria Rilke, *The Notebook of Malte Laurids Brigge*, intro. Stephen Spender (Oxford: Oxford University Press, 1984), 235–43.

6. See Tertullian, *On Purity* 78; Jerome, *Epistulae* 21, in *Patrologia latina* (*PL*) 22, ed. J.-P. Migne (Paris, 1845), cols. 379–94; Ambrose, *Exposition of the Holy Gospel According to St. Luke*, trans. Theodosia Tomkinson (Etna, Calif.: Center for Traditionalist Orthodox Studies, 2003), 330–31; Augustine, *Quaestionum evangeliorum libri duo*, *PL* 35, cols. 1323–64; Chrysostom, "When He Returned from the Countryside," in *On Repentance and Almsgiving*, trans. Gus George Christo, Fathers of the Church (Washington, D.C.: The Catholic University of America Press, 1998), 11–15; and *The Gospel Commentary*, trans. Hieromonk German Ciuba (Erie, Pa.: Russian Orthodox Church of the Nativity of Christ [Old Rite], 2002), 13–28.

7. Gottfried of Admont, *Homilioe dominicale*, *PL* 174, no. 31, cols 202–10; Hugh of St. Cher, *A Commentary on the Parable of the Prodigal Son*, trans. and intro. Hugh Bernard Feiss (Toronto: Peregrina, 1996). Further examples are

given by Stephen L. Wailes, *Medieval Allegories of Jesus' Parables* (Los Angeles: University of California Press, 1987), 236–45.

8. See Bonaventure, *Commentary on the Gospel of John*, ed. Robert J. Karris, in *Works of St. Bonaventure*, vol. 8, pt. 2 (St. Bonaventure, N.Y.: Franciscan Institute, 2003), 1422–68.

9. See, for example, Joachim Jeremias, *The Parables of Jesus*, trans. S. H. Hook, rev. ed. (London: SCM Press, 1963), 128; Brad H. Young, "The Father of Two Lost Sons," in *The Parables: Jewish Tradition and Christian Interpretation* (Peabody, Mass.: Hendrickson, 1998), 130–57; and Arland J. Hultgren, *The Parables of Jesus: A Commentary* (Grand Rapids: Eerdmans, 2000), 70–91. Heidi J. Hornik and Mikeal C. Parsons point out that the word "father," in different forms, occurs twelve times in the parable and would have conditioned the audience's response to it; see their *Illuminating Luke: The Public Ministry of Christ in Italian Renaissance and Baroque Painting* (London: T. and T. Clark, 2005), 139. This is the second volume of their three-volume series on Luke. For a different view of the parable, see Dan Via, *The Parables: Their Literary and Existential Dimension* (Philadelphia: Fortress, 1967), 164.

10. For followers of the "L" hypothesis, see, for example, J. A. Fitzmyer, *The Gospel according to Luke* (New York: Doubleday, 1983), and David A. Holgate, *Prodigality, Liberality and Meanness in the Parable of the Prodigal Son: A Greco-Roman Perspective on Luke 15:11–32* (Sheffield, UK: Sheffield Academic Press, 1999). The "L" hypothesis was ventured by Burnett Hillman Streeter as part of his "four document" hypothesis in his *The Four Gospels: A Study of Origins, Treating the Manuscript Tradition, Sources, Authorship, and Dates* (London: Macmillan, 1924), chap. 9.

11. See Young, "Father of Two Lost Sons"; Eckhard Rau, *Reden in Vollmacht: Hintergrund, Form und Anliegen der Gleichnisse Jesu* (Göttingen: Vandenhoeck and Ruprecht, 1990), 216–408; and Michael Fuss, *Buddhavacana and Dei Verbum: A Phenomenological and Theological Comparison of Scriptural Inspiration in the Saddharmapundarika Sutra and in the Christian Tradition* (Leiden: Brill, 1991).

12. On this theme, see Kenneth E. Bailey, *The Cross and the Prodigal: The 15th Chapter of Luke Seen through the Eyes of Middle-Eastern Peasants* (St. Louis: Concordia, 1973).

13. On "accountable silence," see Harvey Sacks, Emmanuel A. Schegloff, and Gail Jefferson, "A Simplest Systematics for the Organization of Turn-Taking in Conversation," in *Studies in the Organization of Conversational Interaction*, ed. Jim Schenkein (New York: Academic Press, 1977), 7–55; also see Stephen C. Levinson, *Pragmatics* (New York: Cambridge University Press, 1983), 294–329, and Paul Drew and John Heritage, "Analyzing Talk at Work: An Introduction," in *Talk at Work: Interaction in Institutional Settings* (New York: Cambridge University Press, 1992), 3–65.

14. If either son is married, we know nothing about it. One presumes that the younger son is unmarried. Alicia Batten argues that the parable "demonstrates

a gynecocentric point of view," though I find her argument unpersuasive; see her essay "Dishonour, Gender and the Parable of the Prodigal Son," *Toronto Journal of Theology* 13 (1997): 187–200.

15. See Eta Linnemann, *Jesus of the Parables: Introduction and Exposition*, trans. John Sturdy (New York: Harper and Row, 1966), 75. For the legal situation, see *Baba Bathra* 8f, and Joachim Jeremias, *Parables of Jesus*, 128.

16. For purity laws, see Jonathan Klawans, *Impurity and Sin in Ancient Judaism*, part 1 (New York: Oxford University Press, 2004).

17. On this theme, see Jean-Luc Marion, *God without Being: Hors-Texte*, trans. Thomas A. Carlson, foreword by David Tracy (Chicago: University of Chicago Press, 1991), 97.

18. Richard L. Rohrbaugh over-reads the parable in order to make a case that the entire family is dysfunctional; see his "A Dysfunctional Family and Its Neighbours," in *Jesus and His Parables: Interpreting the Parables of Jesus Today*, ed. V. George Shillington, forward Seán Freyne (Edinburgh: T. and T. Clark, 1997), 141–64. James Breech makes much of the analogy with King Lear in his *The Silence of Jesus: The Authentic Voice of the Historical Man* (Toronto: Doubleday, 1983), 207–10.

19. *The Talmud of Babylonia*, trans. Jacob Neusner, vol. 20, *Baba Qamma*, chaps. 4–7 (Atlanta: Scholars Press, 1992), 82b.

20. T. W. Manson quotes a rabbinic saying, "When a son (abroad) goes barefoot (through poverty), then he remembers the comfort of his father's house," in *The Sayings of Jesus as Recorded in the Gospels according to St. Matthew and St. Luke Arranged with Introduction and Commentary* (Grand Rapids: Eerdmans, 1957), 288.

21. On "without why," see Martin Heidegger, *The Principle of Reason*, trans. Reginald Lilly (Bloomington: Indiana University Press, 1991).

22. See John Calvin, *Commentary on a Harmony of the Evangelists, Matthew, Mark and Luke*, trans. William Pringle (Edinburgh: Calvin Translation Society, 1845–46), 2:342–51.

23. See John Dominic Crossan, *In Parables: The Challenge of the Historical Jesus* (San Francisco: Harper and Row, 1973), 66–74.

24. See Eberhard Jüngel, "The World as Possibility and Actuality: The Ontology of the Doctrine of Justification," in *Theological Essays*, ed. J. B. Webster (Edinburgh: T. and T. Clark, 1989), 121.

25. On the canonicity of the Vulgate, see Heinrich Joseph Denzinger, *The Sources of Catholic Dogma*, trans. Roy J. Deferrari (St Louis: Herder, 1957), DS 785. On the teachings of the magisterium regarding the inspiration of the canon, see DS 348, 706, etc.

26. See Theodore of Mopsuestia, *Commentaire sur les Psaumes I–LXXX*, ed. Robert Devreese, Studi e Testi 93 (Vatican City: Vaticana, 1939), 282.

27. See Maurice Blanchot, "The Narrative Voice (The 'He,' the Neutral)," in *The Infinite Conversation*, trans. and intro. Susan Hanson (Minneapolis: University of Minnesota Press, 1993), 379–87.

28. See Edmund Husserl, *Ideas Pertaining to a Pure Phenomenology and to a Phenomenological Philosophy*, vol. 1, *General Introduction to a Pure Phenomenology*, trans. F. Kersten (Dordrecht: Kluwer, 1983), §24. Jean-Luc Marion points us to a principle of insufficient reason in phenomenology; see, for example, Marion, *The Erotic Phenomenon*, trans. Stephen E. Lewis (Chicago: University of Chicago Press, 2007), §17.

29. I am thinking of Emmanuel Levinas, "Phenomenon and Enigma," in *Collected Philosophical Papers*, trans. Alphonso Lingis (Dordrecht: Nijhoff, 1987); Michel Henry, *I Am the Truth: Toward a Philosophy of Christianity*, trans. Susan Emanuel (Stanford: Stanford University Press, 2003); and Marion, *The Idol and Distance: Five Studies*, trans. and intro. Thomas A. Carlson (New York: Fordham University Press, 2001). Special attentions should be given to Henry's reading of Luke 15:11–32 in *I Am the Truth*, 163–64.

30. Heidegger, *Four Seminars*, trans. Andrew Mitchell and François Raffoul (Bloomington: Indiana University Press, 2003), 80.

31. See, for example, Levinas, *The Theory of Intuition in Husserl's Phenomenology*, trans. André Orianne (Evanston, Ill.: Northwestern University Press, 1973), 157.

32. See Eduardo Cadava, Peter Connor, and Jean-Luc Nancy, eds., *Who Comes after the Subject?* (London: Routledge, 1991).

33. See Eugen Fink, *Sixth Cartesian Meditation: The Idea of a Transcendental Theory of Method*, trans. and intro. Ronald Bruzina (Bloomington: Indiana University Press, 1995), §11.

34. See Jean-Yves Lacoste, *Experience and the Absolute: Disputed Questions on the Humanity of Man*, trans. Mark Raftery-Skehan (New York: Fordham University Press, 2004), §65.

35. It is always possible for Catholics and Protestants alike to complicate the schema by adding that contrition, confession, and atonement must precede the act of forgiveness.

36. See Henri J. M. Nouwen, *The Return of the Prodigal Son: A Story of Homecoming* (New York: Doubleday, 1992), 99.

37. See Barth, *Church Dogmatics*, 4.3.1, ed. G. W. Bromiley and T. F. Torrance, trans. G. W. Bromiley (Edinburgh: T. and T. Clark, 1961), §69.

Phenomenology as *Lectio Divina*
Jesus and the Woman Caught in Adultery

ROBYN HORNER

Hors-texte

We have been invited to read a text "phenomenologically," yet to read it without reference to the phenomenological and other debates that might inform such a reading. That is the brief—just to let the text speak for itself, without interfering in that speech. So, with apologies to the commissioning editor, I must warn the reader in advance that these preliminary comments are to be excised from my reading of a passage from the Gospel of John.

To read phenomenologically is to begin with an attempt to put in brackets "the natural attitude"; it is to try to isolate what appears in immanence to consciousness—or lived experience—without first presuming its character as object (first reduction) or even as being (second reduction), but simply to accept what gives itself from itself (third reduction). At its most radical, to do phenomenology is to allow a phenomenon to appear according to the horizon of givenness, which some might say is almost no horizon at all. Of course, I follow a particular phenomenological thread here. In following that thread, I am bound to add that what gives itself to lived experience potentially exceeds the bounds of that experience or, better, gives itself otherwise than in presence to lived experience. The phenomenon appearing according to the horizon of givenness might thus give itself only as excess.

While phenomenology in its pure form seeks to arrive at the essence of what is given—an ideation that is in some sense universal—it is clear from the very mention of horizons that what is given must somehow be contextualized in order for it to be given as such. The phenomenological act itself is historically and culturally situated. So, while the horizon of givenness might reflect the ultimate attempt not to precondition what appears, we cannot ignore the way in which hermeneutics plays its part. To be given is always to be given *as*, although this becomes a more complex issue when we seek to remain open to the possibility either that the given exceeds the horizon altogether or that it exceeds any single horizon. The reduction to givenness, then, can be a complicated maneuver, since it might operate negatively with respect to the horizon, opening up little more than a gap or an interruption. If that is so, then context becomes important in a different way. What contexts does the phenomenon exceed or interrupt? A negative hermeneutic becomes necessary: how can we bring the given phenomenon to visibility by way of this interruption without distorting it?

A phenomenological reading is an attempt to bring to light; it should only bring a light to bear on a text in order to show what is given there. While such a reading would not prohibit the investigation of "the world behind the text," as they say, that will not be the focus here. And while we are working within the world "of" the text, so to speak, our questions will not be typical to that kind of investigation. We are reading a gospel pericope that might not have been in the first edition of John—but this is not our primary concern. We are not trying to trace the origins of the text or to say anything profound about its authorship. We are not trying to identify how this text functions in the context of the whole gospel. Significantly, we are reading in English, not in Greek. In that sense, this is not a commentary in the manner that one might expect, and in any case, I am not qualified to give a commentary.

This brings us to observe that it is the world "in front of" the text that will need to be further specified. As such, it is not the world of the philologist, but the world of the believer. Let us make no apology in that regard: we read here, I read here, as one who *listens to* the text in the context of the Christian community—quasi-liturgically, as it were—and tries to see or strains to hear or perhaps feel the weight of what gives itself and struggles to bring itself forth in manifestation. This is *lectio divina*: in prayerful attentiveness, one seeks to be open to what might show itself. As prayer, it takes the form of confession. That it is *lectio divina* is not to say that it is a movement of *eisegesis*: in fact, the opposite must be the case. And while I confess, from the start, belief in the Christian God, the phenomenological limits to my reading of the text are observed. It is my task only to describe what is given there, even if that description takes place in the context of prayer. In that, however, there is no avoiding that the debates about what constitutes phenomenology—particularly the French ones—will reassert themselves. There is no simple reading of the text, for we will inevitably be haunted by other questions as we read. It will be no surprise to find that I am constantly troubled by Jean-Luc Marion reading Augustine as I read John, even as I resist the urge to insert footnotes.

The Text: John 8:2–11

Early in the morning he came again to the temple. All the people came to him and he sat down and began to teach them. The scribes and the Pharisees brought a woman who had been caught in adultery; and making her stand before all of them, they said to him, "Teacher, this woman was caught in the very act of committing adultery. Now in the law Moses commanded us to stone such women. Now what do you say?" They said this to test him, so that they might have some charge to bring against him. Jesus bent down and wrote with his finger on the ground. When they kept on questioning him, he straightened up and said to them, "Let anyone among you who is without sin be the first to throw a stone at her." And once again he bent down and wrote on the ground. When they heard it, they went away, one by one, beginning with the elders; and Jesus was left alone with the woman standing before him. Jesus straightened up and said to her, "Woman, where are they? Has no one condemned you?" She said, "No one, sir." And Jesus said, "Neither do I condemn you. Go your way, and from now on do not sin again."

Reading/Confession: *Au Lieu de Soi*

The people have come to Jesus, and he sits down and begins to teach them. We do not know what he says, but we see him sitting there, teaching.

Actually, I don't see him very well at all. I am struggling to see any more than my Sunday-School portraits of him—I can't see him as such. As much as I want to picture him, no gospel tells me what he looks like; 30,000,000 portraits of him arrive in Google in 0.19 seconds (about 6 times the number of images of Plato), but I get no traction. *Blessed are you who have not seen, and yet believe.*

Jesus is sitting there in the narrative, teaching, but he resists my gaze. In part this is because we know that we can do no more than guess at his appearance—more than that, let's face it: we cannot even begin to imagine who he is, not just how he appears. He resists the gaze (but not yet, perhaps, in any way that would make him unique). Jesus is not made an object for us here—as he might have been if he were pictured in a newspaper, or if he were delivered as an image in Google, or even if he were the focus of a column in a gossip magazine. Yet neither is he given as a subject *as such*, for subjects resist our inquisitive, acquisitive eyes even more, and he more than most. He is not a subject for me in the sense that he is simply another like me: he is no Husserlian *alter ego*. And he is not given freely to my imagination as if he were simply a character in a play or a story, no matter what we might say about the textual context in which we are meeting him. As I listen, as I try to see, Jesus is over *there* somewhere, removed from me, not invisible exactly, but *invisable*—I cannot focus my intentional aim on him as such.

At the same time, he is the focal point of the narrative. Our hearts, if not our eyes, are drawn to him in the same way that the people who have come to listen to him have been drawn to him. What we are given here in this text is his intense attractiveness to others: *all the people came to him.* Jesus draws them to him; he draws us to him—perhaps this is only mimetic desire (isn't all desire supposed to be mimetic?). We want to see and hear him, at least because they want to see and hear him. I want to see and hear him, here, now. So, do *I* desire him, this Jesus whom I cannot see—and do I desire *him* as such? What if—as it appears—I am not given him *as such*? Further, would desiring be authentic, if it were only borrowed? And who am I, reading, listening, desiring, in a way that is not my own?

To desire in a way that is not my own—can I not even desire for myself? This question, the question that troubles the intellect in such an abstract way ("who comes after the subject?"), this question about grounds, about finding a ground, about knowing that there is something on which I can stand, traditionally expressed in the conjunction of an essence and a substrate (*substantia*)—here we find it emergent much more existentially. What if there "is" no *I* to speak of? What if, in the end, the boundaries blur and the thoughts and feelings dissipate to such an extent that there is no one singular, no one remaining when the supports are taken away? What if there is no self to be known, not even the shade of a self-in-loss? If I hang onto the last shred of hope that my desire ultimately defines and individualizes me, yet my desire is only the simulacrum of desire, then I am lost doubly.

It is no small thing, in this light, to beg for the grace of desire, the desire to desire truly. Perhaps the truth is not so much that all desire is simply mimetic, but that all desire is given, in one way or another. (I confess—if it is not my desire, then let it not merely be their desire imitated but your desire in me, that this may become my own. Not that I may only desire to become myself, but that I be given my desire and, therefore, given my true self.) *Not I, but Christ who lives in me.*

As I look for him among the crowd, for the one who draws the focus of the crowd, I do not see him. Yet slowly, strangely, I find that he has already been there. Becoming still, calming my anxiously searching, overly intellectual gaze, I become aware that he is already there, yet that he is not before me. He gives himself *within*, almost *behind* me, as I gaze forward by default. I cannot turn to see him; I cannot cast my eye upon him. I cannot even glance there where he is to be found, cannot hope to expose his presence, to draw him into the present of an *I think*. Yet I am aware that he is already there. Here I really struggle to find a way to express that recognition. Let me signal my borrowing from Levinas and Derrida if only to the extent that they provide me with an idiom as I come up against the absolute limits of the language of the present: if Christ is there, within me even now, he has already passed immemorially (in a past that was never present) or, better, in the future perfect (he will have been present). My awareness of his self-givenness is not seeing, then, but it is almost as if he has momentarily taken my breath away. There is a fracturing of time as if in the moment of finding oneself suddenly known from the inside. *Tu autem eras interior intimo meo*, indeed.

Let me reflect on this in the cold, hard, light of day. How do I know that it was him? How do I know that the interior otherness that so took me by surprise is anything other than the product of my wishful thinking, or any more than the otherness that I am to myself? There are a number of things that strike me about this experience, if I am able to call it such (and Marion's accounts of counter-experience cannot but come to mind).

There is no evidence, other than my witness to it, of the event of Christ's self-givenness in my listening to this text. That self-givenness took place otherwise than according to any categories one might expect to associate with cataphatic religious experience: I did not have a vision; I did not hear voices; I do not even have a particular message to impart as a result. While it was a positive experience of givenness, it might be described, then, more apophatically, as an experience of the "interruption" of experience. We could suggest it was the in-breaking of what Marion would name a saturated phenomenon: I was aware of "someone" there, but without seeing or knowing as such. Nevertheless, I have no doubt that my identification of this saturated phenomenon with Christ is dependent on a very particular hermeneutic context.

In that moment, upon which I have reflected often since, I recognized the one interior to me as the same one upon whom I was trying to focus in the narrative and, in fact, as the same one who passes through every Christian narrative. There was something about the givenness in each case that was the same, even and perhaps especially to the extent that such given-ness was resistant to object-clarity, for example. To say "I knew it was him" does not mean that I could give an objective account of his presence (*savoir*) but that there was a sense of unmistakable familiarity about it (*connaître*), almost like one has when a scent reexperienced evokes a place or a time long past, issuing forth feeling of such magnitude that it can no longer be called simply "feeling" and winds like a blow.

Rereading the text, I cannot reproduce this experience at will, even though faith might tell me that Christ is somehow always within me (and in the reading of the biblical word), whether I am aware of it or not. In the context of phenomenology, one might expect that the given would give it-self repeatably (this is, after all, the test of the scientific): I listen to the text, and as I become still, I become aware that Christ is within me as I listen. But this is not the case. That I cannot depend on this occurring suggests that it is not simply an awareness of the "generic" otherness that I find al-ready within myself. That I have no control over it happening confirms the prerogative of the given to give itself.

All this leads me to observe something further about the nature of phe-nomenology. Insofar as phenomenology is restricted to the field of imma-nence, all I have phenomenologically is an experience of interruption (the uncanny sense that someone is there)—the effects of which I have described as the feeling of momentarily having had my breath taken away or of a fracturing of time. Hermeneutically, it is essentially open. It is open in one sense to the extent that another interpretation—devoid of the context that provides it with such religious significance—might be different: there is a given phenomenon, but it is ultimately explained as a phenomenon of the imagination, for example.

Yet we cannot separate out the hermeneutics entirely from the given-ness of the phenomenon. For another person, the phenomenon might give itself, but that person might not find such an event interruptive of his or her horizons because there may not be a relevant hermeneutic context to be interrupted in the first place. In this instance, it would not even qualify for that person as an event, especially if we use Romano's sense rather than Marion's—that is, where an event is what overturns our being in the world and somehow transforms it. In that light, we respond to Benoist's question—what if where you say you see God, I see nothing?—by qualifying the "nothing." You may well see "nothing," but that may actually be because you don't notice it or are not able to recognize it, not because it is not given.

In both these instances, it is clear that the starting point for phenome-nology is significant. Religious phenomena are not to be a priori excluded as a possibility. At the same time, there is still room for discrimination and discernment. That the phenomenon is ultimately explained theologically with recourse to the transcendent does not mean that such an explanation is not subject to any sort of test. But what is the appropriate test? At this point, it is a theological one, having its own coherence within theological discourse.

Let us return to the text. Someone named Jesus sits there, in the narrative, teaching. He is not up high, not on high, not at a lectern. Does he stand up when the woman enters the temple with her accusers? (He was sitting down, but later he bends down, which is harder to do if you are already sitting. . . .) With the interruption of the accusers the focus shifts from sitting to standing level.*

Now, we do not see Jesus (or any of the other characters, in fact) in photographic detail, and yet this is a text that is in some ways all about visibility. The woman's accusers *make her stand before all of them.* That's the thing. She had been caught in the act of adultery, and they bring her and make her stand there in front of everyone. She can be seen; her intense visibility is all the more striking when she remains in so many ways invisible to us (she has no name, no features). If there is any light to be shone in this text, it is upon her—such a powerful light that it exposes her from the inside out. There is no barrier to shield her from the probing looks of the assembled people; there is no resistance to their seeing because she has been caught in her utmost intimacy. It is all there, and she is more than naked, to be seen. This is because what is typically least visible—what is largely internal to her—is somehow exteriorized by way of the shaming condemnation: she has been caught in adultery, and so we have not only her by-now-very-sordid act before us but also her feeling, no named feeling, but feeling as such, whatever feeling has motivated her liaison with this partner. In this way, the invisible woman almost burns with interior visibility, which is the essence of shame. We are not told how she feels, this woman, as she stands there before them and before us, yet we see her shame. What belongs inside her, that which is most secret, is now on the outside, exposed. There is no longer a border between inside and outside to protect her; her skin is breached all over and all at once. There is no place of invisibility into which she can retreat.

(Given only in the harbor of invisibility, of course, is the woman's sexual partner. She had been caught *in the act*; *ergo*, they had been caught in the act together. She has been dragged here; for some reason, he remains elsewhere. He is given, but he does not appear.)

As much as this is a text about visibility, it is a text about looking. Frankly, I don't really want to look at this: it is all too much information. I don't really want to see what shames another, lest I become a *voyeur* and complicit in putting her there, lest I participate in her shaming. Are the assembled people looking? The woman is made to stand *before all of them*, and her accusers highlight her visibility as they address Jesus (*Teacher, this woman was caught in the very act of committing adultery*). But are the people really *looking*? It is evident that the woman is there to be seen by them in all her heightened visibility. Perhaps they are looking. Perhaps they are less squeamish than I; perhaps they want to look; perhaps the temple has momentarily become the stadium, *il Colosseo* for sinners. Yet these are the people who have been drawn to Jesus. Are they looking at the woman, or are they averting their eyes?

More than that, if I look at her she confronts me with sin—not hers, but mine. There but for the grace of God. . . . All that remains unseen, for the most part, so easily dragged into the light (*and people loved darkness rather than light because their deeds were evil*). Lewis is right, I think, that murder begets murder because the sin gets harder and harder to hide from oneself. We don't want to look at sin, or if we do, we want to make sure it belongs to someone else and that we destroy the carrier of the infection. The woman acts as a mirror: only throwing stones will appropriately deal with what she represents to her accusers (and, ultimately, the onlookers). In the *dénoument* to the story, Jesus calls this for what it is. If anyone is prepared to look in the mirror, then he or she may throw first.

What are we given of the accusers, these men who bring the woman to be humiliated (on her way to being stoned)? They are named in code: *scribes and Pharisees*. Let us leave it to the biblical scholars to explain what this means and ask first what the accusers are doing as we watch. Their reference to the woman in their address to Jesus suggests that they look at her, but perhaps only momentarily. If they were really looking, would they be able to do this to her? Their bringing her in seems so callously done—in a sense, almost casual. The woman's accusers have brought her here with an end in mind, apparently, which is to catch a much bigger fish, to draw Jesus into a discussion that will trap him. The woman is merely instrumental to that end. Are they really here for the sport of shaming her, or is that incidental to the main game? Are they looking at her—do they really see *her*? Their use of her suggests instead that she remains an object to them and not a person. Their focus is, in any case, more upon *him*, their opponent. Yet when they look at him, what do they see? What does anyone see when there is a threat? What do we see other than a threat? Not a person, certainly, but the projection of our fear, which becomes the object of our hate. In the accusers, we are given Jesus as a screen onto which is projected all their own demons. He comes to represent one who judges; who would not be afraid? Who would not be afraid that this might all lead to personal annihilation? In a text that is apparently about visibility, the accusers do not see the woman, and they do not see Jesus: all they see are their own selves.

One thing is clear, which is that Jesus seems to be doing his best for most of the narrative not to look at the woman. He shifts the plane of action once again; bending down and writing on the ground, he draws the attention of the onlookers away from the woman. Given that he is writing on the ground, then, it appears that his gaze is down for much of the time (and we can say no more about this than that it serves as a point of focus). Refusing to respond to the accusers, he prolongs the awkwardness of the moment. The question—*what do you say?*—hangs there in the air, with no quick agreement from Jesus with their condemnation on the basis of the law of Moses. (Does anyone feel uncomfortable or embarrassed here? Might the onlookers feel uncomfortable because they are not quickly reassured that it is just to condemn the woman? Or might they feel uncomfortable because they think Jesus can't respond to the challenge?) In any case, the accusers get right on with it. Like children, who have tunnel vision when it comes to pursuing a satisfactory outcome to an issue and apparently cannot see what else is going on around them, they keep on questioning him.

When Jesus finally stands and responds, he suddenly comes sharply into narrative focus. Still, we may not see him as such, but his words concentrate his person. This happens twice. He rises and speaks for the first time, with a force and an authority that is striking because of its context. The one who has placed himself at the lowest level, hands in the dirt, and who appears to be without answers, arises to speak powerfully and unambiguously. The air of unease or embarrassment around Jesus's capacity to respond is almost violently dispelled; the trap has been more than neatly avoided; the response is devastating. Jesus becomes the mirror to the accusers and to the crowd: see here your own sin; see here how you participate in the sin of the woman. The spotlight is suddenly shone upon everyone, and a new sense of embarrassment arises to thicken the air once again. For all of an instant, the scene is overexposed.

What does sin look like out in the open? We have already been shown something of the sin of the woman and her shame in her appalling visibility. The sins of the multitude are not named; all we are given to see, in fact, is the sin of their preparedness to sacrifice her without thought to their own need to repent. Yet that is enough. The givenness of sin saturates intuition in its own way: even as the sinner becomes more visible, sin is given in a kind of conceptual darkness. I am not presuming to personify it here, but only to observe how it somehow escapes rationality, emerging from and at once retreating into a depth that is unfathomable. Imaginatively, while there is—on the one hand—a kind of scale to sin, stretching from the least venial to the most mortal, there is also—on the other hand—never more than a hair's breadth between any single point on that scale and any other. It is all of a piece, which is why being confronted with sin is not only absolutely humiliating, but can be truly terrifying.

The challenge given, Jesus withdraws again, returning in a downward movement to the narrative dust. The crowd dissipates, and at last the scene becomes personal. For all the obscene exposure encountered in the text thus far, there has been nothing intimate about it: for all that it evidently puts on display what is most personal, the pornographic obliterates the personal in the same move. So, finally we enter a space of real intimacy. When the crowd has gone, *Jesus* [is] *left alone with the woman standing before him.* He rises a second time, and addresses her directly. *Woman, where are they? Has no one condemned you?*

Speak, Lord, your servant is listening. There is a marked contrast between Jesus's address to the woman and his earlier address to the crowd. Where that had taken the form of something like a juridical pronouncement (*let anyone among you who is without sin be the first to throw a stone at her*), his address now reflects the beginnings of a personal relationship. Jesus's address to the woman starts, not with his assessment of her or of what has taken place, but with two questions for her to answer. This effectively means that she first has to assess the situation for herself. She cannot make this assessment with her eyes downcast (have they been downcast?), but must look up and around to see that the crowd has, in fact, gone, and that no one remains to condemn her with a stone. And so, she responds: *no one, sir.* For we who see her now, who have been reluctant witnesses to her utter nakedness before, there is a dramatic shift. Suddenly she becomes more herself than she was then, in spite of the fact that we had already viewed her completely exposed, as if there were nothing more we could possibly have seen. The woman is addressed, and she responds, and she is given a dignity that is all the more profound for the way that she remains, as it were, unclothed, not hiding anything. Jesus addresses her, and she becomes herself: in Jesus's address to her she is given herself, and she responds as herself at last.

It is *as* herself in this way that the woman finds she is not rebuked by Jesus (*neither do I condemn you*) and perhaps experiences for the first time the possibility of fulfilling his otherwise seemingly impossible command: *from now on do not sin again.* The self regiven in being personally addressed by Jesus, the self thus invested with a new dignity and enabled to respond, is the self able to move forward as itself, the respons-*able* self, the self able to desire the good instead of being dissipated in sin.

Class dismissed. *Go your way. . . .*

The narrative ends abruptly. The woman has been transformed, and we might want to dwell with her on the great mercy she has been shown and the kindness of Jesus himself. She—and we—might wish to linger in his presence, to enjoy the moment, to enjoy *him* in her newfound identity. Instead, just as she comes face to face with him, she is told to leave. We do not get to hold on to Jesus, to grasp him (as if we *could*), but only to remember that he has been there and to desire that he might come again. He never becomes ours. It is a severe mercy, a costly blessing. However, if we are prepared to be found in the deepest dark of our secret lives and come into the light—not only adulterers, but inquisitors, spectators, people who have been prepared to sacrifice others to protect ourselves—the offer remains for us to become his.

Split Interpretations of a Split I
Romans 7:7–25

JEAN-LOUIS CHRÉTIEN

The writing of St. Paul's Epistle to the Romans is exceptionally dense and profound. Martin Luther opened the important preface to his German translation of the epistle with the following assertion: "This letter is truly the most important piece in the New Testament. It is purest Gospel. It is well worth a Christian's while not only to memorize it word for word but also to occupy himself with it daily, as though it were the daily bread of the soul.'"[1] For Luther, this epistle was a sort of canon within the canon, insofar as this biblical book (along with others, such as the Gospel of John) provided him with the key to the comprehension and interpretation of all the others. The Christian doctrine of grace is there given one of its essential foundations. But the density of the writing presents a notable challenge for interpreters. From the origins of Christianity up until this very day, the Epistle to the Romans, in its entirety and in individual passages, has provoked debates and controversies among its interpreters. A particularly acute example is found in chapter 7, from verse 7 until its conclusion in verse 25—the passage upon which the following study will meditate:

> What then should we say? That the law is sin? By no means! Yet, if it had not been for the law, I would not have known sin. I would not have known what it is to covet if the law had not said, "You shall not covet." But sin, seizing an opportunity in the commandment, produced in me all kinds of covetousness. Apart from the law sin lies dead. I was once alive apart from the law, but when the commandment

came, sin revived and I died, and the very commandment that promised life proved to be death to me. For sin, seizing an opportunity in the commandment, deceived me and through it killed me. So the law is holy, and the commandment is holy and just and good. Did what is good, then, bring death to me? By no means! It was sin, working death in me through what is good, in order that sin might be shown to be sin, and through the commandment might become sinful beyond measure. For we know that the law is spiritual; but I am of the flesh, sold into slavery under sin. I do not understand my own actions. For I do not do what I want, but I do the very thing I hate. Now if I do what I do not want, I agree that the law is good. But in fact it is no longer I that do it, but sin that dwells within me. For I know that nothing good dwells within me, that is, in my flesh. I can will what is right, but I cannot do it. For I do not do the good I want, but the evil I do not want is what I do. Now if I do what I do not want, it is no longer I that do it, but sin that dwells within me. So I find it to be a law that when I want to do what is good, evil lies close at hand. For I delight in the law of God in my inmost self, but I see in my members another law at war with the law of my mind, making me captive to the law of sin that dwells in my members. Wretched man that I am! Who will rescue me from this body of death? Thanks be to God through Jesus Christ our Lord! So then, with my mind I am a slave to the law of God, but with my flesh I am a slave to the law of sin. (Rom. 7:7–25)

Entire library stacks could be filled with treaties discussing the correct interpretation of this passage. There the best-known authors of the Christian tradition would be found, from Origen to St. Augustine, from St. Thomas Aquinas to Luther and Calvin, and beyond. This study will not recount the history of these debates nor claim to decide them, but it will focus on certain philosophical aspects of this hermeneutical conflict by privileging the study of the first person singular, of the "I"—that is, the "I" of the speaker in the epistle as well as the I of the reader, which interact with each other.

Indeed, the lively and dramatic intensity of this passage, which grabs hold of any reader, arises from the constant usage of the first person singular and of the pronoun *me*. In fact, the contrast with the preceding passages is stark: in the whole of chapter 6 as well as in the first six verses of chapter 7, St. Paul expresses himself insistently in the first and second person plural (*we* and *you* [*vous*]), the *we* of the Christian community and the *you* of his addressees (called "brothers"; Rom. 7:2). There are only two uses of the first person singular in authorial comments (Rom. 6:19: "I am speaking in human terms because of your natural limitations," and Rom. 7:1: "for I am speaking to those who know the law") and a single use of the pronoun, in Romans 7:4, "my brothers" (literally in Greek, "brothers of me"). Then, in Romans 7:7 the passage to the first person singular is sudden and remains in force, nearly exclusively, until the end of the chapter. Apart from "our Lord" (Rom. 7:25), the only use of the first person plural ("For we know that the law is spiritual"; Rom. 7:14) is exclusive rather than inclusive—that is, it serves to oppose the I to the we instead of joining them: "but, *me*, I am of the flesh. . . ." For readers who are not familiar with ancient Greek, it is necessary to explain that unlike English or French, but as with Latin, this language does not require in normal usage that a pronoun precede the verb: the person is indicated by the verbal form itself. Thus when the pronoun is written or pronounced, it signifies an exceptional emphasis on the person in question, as in the English form "*as for myself*, I think . . ." or "you *yourself* said. . . ." Now in this short passage, twenty-three occurrences of the pronoun *me* can be noted in its various cases (me, of me, for me), and this extraordinarily high frequency indeed discloses the main purpose of the writer.

In a famous phrase opening a reflection on identity, the philosopher Plotinus says, "But we ourselves, what are We? [*Mais nous—qui nous?*]"[2] In our case, since the church fathers, the question is exactly *who* says "I" in this passage of the Epistle to the Romans: *which* one is this *me* who seems to confess to us the tearing of his interiority and his intimate, personal struggle? As soon as this question is raised, one of the many paradoxes elicited by this passage surfaces. Certainly, upon discovering these verses, the ordinary reader may have an impression of familiarity. To recount one's difficulties and torments by repeating "me" would appear, on the one hand, from our contemporary point of view, as the most direct and most ordinary mode of self-expression. On the other hand, the reader could believe that he is recognizing something of his own experience (in confronting his "I" with the "I" of the speaker) in at least certain phrases of this passage. After all, who has not known the fascination of a prohibition when we are attracted to and seduced by an act precisely because it is forbidden? Who has not known the wretched failure of good resolutions when we fail to accomplish that which we—sometimes solemnly—set out to do, and we persist, despite our decisions and shame, in a habit that we know is bad or harmful? This feeling of an immediate communication between the speaker and the reader is, as is often the case, a gross misperception. If, in fact, this passage raises questions of a universal scope, we can only grasp them as such after the many reflections and mediations required in order to draw out the exact meaning and not upon the first glance at the words. Precisely that which appears the easiest to comprehend in this passage is in reality the most difficult and problematic.

It may be true from a rhetorical and literary perspective that a first-person speech touches its listener or reader in a characteristic way. After all, such speech does deliver a call, from which it is difficult to withdraw, at least when it is not simply an anecdote. It evokes essential conflicts of human existence by inviting one to ask oneself, "And as for me, where am I in regard to this matter? Is this test also mine or is it alien to me?" Nevertheless, the meaning and nature of this call varies greatly according to how I perceive the personality of the one who is expressing himself and the human situation in which he finds himself and from which he derives his meditation. The failures of a weak man before miniscule difficulties of everyday life do not move me in the same way as the shipwrecks of a strong man in great trials. For this reason, the interpretation of this passage presents considerable complexity.

Without its being either possible or desirable to set forth the complete history of the exegesis of this passage, it suffices to note for this essay that its exegetes always begin with a first alternative. They seek to determine whether the "I" who speaks ought to be considered that of Paul, an "autobiographical I," as it is called today, or whether this "I" is another, whose experience Paul describes by taking on his role, by inhabiting his character, in order to describe the experience from the inside. But once one of these two interpretative choices has been made, the question of meaning has not yet been answered, because then a new question arises, the decisive one. If Paul speaks in his own name: what moment of his experience, or what period of his life, is he describing? If Paul speaks in the name of another type of person: *what* type of person and in *what* situation, with respect to his relation to God? Two recent authoritative commentaries on the Epistle to the Romans, one by Cranfield, the other by Witherington, illustrate this hermeneutical knot. Naturally they divide this passage in two sections according to the verbal tenses employed (Rom. 7:7–13 in the past and 7:14–25 in the present). In the first section Cranfield distinguishes six interpretations (that is, identifications of the "I") and Witherington five, and in the second section seven and eight respectively.[3] Yet their interpretations of the second section are diametrically opposed.

At least one certainty imposes itself: to consider one part autobiographical and not the other, and thus that St. Paul, in the same passage, would move suddenly from one use of "I" to another without warning and without indication, is somewhat violent and incoherent. The past and the present tenses form a meaningful whole and refer to each other. Either the entire passage must be understood as referring to Paul, or throughout, Paul must be assuming another character than his own person. Moreover, what is understood by "autobiographical" must be made explicit, and defining criteria must be given. A number of features noted since Christian antiquity contradict the interpretation of this passage as an account of the individual Paul's private experience. At what moment was Paul, a Jew circumcised from a young age, "without law"? And if the second part is supposed to describe his life in Judaism, how does one reconcile this torn and tormented experience with other speeches by St. Paul, pronounced beyond doubt in his own name, that do not offer even the slightest characteristics of a similar vision (for example, Phil. 3:6 and Gal. 1:14 cited by numerous exegetes)? Even so, that Paul speaks in the name of a general possibility of human existence, of the way a person stands before the law or lives in the law, does not mean that this human possibility is completely foreign to him or that he never adopted it in one way or another. The choice is not between the singular account of a private experience and the evocation of that with which I bear nothing in common. To speak, for example, of human anguish in the face of death, as may take place in a philosophy course, is indeed not to recount one's own anguish and the manner in which one experiences it, but neither is it to affirm that it is foreign to oneself. My particular relationship to this anguish can remain undetermined, and nothing can de deduced in regard to my interior life, since I may be describing a possibility that I have surpassed or overcome. A famous and concise example of this hermeneutical difficulty in identifying the "I" is the sentence of the great seventeenth-century French thinker and scientist Blaise Pascal, found in his *Pensées*: "The eternal silence of these infinite spaces frightens me [Le silence éternel de ces espaces infinis m'effraie.]"[4] Everyone recognizes its formal and rhythmic perfection in French. But is this a fear that the individual, Pascal, experienced, and that he confides to us with a stroke of the pen, in which case we would be cast into interminable speculations about Pascal's personality and spirituality? Or rather is the sentence to be found in the mouth of a human being without God, in an apologetic design, in order to show his dereliction and fragile solitude? The sentence's meaning and the speech toward which these words direct us are not at all the same in these two cases. To move forward with these questions, this study will focus on the second part by accentuating both the interaction between the speaker and the reader and that which the interpretive variations, St. Augustine's in particular, tell us about the changes in the determinations and defining dimensions of Christian existence.

But, before turning to the second part, it is best to approach the first section. To see it as a singular and empirical confession is manifestly untenable when one perceives the universal scope of its newly opened dimensions and of the concepts that tie themselves within it in a tight and dramatic knot in order to describe the advent and the event of evil through the (divine) law: life and death, law and sin, desire understood as covetousness or concupiscence. It is a matter of an inaugural and catastrophic event by which the very meaning of life and death is altered and overwhelmed. These terms are some of the most general ones used with respect to human existence: that which was for life ends up serving death; that which is not only good, but just and saintly, becomes an occasion for the eruption and outpouring of evil. "And I died" (Rom. 7:10): the paradox of this sentence, in principle impossible, expresses the unprecedented [*inouïe*] force of the matter at hand. It is undeniable that the narrative of the Fall of Man in Genesis 3 underlies these words, as many exegetes have insisted, and that these sentences have us live, by their form, this "Fall" in some way from the inside, even if it is possible to imagine a number of different relationships between this fall that is a spiritual death and Adam's Fall. Philo of Alexandria (*Legum Allegoriae* I, §§ 105–7), had already affirmed, prior to the church fathers, that Adam and Eve had begun to die at the very instant when they committed their sin, in accordance with Genesis 2:17 ("in the day that you eat of it you shall die").

It is important to note that, in this first section, neither the name of God nor the man's name is pronounced. (They will be in the second section: "the law of God" [Rom. 7:22] and "Wretched man that I am" [Rom. 7:24]). In this first part, the presentation is purified, even rarefied [*raréfiée*] to an extreme. This major and significant catastrophe that transforms the economy of human existence from top to bottom is described concisely, in a few lines, in an utterance that is dedicated exclusively to the *logic* of this event, to its underlying *structure*. The *form* bears no commonality with an empirical account of a particular experience. Only a blind person could believe that he perceives therein the self-description of private emotions as such. This *drama is a three-person drama*: the law (or the commandment), sin, and "me." The effect of sin is concupiscence or covetousness. The event is an inversion of life and death: the power of death comes to life and to an intense life; the power of life is used by the power of death, for death—that is, for itself—and "me," I pass from life to death.

The fact that the law is said to be "holy" signifies that it is God's law, that God alone gives it and commands in it; yet grammatically and literarily, it seems to exist in and by itself: the law "says" or proffers (Rom. 7:7).[5] In the same way, sin is the subject of a number of action verbs, as if it were an existing, personal power (Rom. 7:8–10, 13). The implication is not that St. Paul hypostatized evil but rather that this agency underlines the dramatic character of this transformation and presents it in the form of lively, quick, and nearly instantaneous events, as a fight between the law and sin, in which "me, I" am, at one and the same time, the battlefield and the victim. In this passage, by means of the law, evil *becomes* a force that acts on me as well as in me. Once again, the universal dimension of the powers at work in this drama exclude the possibility of considering these sentences as bearing a strictly individual value and as communicating a particular and uncommon experience—over and beyond the fact that such interpretations would require attributing an untenable egocentrism to St. Paul. Rather, this part offers us terms and a dramatic schema in order that each one can articulate the meaning of his personal existence and of his captivity. In fact, such a reading is implied by definition by the literary genre of a pastoral epistle, which is not a private letter confiding in a friend.

This drama is the drama of *the manifestation and the revelation of evil as evil* by means of the interdict pronounced by the law. The interdict states what it proscribes, and, in so doing, it brings it forth and makes it appear *as* evil. The appearance of evil itself shapes a double-sided event. On the one hand, only when evil itself is identified can one defend oneself, avoid it, and struggle against it—a visible and recognized enemy is a lesser concern than an invisible and unfamiliar enemy whose existence has not made itself known, or whom one considers harmless or even friendly. But on the other hand, when evil itself appears, passes from latent to patent, and becomes a real possibility before me or within me, it truly and properly becomes itself, it is fulfilled as such, it raises itself up upon its own ground: now when I gaze upon it openly, upon its actual form, its power of seduction and bewitching is given all its strength. Only then can it attract me *as evil*. Significantly in Romans 7:14, the *apparition* of sin as sin, far from being the beginning of its decline or a victory against it, is an instrument of its action and the pathway by which it will reach the fullness of its malignancy or by which sin constitutes its empire over us by perverting that which ought to vanquish it.

The word of the law, which forbids me to murder, steal, or lie, reveals such acts as unmistakably bad and at the same time addresses me unmistakably as one who can or could murder, steal, or lie, for that which I ought not to do is by definition that which I could do, otherwise the prohibition would make no sense. In this regard, Søren Kierkegaard's admirable meditation on liberty and the vertigo of the possible in *The Concept of Anxiety* is well known. As Origen and St. Augustine both noted, the Epistle to the Romans does not claim that there are no evil desires or sins before the law, but that we come to know them and recognize them only by the law and in its light (Rom. 7:7). The light of the law makes the darkness visible as darkness; the holiness of the law shows evil and injustice as they are and as that which revolts against God. Thereby the law brings it to pass that, for our conscience, the revolt of evil and injustice, along with their power for death, can rise in an action that is properly their own. They enter into a veritable open war against justice. They set themselves up as a party or camp—that is, a side that one could join or a choice that one could make, with full knowledge of the facts. In a manner of speaking, evil comes of age—as is said of a human who reaches adulthood—and becomes a power acting in its own name. (An example of this reversal, albeit unquestionably less serious and less wide-ranging, yet very significant, is found in certain modern, post-Romantic interpretations of *Paradise Lost*, which see in Milton's Satan the spokesman for the highest human values of liberty and autonomy, advancing precisely in the opposite direction from that which without doubt constituted the poet's intention: in a novel by Joyce Cary, a character asserts that Milton should not be given as reading for children, for Satan's speeches would be too attractive!)

The law that clearly delimits the distinction between the use and the abuse or between the good and evil usage of our desires, of things, or of words, can itself be that which evil abuses in order to come forth in power. Indeed, every fight, if the comparison with bodily struggles is acceptable, implies contact with the enemy, in which he can also grasp or hold one of our limbs. One cannot touch without being touched. This passage will be foundational for Luther's doctrine of the law, but the text itself does not impose his interpretation. The logic at work here could also be drawn out in an anti-nomistic direction, leading to the rejection of the law altogether, as if it created the evil it reveals, or leading to the dangerous utopian vision according to which the law would no longer be necessary if each human being would purify himself, whether through a religious conversion or through the transformation of the conditions of social existence. I might as well seek to kill the doctor because he reveals to me my sickness or believe that medicine could one day be eliminated because everyone will live in perfect health!

The focus of the most lively and sometimes violent debates within the tradition, however, is the second section of this passage, and their stakes bear the greatest significance for this study. Henceforth the first-person speech is in *the present tense*, and its importance increases all the more, since out of the twenty-three uses of the pronouns "me," "myself," and "I," seven appear in the first section, and sixteen in the second, thus more than double, without counting the first-person verbal forms. Moreover, the very nature of the description is characterized by an increasing interiorization: the speaker presents in a much more developed way, from the inside, as he sees and feels them, the consequences of the drama exposed in the preceding section. In the first part, the "law" or the "commandment" is four times the subject of a verb but in the second part, only twice (it is "spiritual" in Rom. 7:14 and "good" in 7:16, where its *nature* is so described and not its *action*), and thereafter it is no more than an object or is located in some other phrase (Rom. 7:16, 21, 22). The "law" also splits in two: another law opposes itself to "the law of God" and the "law of my spirit"—this "other law" is bad (Rom. 7:21–23). This innermost conflict and rift, described in the present in the first person, might appear naturally in an epistle to be attributed directly to its author, Paul, exposing his own situation. But major difficulties then arise. If the conflict concerns the current life of the Apostle Paul, it would concern his life as a Christian, in the dimensions of grace and redemption received in the death and resurrection of Christ. In addition to the fact that it would be strange to proclaim that Christian existence is characterized by powerlessness and enslavement in regard to evil and torment, which would not be an apostolic message, how can one understand that the same man, in the same time and from the same perspective, may depict himself as slave and as free, as carnal and as spiritual, as dead and as alive, as one who bears the law of sin and one in whom God's spirit acts—a question that cannot but be posed upon reading the end of this chapter as well as the following chapter, where the second terms of these oppositions appear?

The Lutheran doctrine of the human being *simul justus et peccator*, at once righteous and sinner, which responds to this question, cannot be immediately adduced as an explication, since it is grounded precisely upon the exegesis of this passage and thus cannot serve as a preliminary guide for the interpretation of this passage without creating a vicious methodological circle. Redemption is the sovereign act of God, liberating the human being from captivity to unrighteousness (injustice) and sin: how could the man who says of himself in an extremely powerful statement, "but I am of the flesh, sold unto slavery under sin" (Rom. 7:14), be liberated and ransomed from slavery? How can the man who here writes, "now if I do what I do not want, it is no longer I that do it, but sin that dwells within me" (Rom. 7:20) also be the man who at the same moment in a similar situation says, "it is no longer I who live, but it is Christ who lives in me" (Gal. 2:20a)?[6] How can the joy of redemption and of liberating resurrection be reconciled with the exclamation "Wretched man that I am! Who will rescue me from this body of death?" (Rom. 7:24)? These are a few of the arguments that led a number of church fathers to consider that St. Paul is not describing his (or the) baptized Christian life, but human life before the grace of Christ and redemption. The most widespread biblical translation in France at this time—the *Bible de Jérusalem*—adopts this vision by introducing an editorial subtitle for this passage currently under examination: "The human without Christ under sin." In short, is the speaker here dead or resurrected? As it would be redundant to make a list of the many renowned thinkers who understood the passage in this way, it is sufficient to recall Origen's powerful claim in his *Commentary on the Epistle to the Romans*: "But whoever understands these words by attributing them to the Apostle seems to me to be evoking despair [*desperationem*] in every soul" by pointing out that we are always enslaved to the law of sin.[7] In Christian thought, despair is the worst state that may befall the human. In other words, for Origen, understanding these words as ascribed to St. Paul and the Christian life would be *to invert* radically the focus of the epistle and, in the fundamental sense, *to destroy it as gospel*, as Good News, and to make of it bad news, by indicating the inescapable character of our imprisonment in evil, from which St. Paul himself, according to the interpretation that Origen rejects, would never have been freed.

The central question arises for us right here: how can one comprehend the movement of thought, wherein the possibility that this passage describes the human in the grace of Christ becomes the dominant interpretation? In fact, despite the horror of the great thinker and most important exegete Origen, did not St. Augustine's move from the first interpretation (the human before grace) to the second interpretation (the human in Christ's grace) authorize the dominance of this interpretive possibility up until today, when it is contested anew? One ought to consider how, in what sense, and why this interpretation could come to be understood as describing the *Christian life* in its most singular character. The majority of studies of this passage are busy trying to have their interpretation prevail and to gain further arguments against advocates of a different reading without inquiring about the meaning of the historical movement from the first interpretation to the second or about what is revealed with regard to this changing understanding of Christian existence.

John Cassian, one of the pioneers of monastic life and thought in Europe, sets up an in-depth debate between these two interpretations and settles on the second. His foremost work, *Conferences*, presents itself as dialogues between monks on questions of spiritual theology. At the end of chapter 22 and throughout 23, the discussion turns to the meaning of chapter 7 of the Epistle to the Romans in the context of a reflection on impeccability, an ideal of certain monks that Cassian clearly rejects. For him, Christ alone is without sin, although a person may overcome any serious sin by Christ's grace. The monk Theonas cites a number of verses from the end of chapter 7 (19, 20, 22–23), explicitly attributing them to the Apostle Paul's very person, and comments on them as follows: "Upon contemplating the full extent of his fragility or that of his (human) nature, he became terrified by the scale of such immoderate [*démesurée*] depths and fled to the haven of divine succor"—that is, toward grace. Previously he had asserted that the sentence from the book of Proverbs 26:16, "for though [the righteous] will fall seven times, they will rise again," can be attributed to Paul. John Cassian even has his character enumerate the nature of the seven falls (a distraction, a hesitation, an unexpected thought particularly during prayer), while distinguishing them from all "mortal sin." Faced with these assertions, his interlocutor, Germain, exclaims and protests, affirming that many understand these words by attributing them not to Paul himself, but to sinners who, being prisoners of their carnal habits and captives of the tyranny of evil, would like to abstain and not yield to evil, but cannot. Paul then speaks not in his name, but in their name (*non ex sua, sed ex peccantium persona*).[8] He is only giving them voice and is drawing on the classical arguments that were highlighted previously: "the elected jar" that Paul had become could no longer be a "captive" borne along by the law of sin, despite himself, toward evil actions.

Regardless of the interpretation adopted, the interpreter should not blunt the cutting edge of the passage's language. For example, Father Lagrange, a famous Dominican exegete, wrote the following comments on Romans 7:15 ("For I do not do what I want, but I do the very thing I hate"): "It is prudent not to stick too closely to terms that are not exempt from a certain literary exaggeration."[9] After all, St. Paul ought to be credited, a fortiori in this essential work, with knowing what he is saying and with choosing his words, and their more or less powerful force, with discernment. To distort and change the weight of his words by decreeing (in the name of what criteria?) that they do not have their customary value is, on the interpreter's part, to exchange gold for straw.

Returning to John Cassian, the debate further deepens in the next dialogue and even reaches a sort of extreme boundary. Indeed, Theonas completely reverses the thesis exposited by Germain: far from suiting "the sinful person," the second section of the passage here under examination concerns none other than "the perfect ones alone," those who conform to the life of the apostles of Christ. Only they could speak such utterances. It would be impossible to imagine a more complete reversal of Origen's interpretation, cited previously, according to which the attribution of these words to apostolic life would push everyone to despair. But in what sense can these utterances reveal the perfect Christian? For to declare oneself captive to the power of sin is assuredly a highly paradoxical sign of such perfection. Theonas's propositions put forward two arguments, the one negative, the other positive. The heart of the negative argument is that if there is a struggle and conflict within me, if I yield despite myself to the "law of sin" and accomplish evil while willing the good, I must yet know and love the good, and thus I am not utterly corrupt, nor evil through and through.[10] This may be indeed true, but it also raises some difficulties with significant consequences. Furthermore, a significant fault line lies between not being completely evil and being perfect.

The first difficulty is in some way identifying evil with the extremity of evil, with a radical and total evil. Evil then is our only possession, our only good, and becomes identified with pure amorality and not with immorality in a figure that could be called diabolical. The second difficulty lies in bracketing the question of knowing whether or not I am committing a more serious evil by carrying out an evil that I recognize as such than by failing to imagine other possibilities. Do I not profane justice more seriously by acting against my conscience and against that which it recognizes as just than by having a completely false and shadowy conscience, where I obey without hesitation nothing but my desire? For our humanity, the second case is more frightening when it is witnessed; but the first case bears in itself the measure of its weighty culpability. The third difficulty, the decisive one for our argument, consists in the fact that this interpretation leads to a deep *metamorphosis* of evil and of its exact nature, which is here in question: the sins against which St. Paul, or those who are as perfect as he, struggle (in this reading) are venial and not mortal sins, which *nothing* in the text of this epistle indicates. The contrary would be more likely given the forcefulness of the writer's expressions. Yet this interpretation will have a lengthy posterity as attested by John Calvin's firm repetition: "we must observe, that this conflict, of which the Apostle speaks, does not exist in man before he is renewed by the Spirit of God: for man, left to his own nature, is wholly borne along by his lusts without any resistance."[11] All natural law, upon which to the contrary Origen depends, is then excluded.

The positive argument is expressed by John Cassian in a beautiful parable, summarized as follows. . . . Imagine that two individuals enter a spacious dwelling in which is found a profusion of furniture and things. The one has a clear and piercing vision, the other, such as a nearsighted person, a poor and blurry vision. The second will only see large masses; all the details will escape him, whereas the first will distinguish clearly the least recess and the smallest detail. The "saints" are the "sighted" [*voyants*]: when they look into the dwelling of their soul, nothing escapes them, and thus they see all types of little sins that others do not perceive.[12] The aforementioned examples of sins that St. Paul (according to this interpretation) attributes to himself are in fact extremely significant: a momentary slackening of attention, a fleeting thought or image that crosses his mind while he is praying. Literally, they are *minutia*, what John Cassian calls "the dust [*minutiae*] of multiple stains accumulated on us." St. Augustine, in his great examination of conscience at the end of book X of the *Confessions*, also describes this intermittent character of one's attention: the sight of a spider capturing a fly, albeit merely an instant, can distract us from a weighty task.

The higher our expectations, the more we see with acuity all the ways in which we go astray, the more God's grace purifies us, the more our vigilant gaze notes all that is impure in us, although it may only have lasted an instant and was produced without our explicit consent. From a purely descriptive point of view, this is undeniably true, and everyone knows that the saints considered themselves the worst sinners on account of thoughts that would appear without any serious consequences to those of us who are not saints. Such vigilance is most certainly demanded by the gospel itself, as is seen in the Sermon on the Mount (with its invitation to be perfect "as your heavenly Father is perfect"—Matt. 5:48): to gaze with desire upon a woman who is not mine is already to commit adultery (Matt. 5:27). The issue is thus not at all that of contesting the pertinence of this description in itself for the life of the saints; it is to know if that is really what St. Paul is aiming at toward the end of chapter 7. The center of this hermeneutical controversy therefore becomes the profound, most fundamental question of the nature of the evil that persists in us and of the manner in which it is to be characterized.

If Origen refuses to attribute the conflict of chapter 7 to Paul's personal description of his own Christian life, it is definitely because he sees described therein much more serious and grave faults. Yet evidently he did not ignore the existence of distractions in prayer, since in his treatise *On Prayer* (XII.2) he furnishes the classical principle that enables the reconciliation of the intermittent character of our attention, on the one hand, with the evangelical expectancy of perpetual prayer, on the other hand ("pray without ceasing"—1 Thess. 5:17). Origen writes, "We regard the whole life of the saint as one great continuous prayer. What is usually termed 'prayer' is but a part of this prayer."[13] If we perform an action for the love of God, it is prayer even if we do not think of God at each instant that we act. We might conclude that John Cassian and John Calvin's interpretations both *beg the question* [*petitio principii*]: first, the words about slavery to sin are attributed to St. Paul, and second, since St. Paul is speaking, these sins are interpreted as minutia.

The direction and meaning of this movement, however, is very important. It is one of *increasing interiorization*, which becomes more and more pronounced with the growing hold and influence of conscientious self-examination, with an ever-sharper gaze upon oneself, a gaze that eventually becomes the norm of Christian life—its very signature. Combat against the forces of evil at work in the world, and in our acts performed within the world, tends to be replaced, in a world dominated by Christian faith, by an increasingly violent inner combat. "Peace also has its martyrs" was a patristic saying that appeared when public persecutions were decreasing or disappearing. To wrestle with the internal enemy of faith requires no less courage than to wrestle against its external enemy. The more sin's "pockets of resistance" (if military language is appropriate) are limited and circumscribed within us, as in the life of saints, while appearing all the same impossible to reduce or eliminate altogether, the more their presence appears severe and their persistence oppressive. Combat moves into the most hidden corners, the most inaccessible parts of the inner person. The fight against the "good conscience" and against pride replaces the fight against apostasy and public denial of faith. Many centuries later, Kierkegaard's entire movement of thought, including its polemical vigor, rests upon the fact that he lives in an officially Christian society, where "being Christian" is supposed to be self-evident and appears clear. Moreover, the Christian language itself changes. Expressions previously reserved for mortal sins now designated venial sins. This shift was not a "literary exaggeration," but the sign of a heightened vigilance, of a tracking of sin within us—a development to which monastic life contributed. The implication is not that the earlier writers were less demanding, but that they were not exactly speaking the same language, and above all that they did not see human *finitude* in the same light. This latter point is the other major dimension of our reading.

It is worth meditating on the fact that not only does this passage in the first person take on the forcefulness of a call and a request for the very person of the reader, which is the basis and goal of its form, but, in addition, that this passage on the division and the tearing of the "I" between two dimensions or directions, corresponding to two laws, comes to divide the interpreters into two groups and to tear them apart violently. To attribute what, in our eyes, is an interpretive mistake to the moral or spiritual shortcomings of the interpreter was widespread in prior periods, in the context of violent religious polemics, but fortunately enough has nearly disappeared from contemporary exegesis. A judgment upon the *human* who interprets is no longer customary, even if his insight and rigor of method are questioned. Yet this passage still sometimes elicits such judgment, as under the pen of Cranfield in an otherwise excellent commentary. In regard to the expression of Romans 7:14, he writes, "We ought to ask ourselves whether our inability to accept this expression as descriptive of a Christian is not perhaps the result of a failure on our part to realize the full seriousness of the ethical demands of God's law (or of the Gospel)."[14] He is writing in the first person plural, but he is not speaking of himself, since he maintains the exact opposite interpretation. He is engaging in the same practice to express his thought as the one that his adversaries assign to St. Paul in this passage (speaking in the first-person present tense in the name of someone else or of another type of person, other than oneself). Indeed, this "we" signifies "you" [*vous*]: you should ask yourselves if. . . . As such it introduces a reproach of extreme severity. In fact, it is an intimidating criticism that also bears a kind of trap: if I am accused of a poor reading because my religious experience is narrow and superficial, how can I assert on the contrary that I am a much more discerning Christian without being immediately caught in the act of pride? But the trap also closes on the one who set it. To reverse the proposition would be to say, "I interpret better than you, for I am more spiritually advanced and discerning," while at the same time affirming that the more elevated one is spiritually, the more one sees forcefully the evil within. It is precisely this that leads Cranfield to ask that rhetorical question (after all, he had already answered it de facto).

The gravity of the stakes in this debate has now been made manifest. It is significant that that against which John Cassian is fighting, in the passages previously cited, is a certain monastic ideal of impeccability, just as it is also significant that the controversy with Pelagius and the Pelagians—for whom the Christian can attain moral perfection and therefore must do so, up to the point of being able truly to call oneself without sin—is, in everyone's eyes, a decisive factor (albeit not the only one) in the movement by which St. Augustine passes from the first to the second interpretation of the epistle's chapter 7, identifying in this way the internal struggle with Christian life itself, a move from which most exegetes turn away today. Revisiting the often-studied history of this shift is not the present task.[15] St. Augustine has explained himself, justifying this hermeneutical change, but the kick of his argument is really the fact that he criticizes vigorously an interpretation, putatively penned by the Pelagians, that had long been his own and that he frequently advanced in distinct explications and various arguments. Besides, it figures in his best-known work. In the *Confessions* (VIII.5.11–12), he describes his past life with great, forceful expression, making use of the words of St. Paul; yet this passage addresses his life immediately *prior* to his conversion.[16] Moreover, it is noteworthy that in a few places, St. Augustine does not present these two interpretations as absolutely exclusive but describes the second, the one ascribed to the Christian under grace, as *probabilius*, more probable than the first, which does not render it absurd or impossible.[17] St. Thomas Aquinas, noticing the two successive interpretations of St. Augustine, constructs his own commentary by presenting the *two* interpretations one after the other, sentence by sentence, all the while considering the second "better," flowing more easily from the text. He thus accepts that both are meaningful—though unequally so—and that both call for much thought. Nevertheless, polemics lead St. Augustine to harden his tone and affirm that he had understood (in his first interpretation) otherwise or, rather, that he had *not* understood altogether (*aliter intellexeram, vel potius non intellexeram*) and that finally he "yielded to better and more intelligent interpreters, or rather, if it must be said, to truth itself," such that the first interpretation is now denounced as positively false (so also argued John Cassian and, later, Luther and Calvin).[18]

What are the results? This passage—heavy with stakes of great consequence for the comprehension of existence, specifically Christian existence, on account of the dimensions put into play (even if certain isolated expressions have been identified with pagan sentences when the logic of the whole is ignored)—is a fruitful place to meditate on the tensions and difficulties of biblical hermeneutics as illustrated by the enduring controversies on the subject. It shows, first, that the first person singular, which appears spontaneously to be such a clear mode of expression that it does not even require any interpretation, constitutes in reality, by its fluidity, by its plasticity, by the diversity of its possible usages, a powerfully enigmatic and, as the case may be, ambiguous form. Whatever may be drawn from a written work in the first person that presents a dimension of experience can be intensely problematic. Immediacy is often illusory. Moreover, reading such a written work puts in play and in question [*en jeu et en cause*] one's own "I"—that is, one's interpretation of himself and of his personal experience—which opens or closes him in various ways to the meaningful horizons of that which he is reading, in other modalities than those called for by an impersonal writing. My own real or possible tearing is evoked by a passage that speaks of the tearing of the I: I appear [*je comparais*] with my own obscurity before the writing that speaks of human obscurity. There is here a *critical* aspect, in the original Greek sense of *krisis*: what I read discerns the possibilities within me, even divides my possibilities. This is one of the reasons this passage of St. Paul's has been able to arouse such passions among its interpreters: what conflicts may I recognize eventually as mine or as belonging (or not) to my existence in faith?

This hermeneutical fact and question indicates that a pure exegetical approach, appealing to neutrality and objectivity, is insufficient: an extraordinary deepening of experience has been carried out in each one of the interpretations, and schemata have been clarified, which neither paganism nor Judaism had seen, at least with this precision. Even though one of them might be judged not to correspond to St. Paul's intention, all the surplus of meaning that has been built upon it belongs forever to Christian thought and cannot be purely and simply set aside on the grounds that it would be false. (As far as I am concerned, I have only come lately to think that this passage pertains to the human being before grace, and I have thus followed, despite myself, in the opposite direction, the pathway taken by Augustine, for whom I have such great veneration.)

At issue in this debate over the identification of the I who speaks in this chapter of St. Paul's Epistle to the Romans, and in the reversal of the dominant interpretation in the Latin tradition, is *the accentuation of the drama* present in Christian existence and experience. Instead of emphasizing above all the extraordinary liberation given in baptism by confronting it with non-Christian forms of existence, we focus on the fact that this liberation, for whoever sees himself called to saintliness, is the opening of a more acute and more violent interior combat that will only end with our temporal life. The human being's interiority comes under the scrutiny of an ever-more-acute gaze, and thereupon a greater sense of human finitude and fragility, even within the freedom of the Spirit, takes root in and deepens thoughts and practices. Grace, then, is not first that which gives life and serenity, but that which gives strength to fight (evidently this is not an alternative but a shift in emphasis). An *agonistic model* of Christian existence prevails, freed from the dream of impassibility, inherited from stoicism, and present in certain church fathers or from the ideal "Gnostic," St. Clement of Alexandria. The most elevated mystical life is no longer the one that escapes from conflict, having overcome it by the grace of God, but the one that has continued to fight when others quit, believing they no longer had to fight. In this version, war is and always will be within us, at least within time: the inner space will never cease to be a battlefield, where the enemy's resistance increases in proportion to the territory conquered.

Feelings, passions, movements, or acts of the spirit cannot be described in the same manner as material things. The words, the concepts, the schemata that we forge to outline define [*cerner*] and distinguish them, powerfully structure our very experience, and open new possibilities for how I get a grip on myself. The interpretation of this passage not only *described otherwise* Christian interiority, it *produced interiority*, another Christian interiority, and left its mark on Western history. In the abounding contemporary debates on the "sources of the I [*moi*]" and on the history of the conceptions of personal identity, the focus is primarily on the theoretical definitions that have been given. But the existential sites where this identity forges itself, the nature of the conflicts where it is reinforced or weakened, are no less important. The debate over the interpretation of chapter 7 of the Epistle to the Romans, unknown or ignored by philosophers, is in this matter determinative. To overestimate its role in the history of the spirit would be impossible. The preceding pages make no claim to exhaust its meaning but rather to set forth its importance and to define more carefully the fundamental questions it raises.

Translated by Reuben Glick-Shank

Notes

1. Martin Luther, *Commentary on Romans*, trans. J. Theodore Mueller (Grand Rapids: Zondervan, 1954), xiii.

2. Plotinus, *Enneads* VI.4.14, trans. A. H. Armstrong (Cambridge, Mass.: Harvard University Press, 1988), 317.

3. C. E. B. Cranfield, *A Critical and Exegetical Commentary on the Epistle to the Romans* (Edinburgh and New York: T. and T. Clark, 2001), 1:342–44; Ben Witherington III, *Paul's Letter to the Romans: A Socio-Rhetorical Commentary* (Grand Rapids: Eerdmans, 2004), 187.

4. Blaise Pascal, *Pensées*, ed. M. Le Guern (Paris: Gallimard, 1995), 161; English translation: Blaise Pascal, *Pensées*, trans. Roger Ariew (Indianapolis: Hackett, 2004), 64.

5. S. Legasse, *L'Epitre de Paul aux Romains* (Paris: Cerf, 2002), 452; the best recent commentary in French.

6. St. Augustine, in his second period, contests this objection made by the Pelagian Julian, grounding himself on Galatians 2:20: St. Paul is only speaking of desires to which he does not consent and that never become acts, because the presence of Christ's Spirit within him reveals to him their evil; *Contra Julianum Pelagianum* VI.23.71ff.

7. Origen, *Comentarii in epistulam ad Romanos* VI.10. 2; my translation.

8. John Cassian, *Conférences*, ed. E. Pichery (Paris: Cerf, 1959), 3:131–35; my translation.

9. M. J. Lagrange, *Saint Paul: Epître aux Romains*, 7th ed. (Paris: Études Bibliques, 1950), 175.

10. Cassian, *Conférences*, 3:138–39; my translation.

11. John Calvin, *Commentaries: Epistle of Paul the Apostle to the Romans*, trans. John Owen (Grand Rapids: Baker, 1989), 19:262.

12. Cassian, *Conférences*, 3:147–48; my translation.

13. Origen, *Prayer: Exhortation to Martyrdom*, trans. John Joseph O'Meara (Mahwah, N.J.: Paulist Press, 1954), 47.

14. Cranfield, *Critical and Exegetical Commentary on the Epistle to the Romans*, 1:346.

15. See in particular the work of M. F. Berrouard, "L'exégèse augustinienne de Rom. 7, 7–25 entre 396 et 418," *Recherches augustinienne* 16 (1981): 101–95.

16. Contrary to Witherington's assertion in *Paul's Letter to the Romans*, 188

17. See, e.g., Augustine, *Retractationes* II.1 or *De praedestinatione sanctorum* IV.8.

18. Augustine, *Contra Julianum Pelagianum* VI.23.70; my translation.

Love and Law according to Paul and Some Philosophers

JEFFREY BLOECHL

I

At a time when there is no lack of surprises in philosophy and theology, there is nonetheless something uncommonly provocative about the recent interest certain philosophers have taken in the letters of St. Paul.[1] It will not do, in the face of this, to reject out of hand the use of reading these texts as if the faith that moves them is somehow secondary to their potential to fuel the programs of philosophers who start from a position that is at most indifferent to the question of God. Let us restrict ourselves to two of them. Neither Giorgio Agamben nor Alain Badiou addresses Paul essentially as a theologian, but instead attempts to mine from his letters new resources for freeing a conception of the human condition, and specifically our subjectivity, from containment in political order. From the fact that this concern is hardly alien to those letters, one is led necessarily to wonder about the difference between the religious roots of Paul's resistance, above all to the Roman Empire, and a much more contemporary concern with politics of a somewhat different sort. If then one looks slightly further, one finds that both Agamben and Badiou press their concerns with a particular focus on our relation to the law, which is again plainly within the purview of Pauline thought. But is Paul interested above all, as they are, simply in liberating us in our worldly condition from this or that oppressive regime (let alone, as one finds them contend, from order as such)? Let us agree to inquire after these differences, wishing to hear Paul on his own terms and asking ourselves, wherever discrepancies might appear, just what is afoot in contemporary experience.

Agamben: Paul and Messianic Subjectivity

Already long before taking up Paul, Agamben has held a view of the state as a repository of oppressive force and of the law as its extension into human life. In his view, every political order, as an order, has an abstract form that is essentially indifferent to the uniqueness of each living person. The law by which that order extends over and envelops human relations therefore subjects each person and each relation to what are in fact generalizations. Under these conditions our subjectivity is defined by our subjection to the law, and our "life," in its pristine uniqueness, is found at the underside of the rules of oppression. An entire series of works has attempted to concede all of this to politics and at the same time liberate life. In his book on Paul, *The Time that Remains*, Agamben takes particular interest in the conception of time as messianic, which he defines by a futurity that would transcend the worldly future that is never more than not-yet-now. The way of life that is oriented to such a futurity is not, at root, restricted by any worldly order. Agamben's Paul will have discovered this in himself, thanks to his encounter with Jesus, and then proclaimed it as the general condition for all human life. For his part, Agamben proposes to extend the critical implication of the Pauline mission by making messianicity the vantage point and basis from which to criticize any order that does not recognize it— and indeed, there is no mistaking his thought that every order must by definition fail to do so.

In order to glean this general thesis from the letter to the Romans, Agamben first has to identify the discovery of messianic time in its full significance with Paul and not with the Jesus whose life and teachings will have made this possible. This requires him to propose that when Paul uses the word *christos*, he does not associate it exclusively with the person named Jesus.[2] Let us not overlook the elevation Paul receives and the diminishment that befalls Jesus in Agamben's interpretation. It is with this shift that the messianic uniqueness of Jesus is evacuated, through Paul, into all humanity.

As for the specific nature of the salvation that this would involve, Agamben considers it to lie in the possibilities opened up by a realization that in our original condition, as life, we are not one with the identity imposed on us by order and law. He is thus in position to hear Paul's call to live "as if not" (*hōs mē*) attached to the world as a matter immediately for our relation with the law. For Agamben, the messianic person—which, again, can be any and all of us—would act as if neither subject to the law nor defined by an urge to negate it. And this would apply to one's relation with any other principle or division, which in all cases otherwise have the effect of ordering us and, on Agamben's definition, oppressing us. Of course, this suggests that individual life is essentially decentered or at any rate must maintain itself in that position or else submit to totalization. Evidently, the effort that this would involve is both the price and the very definition of salvation. This is especially clear with respect to the law. According to Agamben, when Paul speaks of a deactivation (*katargein*) of the law, we are to understand that this would result from an active engagement by the messianic subject in its decenterment. Our messianism conducts us beyond the rule of the law according to a prior condition in which we are not yet defined by that rule. In the innocence of our deepest condition, we are without law, *anomial*—and yet the law has already been imposed. We may nonetheless be saved if in heeding Paul's call to faith we liberate ourselves.

Two features of this argument for a Pauline conception of anomial, messianic life signify a break with the more familiar, theological conception of Paul. First, there is no mistaking the fact that for Agamben Paul will have equated the gospel strictly and simply with a means to transcend law. There is, of course, good reason to think that this is an important part of the gospel, but considered solely in itself it constitutes a remarkable impoverishment. Second, it is also clear, though this time by subtraction, that one would transcend the law only by single performative acts, which is to say by one's own efforts and, as it were, essentially in isolated moments. Here we have to recognize a theory of grace that goes without any positive sense of the relation with Christ as an ongoing way of living and that has no need of the divine love that believers consider him to embody.

Badiou: Paul and the Christ-Event

Like Agamben, Badiou comes to Paul with an interest in liberating us from totalization. His previous work has already developed a sophisticated ontology on which to base a claim that radical and irreducible particularity is in fact the universal condition of our humanity. His attempt to verify such a claim centers on an attempt to account for newness, as the index of particularity, without reducing it to a variation or improvisation on what is already familiar. Thus, particularity is disclosed in events of newness that are, however, quickly absorbed into the pattern of what is already familiar and in that sense old. In the terms of Badiou's ontology, "event" therefore signifies the eruption of newness into the domain of "being," where it appears and is named. It is not difficult to detect the critical, even revolutionary potential of this distinction: being—*that* we are and *what* we are—is always susceptible to the emergence of what it does not contain, whereupon its claim on us is no longer evident. But this can make a lasting difference only if the interrupting event is named in a manner that does not immediately falsify it by submitting it to a totalizing interpretation. According to Badiou, history does include instances in which an event has been named without submitting it to totalization, and their presence in our cultural memory raises the possibility of awakening humanity to its fundamental particularity.[3] In his view, one such instance can be found in Paul's fidelity to the event that is Jesus as Christ.

This is already enough for us to understand that Christianity is of interest to Badiou only in its structure and not with regard to its specific content. As he reads Paul, the letters depict Jesus as Christ insofar as Jesus interrupts the familiar cadence of being as it had been defined by Jewish and Roman law. Or, again in the terms of his ontology, Paul names the Christ-event in a manner that makes it available to us by invoking a faith that cannot be reduced to adherence to any worldly principles or set of laws. Naturally, what thus "relieves us of the law" is the promise of a resurrection that defies all worldly order.[4] As Badiou does not hesitate to point out, the thesis of resurrection is neither verifiable nor falsifiable—and as far as he is concerned, not only does this not matter, but in fact it is strictly in accord with the very nature of an event to defy assimilation to what is already known.[5]

This once again grants Paul an importance that rivals that of Jesus, since the event becomes an event in the fullest sense—it becomes available to us as truly salvific—only through the genius of the Pauline discourse. Badiou's notion of its distinguishing features could not be more classical: life, spirit, and grace. But like Agamben, he considers their origin to lie in Paul's sense of a privileged relation with Jesus. But whereas Agamben's Paul, as apostle, is set apart already by hearing a call that comes from beyond every order, Badiou suggests that Paul finds himself truly set apart only when and to the degree that he proves capable of fidelity to the Christ-event. This subtle difference is not without considerable importance. For Agamben, Paul's preaching consists essentially in *witness* to the underside of the law, but for Badiou that preaching is defined by active *refusal*. I have suggested that Agamben understands Paul, and all human life, as fundamentally anomial. Badiou's emphasis is instead *anti*-nomial.

With regard to the longer trajectory of Badiou's thinking, we may leave open the question of whether a revolutionary intention determines the ontology that founds his proposal that Paul's thinking is anti-nomial or instead is the ontology itself that leads Badiou toward such claims. For present purposes, it is more important only to underline the fact that that ontology treats with great suspicion any claim for unity among individual subjects. After all, according to the tenets of Badiou's ontology, unity must be a feature of the known order, as distinct from the newness of what interrupts that order. We will have to wonder, then, about the real prospects for community that does not reduce to atomism. But we will also have to wonder how Badiou will understand Paul's word "spirit," by which Christians define the community of faith *and that, even on Badiou's own account, Paul will have realized in and through his fidelity to Jesus.* Let us begin with the latter concern. Whether Badiou is guided by an interest in defending ontological plurality or a wish to establish absolute equality, when he comes to the notion of spirit, his own argument requires him to understand it as an impulse arising strictly and solely within the person who responds to the Christ-event. Perhaps Badiou might wish to make a claim that Paul was *inspired* to fashion a discourse that includes the excellent word "spirit." Yet nothing in his ontology permits him to understand inspiration as any more than a production and even an achievement of the subject himself. This prepares us for the fact that, indeed, Badiou shows no interest at all in Paul's notion of a community of faith united in the life of the spirit. Badiou's Paul "preaches" to individual subjects, enjoining each of them, as if separately, to resist the suffocating normalization imposed by order and law. The entire apostolic discourse has only an instrumental function. It calls forth in each subject a revolutionary movement toward liberation.

Here again, as with Agamben, the concept of grace is secularized, since the Christ-event that prompts such a movement is neither superior nor inferior to other events that also may tear the fabric of human experience and history (other examples given are as disparate as absolute mathematics and emancipated society). In addition to being secularized, grace is reduced to the possibility of discrete acts committed in the final account by a subject insofar as his or her own powers permit. This would have to be the case already for Paul himself, whose understanding of Jesus enabled him to name the Christ-event. It would also be the case for those of us who respond to his preaching of that event according to a capacity we discover in ourselves to understand it as a call to liberation. Grace, then, "is no more than the indication of a possibility."[6] It remains for the subject to carry out the labor required in order to fulfill it. True enough, Badiou does not fail to observe that this labor will be defined by love and, moreover, love of a distinctive sort that is born in faith. Yet for him, this faith, like every other grace, can only be a possibility that I must realize myself. Such a faith, we already know, would bind me to what cannot be contained with the sphere of everything familiar to me and direct the energy of my commitments away from any return to the familiar. From this perspective, Badiou can make love of neighbor intelligible on his own terms: if the love that defines the labor of faith cannot choose what is known and familiar, it strives first to put in question everything that has been gathered first to oneself. But then it is not clear that such a new love could ever be more than the simple contrary of self-love. Does Pauline thought admit of such a severe alternative? Let us now turn to the texts themselves, as even the most familiar reading would have us understand them.

II

I begin with a well-known passage from Paul's first letter to the Corinthians:

> [For] just as one body has many members, and all the members of the body, though many, are one body, so it is with Christ. For by one Spirit, we were all baptized into one body—Jews or Greeks, slaves or free—and all were made to drink of one Spirit. For the body does not consist of one member but of many. If the foot should say "Because I am not a hand, I do not belong to the body," that would not make it any less a part of the body. And if the ear should say "Because I am not an eye, I do not belong to the body," that would not make it any less a part of the body. If the whole body were an eye, where would be the hearing? If the whole body were an ear, where would be the sense of smell? But as it is, God arranged the organs in the body, each one of them, as he chose. If all were a single organ, where would the body be? As it is, there are many parts, yet one body. . . . . [But] God has so composed the body, giving the greater honor to the inferior part, that there may be no discord in the body, but that the members may have the same care for one another. If one member suffers, all suffer together; if one member is honored, all rejoice together. (1 Cor. 12:12–20, 24–26)

I know of two quite different approaches to understanding the origin of Paul's great hymn to the community of faith as body of Christ. One approach reminds us that the image of the body and its parts is employed to suggest something about unity and plurality at least as early as Plato, who calls the world *zoon* and defines it by a *somā* that is *tou kosmou* and *tou pantos*: the world is a living being, the body of which all other beings, both individually and in their multitudes, are portions (Tim. 32c). We are reminded, further, that a similar notion is applied specifically to politics when, according to Livy, Menenius Agrippa offers a parable in response to a group of plebeians who wish to break with the patricians of Rome and form a new city: let not the limbs [the plebeians] deprive the belly [the patricians] of the food that it requires, for should the belly begin to weaken, so too shall the limbs (*History of Rome* 2.32.8–12). Surely Paul would have known of these images, or at least of some lesser version of them in circulation among the learned Roman citizenry of his day. Moreover, this would have been neither the first nor the last time that Greek and Roman thought came to his aid when in his preaching he wished to convey an especially difficult notion.[7]

A second approach finds Paul intent on conveying to the Corinthians—for it is in his letters to the Corinthians that he first writes of the body and its members—a sense of the higher spiritual unity that does not pretend to look past the fleshly particularity that was all too evident to them in a city that was well known at that time for its inclination to debauchery (and long passages of the letter seem to address specifically this concern). In Corinth there was an asclepeion where those who had fallen ill went in search of healing. And, according to custom, those who recovered left behind, as testament to the god, an image of the body part where the newly vanquished affliction had been lodged. To the ruins of ancient Corinth has been added a museum that now includes a small room full of these images—some in simple stone and quite small, others in marble and quite large. There are hands and feet, ears and eyes, and, informing us of the specific expertise of Corinthian healers, many breasts. According to the second approach to understanding the origin of Paul's hymn to the community of faith, his memory of something like this spectacle would have provided him with a vivid and effective means to address the relation between our fleshly existence, in which each of us has her own attachments, enjoyments, and afflictions and our universal participation in something higher that deserves the word "spirit" (*pneuma*).

It is not necessary to choose between these two approaches, since they are not actually opposed so much as complementary. But I am drawn more to the second, archeological approach because it better highlights something essential in Pauline thought that is easily missed by attempts to make it serve modern contemporary concerns. In order to see this, it is first necessary to see that the passage with which I began stands somewhat apart from others in the Pauline corpus where the image of body and members clearly is brought into contact with certain recognizably political themes. Thus, both Colossians 1:18 and Ephesians 1:22 refer not only to the members as the body of Christ (1 Cor. 12:27), but also to Christ as the head from which the life of the community is ordained from on high. Now if we ask about the relationship between these texts and the more extended one with which I began, exegetes tell us that Paul wrote 1 Corinthians while he was in Ephesus at around 54 or 55 A.D.; the epistle to the Colossians was written some years later, possibly by Timothy, after Paul had arrived in Rome; and the Epistle to the Ephesians may well have been written a decade or more after that and not by Paul at all. That said, most experts nonetheless do agree that Colossians and Ephesians are faithful to the teaching of the apostle. The basic unity of these three letters (and others) invites us to consider something like the general form of Pauline thinking without insisting that Paul himself is the immediate source of every line. The difference among the three becomes understandable in context: there is an increased tendency to profile a hierarchical dimension to community, beginning especially when Paul himself encounters the dangerous power of the political order in Rome that soon enough threatens the success of his mission by imprisoning him. It is undoubtedly this that explains the new inflection of the letters to the Colossians and Ephesians. As the power of the political regime comes into view, it becomes important to empha-size to believers that, as far as they should be concerned, the final author-ity in all matters remains Christ—and moreover a Christ whose reign is not merely of this world. After all, as the gospels of Matthew and Luke would later make clear with their accounts of the temptation in the desert, the early Christians were probably already convinced that Jesus himself es-chewed dominion over every worldly kingdom (Matt. 4, Luke 4).[8]

Enough has been said for us to now recognize two guidelines along which to pursue an account of Paul's conception of the community of faith, *before and apart from any need to profile it in an explicitly political manner.* On one hand, we have just touched on the Christological fulcrum by which Paul might be expected to rearrange concepts and deploy images in the service of his mission.[9] On the other hand, we do have available, in 1 Cor-inthians, a rich text in which Paul speaks quite explicitly about community without necessarily promoting the quintessentially political development of hierarchy and authority. What then is Paul's central interest in the first letter to the Corinthians, such as it leads him to speak of the community in terms of a body and its members? We find an interesting answer to this question if we come now to the second point of my interest in the more archaeological approach to 1 Corinthians 12. If, in view of everything we have just observed, we avoid the temptation to think of this passage first of all as a political text and attend instead to the fact that Paul's imagery of body and members appeals directly to our physical, even sensuous, na-ture, perhaps, as what is most familiar to us, we hear Paul calling us most urgently to a conversion of our basic attitude and orientation in the world— again, before any question of the possible ramifications for politics. Many scholars of Paul will find this way of reading the passage rather evident as they will the claim that it is confirmed specifically by the recourse to imagery that probably registered powerfully with the Corinthians, and indeed to any human being: our struggles with what in the vernacular we still call "the flesh." Yet Paul's own conception of "flesh" (*sarx*) is considerably richer than this. His word "flesh" designates something like a dynamism of our being by which we are attached to the world and everything in it—and to that degree precisely not to the God of Jesus Christ. We are helped to understand the proper depth of this idea in Ephesians 2:11–12, where the focus is once again on our unity and distinctiveness as members of one body: "remember that at one time you Gentiles in the flesh . . . were at that time separated from Christ, alienated from the commonwealth of Israel, and strangers to the covenant of promise, having no hope and without God in the world."

Here the important point lies not so much in a contrast between the earlier faithlessness of the Gentiles with their subsequent true faith in Christ as in a manner of distinguishing a way of life captivated by the flesh from another way of life that becomes possible to the degree that one is free of that captivation. What is it to be a Gentile? In Ephesians, it is to be not only without affiliation to the "commonwealth" (*politeias*) of Israel, but also (and depending on our sense of Paul's relation to his own Judaism, we might instead say *further*) to be "separated" (*apellotriomenoi*) from Christ and therefore without kinship to the covenant of promise given first to the Jews and, in their line, to the followers of Jesus. To be Gentile in this sense—to be Gentile "in the flesh"—is to be without hope (*elpida*) and thus, ultimately, *without God in the world*. The Greek word for this phrase is somewhat tighter than the translation indicates (it is also unique in all of the Pauline writings): to be Gentile in the flesh is to live in a world that is *atheos*. To be sure, when the letter refers to "Gentiles in the flesh" (*ethne en sarxi*) a specific group of people is singled out; yet the manner in which this is done plainly indicates a much more general possibility for the human condition. Otherwise, the very aim of preaching to the Gentiles at all makes little sense. They were "Gentiles by birth," as some translations have it, but this circumstance clearly does not rule out another, more spiritual possibility defined by faith in Christ. And this other possibility would be reached by opening oneself to a promise unforeseeable from within the horizon defined by flesh.

Conversely, the call to a new attitude or orientation that I have attributed to Paul in 1 Corinthians would seem bound to entail another horizon entirely. Furthermore, as the phenomenologists have reminded us, a horizon is not merely a frame or sphere within which to know something;

before that, more fundamentally, it is an openness that is always defined by the particular mood through which we see whatever appears there. At the psychological level, the world and everything in it appear differently to us when we are depressed than they do when we are happy. Each mood thus seems to attune our world in a manner that other moods do not.[10] This can also be said of moods, attunements, and horizons that define entire ways of life and not only psychological outlooks. With regard to the Pauline notions that preoccupy us here, the horizon that belongs to the way of life that is captivated by the flesh would proceed from a distinctive mood that is defined by its own attunement—and all of this would give way to a different mood defined by a different attunement belonging to the life of faith in Christ (joy, for example). It probably goes without saying that for the one who comes to believe in Christ the world appears in a new light.

Let us consider for a moment the nature of our relations to the flesh and the world as they appear from the perspective of Paul's mission. Captivated by the flesh, we take the world to be the first and last condition of our being, so that what appears to us shows up solely in the light of our interest and we take ourselves to be the focal point of its meaning. Insofar as we are committed to faith in Christ, those relations are opened up to admit a higher relation with God. This cannot mean that we no longer are in the world, and not even that the faithful would be immune to a recurrent impulse to seize upon the world or parts of the world as if they come before God. Indeed, Paul stops short of such extravagant claims even at his most feverishly apocalyptic moments, when, for example, in 1 Corinthians 7 his exhortation to consider sexual and conjugal relations in view of God's final judgment says only that one should live "as if not" (*hōs mē*) bound in flesh as husband and wife; what he does not enjoin is strictly discontinuing all such relations.[11] So, likewise, does it make sense to think that the flesh is *transformed* in faith, rather than being simply extinguished by it? When we mortals might strip off our old nature, or old self, and put on the new (Col. 3:10–11), we do not kill the flesh, but sanctify it. The flesh is, as it were, inscribed in another register, so that the visceral dimension of our being is also more than visceral. Simone Weil captures this well when in her effort to understand Paul's notion of the old and new self she juxtaposes Philippians 3:19 and Colossians 3:12: there are those among us who are captivated by the flesh and "whose God is in their belly," and there are others who embrace Christ and "put on, thus, bowels of mercy."[12]

Now this manner of taking up the old into the new also defines a Pauline relation to the law that is not simply, as the more strictly political reading is in danger of suggesting, a rejection of one authority in favor of another, higher one. When Paul speaks negatively about the law, he generally has in mind law in the sense of letter and judgment, which is to say the law by which sin is defined by transgression of explicit prohibitions. Such a law, or perhaps better, such a *relation to* the law is deficient in two respects. As Paul himself helps us to see, it leaves us perpetually confronted with our own incapacity to fully justify ourselves—that is, it confronts us with our everlasting sinfulness, so that we are at risk of losing hope. But we might add that it also leaves the law itself exposed to the strange possession by the flesh that issues in moral perversion: the moral masochist, for example, has taken possession of the law in the form of enjoying its severity. Yet for all of this, our relation to the law can also be positive. The law can educate and instruct us in a righteousness that goes further than refraining from transgression. Far from overlooking this, Paul seems to have it presently in mind when he insists on the holiness of the law (Rom. 7:12) and makes clear that he himself does not propose to abolish the law but only to properly uphold it (Rom. 3:31). Needless to say, according to Paul, the passage from bondage to the law that prohibits to willing embrace of a law now properly upheld requires openness to the spirit promised to those who have faith in Christ. To open oneself to the spirit is to breathe new life into the gift of the law. And just as the old self receives a new, positive definition when one becomes a distinctively valued member of the community, so too is the old law, the law of flesh, deactivated only in order to be reactivated by life in the spirit.

All of this enables us to be concise in our understanding of the vision of community found in what I began by calling Paul's "great hymn" to the community of faith. To be joined to the body of Christ is not to cease being oneself in a manner that is recognizably continuous with who and what one had been before. It is rather to still be oneself and yet more than oneself, and moreover as a member of a community that needs one to be precisely oneself. The hand, after all, grasps and possesses and takes things for itself, and it is precisely as such, with that power, that it has its own importance for the whole body. The hand becomes more than a hand that possesses things for itself when it is assimilated to the spirit that is offered in Christ. How does Christ move us from self-assertion and self-gratification to willing commitment to the community? What in Christ accounts for this difference? It can only be the presence in him of love that would hold open the possibility of free commitment—and not the presentation of a higher law enforced by some greater force that commands only a new form of submission. The Christological specification of this thought is well known. For Paul it is the self-emptying Christ who introduces us, in recognizable terms, to the God who is unconditional love. It is also well known that the love of one another for which the Christian community is so frequently noted is incomprehensible apart from a belief in each member that God loves her specifically, personally as herself. And this, let us note, leaves us philosophers to consider the thought that genuine plurality and a notion of absolute goodness are not necessarily opposed. On the contrary, one might even entertain the possibility that each necessarily implies the other.

III

In my accounts of the political readings of Paul developed by Agamben and Badiou, it became evident that in one or another form they rely finally on what can only appear, in this context, as a secularized conception of grace. Let us note that some such conception is bound to suggest itself as soon as one thinks that our own powers are not enough to free us from a condition we find unacceptable. This brings us before the architectonic of a great deal of contemporary European thought, according to which we find ourselves at risk of enclosure by conditions that can be breached only from the outside and beyond our own efforts. In the philosophies of Levinas and Marion, the enclosing condition is Heideggerian being, and the breach occurs in the form of an arresting gaze. For Agamben and Badiou, it is of course order and law that contain us, and we are freed only on the condition of a disordering interruption. In all of these cases—some of which are famously so—a great deal develops from the thought that the risk of enclosure is both real and irreversible. There is no mistaking the echo of certain experiences and of forms of thought that concede everything to them. It is as if our prospects for freedom and transcendence can no longer be thought apart from serious and prolonged reckoning with the menace of a closure, and its darkness, that would be final. It is not for nothing that Levinas, speaking from just this perspective, once characterized our age as "spiritual emphysema."

Paul's outlook is not nearly as bleak as this because his dissatisfaction with the law did not go all the way to a sense of complete subjection to it. Indeed, as I observed, on occasion he even considered that the law itself can be uplifting and energizing as long as we are alive to a sense that it is given in divine love. And this, of course, accounts for the crucial difference between Paul and his contemporary political readers. When the Christian notion of grace is secularized, it no longer defines our relation with the loving God. For both Agamben and Badiou, this appears so evident as to require not even the semblance of argument. The brute assumption that in our wish to escape the totalizing effect of the law we must do without means to reconceive of the law in light of divine love and providence suggests a filiation between the drama of the law and the death of God that is too complex to fully unravel here. Suffice to say that on this point, we might well address the very partiality of their readings of Paul as important signs of the times. And in that vein, we might attend more closely to the fact that the exclusion of God from their philosophies is specifically an exclusion of divine love. This, it may well seem, sketches a somewhat more thoughtful approach to what it might mean to say that God is dead than does the more widespread one that concentrates on the experience of God as nothing more than a helpful concept or comforting idol. Our real problem, it will then seem, is not that we have some trouble reinstating a notion of the absolute, but rather that it is difficult for many of us to truly believe in unconditional love.

But there is more. Absent that belief, Jesus Christ is only a single, momentous historical event, and not necessarily a unique one. This diminishment of the importance of Jesus is especially unfortunate, since a proper understanding of Paul's experience of Jesus is necessary to grasp his sense of what is truly required to join the community of the faithful. For Paul, I have noted, what makes Jesus unique is the presence of the love of God in him (for example, in Rom. 8:39). With this in mind, one might say first, and especially to Badiou, that it is specifically this love that Jesus conveys when he promises resurrection. But one might also say, to Agamben, as well, that this promise is not imposed, but only offered. Or better, Jesus is the proposal of a promise that one takes up only in faith (that is, one accepts the proposal, one believes in the promise). A proposal, of course, leaves one's freedom intact, though accepting it is transformative. We already know the terms of this transformation: one enters freely into the life of the spirit, overcoming captivation by the flesh and bondage to the law. If this is not yet enough to assure the superiority of the Pauline conception of community over conceptions that appear founded on a rejection of its central principles, then at least it permits us to see more clearly into the heart of that rejection itself. Here again, there may be an opportunity to study some of the more difficult signs of the times. What Agamben and Badiou never seem to consider is something close to a truism for the faithful: there is no conflict between the complete exercise of one's freedom and a commitment to the love of God. Now, it hardly needs to be said that it would be one thing to argue against that mistake and quite another to go so far as suggesting that Jesus Christ must become the head of the body politic. Foregoing that idea, we might simply remind ourselves, and ask what it means, that whatever the condition of our political community, it seems certain that it will have to reckon with forces opposed to that other community captured in Paul's image of the body of Christ—even while pro-posing to inhabit some of the same intellectual space.

Notes

1. Earlier versions of some parts of this essay were delivered at the 2013 Simone Weil Lectures on Human Value in Melbourne and Brisbane, Australia. I am especially grateful to Francis Moloney for his helpful response to my reading of Paul, to which I have not yet been able to do full justice. Portions of Parts I and II of this essay will appear in my "Inventions of Christianity: Preambles to a Philosophical Reading of Paul," in *Saint Paul between Ancient and Contemporary Thought*, ed. G.-J. van der Heiden and A. Cimino (Leiden: Brill, 2017).

2. See Georgio Agamben, *The Time that Remains: A Commentary on the Letter to the Romans* (Palo Alto, Calif.: Stanford University Press, 2005), 15–18.

3. These principles are elaborated in Alain Badiou, *Being and Event* (London: Continuum, 2005). In a brief chapter on Pascal, Badiou develops a conception of the "Christ-event" that anticipates a central feature of his interpretation of Paul; see, for instance, 214, 218, 220.

4. Badiou, *St. Paul: The Foundation of Universalism* (Palo Alto, Calif.: Stanford University Press, 2003), 48.

5. Ibid., 45.

6. Ibid., 91.

7. For a comprehensive account, see George H. van Kooten, *Paul's Anthropology in Context: The Image of God, Assimilation to God, and Tripartite Man in Ancient Judaism, Ancient Philosophy and Early Christianity* (Tubingen: Mohr Siebeck, 2008).

8. A refusal of this complication underwrites Jacob Taubes's thoroughly political reading of the letter to the Romans, in which Paul will have at once declared war on Rome and positioned himself as the rightful heir to Moses. To sure, between Rome and Moses, it is undoubtedly a question of the law, and from a depth that Taubes as much as anyone has helped us to recognize. But as Christians necessarily contend, Paul addresses himself to Roman and Mosaic law only on the condition of a faith in Jesus Christ as God by which alone, he claims, the law may be transcended. Yet this objection is not without its own complexity. On one hand, it is not evident that the theological notion of an "obedience of faith" is only a "polemical variant of obedience of laws," as Taubes contends (*The Political Theology of Paul* [Palo Alto, Calif.: Stanford University Press, 2004], 14). When a theologian like Karl Rahner defines faith by *oboedientia* he emphasizes its root sense of receptivity to a revelation that is heard (*ob-audire*). Perhaps this suggests an argument for the distinctiveness of a receptivity that is not, contrary to Taubes's usage, immediately juridical and political (see Rahner, *Hearer of the Word* [New York: Continuum, 1994], and Rom. 1:15 and 16:26). On the other hand, it should not be assumed too quickly that Paul himself ever truly refers to Jesus as God. Within the limits of the one

letter to which Taubes confines himself, the passage in question must be Rom. 9:4. For an account of the exegetical difficulties and debate, see J. D. G. Dunn, *The Theology of Paul the Apostle* (Grand Rapids: Eerdmans, 1998), 255–57.

9. I take this expression from Dunn, *Theology of Paul*, 722–29.

10. See Martin Heidegger, *Being and Time*, §29.

11. For more on this interpretation of the Pauline *hōs me* at the center of his account of world and faith, see Jeffrey Bloechl, "The Principle of the World and the Call of Faith," *Analecta Hermeneutica* 4 (2012).

12. Simone Weil, *Notebooks of Simone Weil* (London: Routledge, 2004), 209–10. Weil's penchant for bold expressions notwithstanding, in the present case her words are taken from traditional piety.

The Affects of Unity
Ephesians 4:1–4

EMMANUEL HOUSSET

Phenomenology and Scripture

As a matter of methodological principle, an authentic phenomenology of religious experience should not place conditions on the manifestation of God, but should understand him only from his Word. Thus phenomenological theology exists only in the context of a radicalization of the requirement to return to the "things themselves" beyond all mental constructions. If the goal of phenomenology, as a project, is to understand everything according to its own standard of knowledge, then it is the same for the knowledge of God. In effect, with regard to theology, we do not apprehend the meaning of God from the structures of our own subjectivity, but God himself becomes the condition of his own manifestation; it is he who prepares his givenness [*prépare sa donnée*] in the space of our interiority. Thus reading the Epistle to the Ephesians does not consist in discovering in the Bible a simple illustration of how to achieve authentic humanity that has already been established by philosophy. What the Bible says is unheard of and impossible to understand without the love of God, which prepares us to hear his Word. "To let appear," so to speak, is the motto that animates phenomenology and gives it its proper character with respect to the entire history of philosophy, of which phenomenology is understood as the secret aspiration: phenomenology is the long and patient work of disclosure with regard to that which is barely there and to that which holds itself back. There is, then, much common ground between phenomenology and scripture, for humility is the very foundation of phenomenological description: phenomenology requires humble submission to the phenomena as they give themselves, endeavoring with the most possible rigor to avoid all theoretical or speculative bias.

The text of Ephesians 4:1–4 is quite remarkable for its density and sums up much of St. Paul's message: "I therefore, the prisoner in the Lord, beg you to lead a life worthy of the calling to which you have been called, with all humility and gentleness, with patience, bearing with one another in love [charité], making every effort to maintain the unity of the Spirit in the bond of peace. There is one body and one Spirit, just as you were called to the one hope of your calling."[1] A phenomenological reading of this passage— that is, a reading directed toward the comprehension of the phenomenality contained in this passage—has the potential to highlight the very important role played by affects. The Spirit is, according to this passage, that which manifests itself in the affects of humility, gentleness, and patience, for those are the affects that enlarge human sensibilities and allow the Spirit to manifest itself in us. It is also clear that not only does phenomenology seek to clarify scripture, but scripture also opens up phenomenology to new dimensions of manifestation inasmuch as it invites us (against a tenacious bias) to attribute cognitive power to affects without thereby substituting affect for reason. In effect, this passage of Ephesians allows us to respond to the following question: what is the affective experience that reveals the presence of God and the gift of the Holy Spirit? Paul's use of humility, gentleness, and patience suggests that it is impossible to know the truth without love, that in order to know God as "the way" it is necessary to walk with him, and that grasping God as life is only possible in the confrontation between one's will and that of God.

Additionally, the texts clearly state that humility, gentleness, and patience make peace possible, which is the affect according to which man is given to himself in unity with other men. In effect, to be at peace is to know [savoir] that one exists in the unity of the Spirit. Peace, therefore, cannot be understood as a simple absence of troubles. Accordingly, humility, gentleness, and patience are not simply means of obtaining peace, but are simultaneously the concrete reality of experiencing the gift of God, his call, and the act of actively receiving it. Put differently, these three affects help us to understand the impossibility of separating contemplation and action: the peace of God is received by being a peacemaker. It is thus possible to highlight the responsive nature of affective experience: humility, gentleness, and patience both recognize the gift and at the same time respond actively to it. Similarly, the unity of Christians ought to be seen as both coaffective, since it is experienced by all [ensemble] as the gift of

God and as communal action, which implies that unity is not an experience of emptiness and resignation.

The force of this passage of Ephesians consists not in an empty exhortation to unity, but in highlighting the path of unity that is long and difficult: without humility, gentleness, and patience there is no peace, and without peace there is no unity. Yet this path toward unity makes sense only if these three affects demonstrate a sensibility that is not a retreat into self or an ignorance of the world and other men. Humility is not submission, gentleness is not cloying, and patience is not placidity, but these three virtues produce sensibilities that illuminate—for these sensibilities are an opening, a "being taken by" something other than the self. Emmanuel Levinas accurately describes the transitivity of experience, which is at heart reflexive: "[it] is to apprehend oneself with the same gesture that already turns toward the exterior to extra-vert and to manifest—to respond for what it apprehends—to express."[2] Accordingly, humility, gentleness, and patience exemplify the reflexive transitivity of experience, in which the other is received in himself, and without which my self-affection would be distinct from my affection for another. Life in communion with the other man is traversed by an obscurity that is not negative, as it consists in accomplishing something together and keeping no account of who did what. In communal life, there is a realization of "being together," of perfection in this human life, which is a preview of the future beatitude.

Humility, Gentleness, and Patience as Tonalities of Christian Existence

Without anticipating a precise analysis of the seven concepts contained in the text of Ephesians 4:1–3 (call, humility, gentleness, patience, love, peace, and unity), it is necessary to further elaborate the question at hand. St. Paul does not in any way propose a psychological or emotional interpretation of the union between God and man. In other words, for St. Paul it is not a question of valorizing *pathos* over and against reason, and it has nothing to do with a religion of "good feelings," which consists only in expressions of self-pride. The call of God does not ask us to choose naively between reason and sensibility, for such a choice is absurd and arises only from an abstract construction.[3] In effect, the call of God entirely transfigures us, and thus our sensibilities, which become transitive in a very novel way.

Heidegger, who is particularly interested in the letters of St. Paul as part of a phenomenological explanation of concrete religious phenomena, has also profoundly transformed our understanding of sensibility by demonstrating the essential link between *Befindlichkeit* and that understanding.[4]

Thus, in showing that sensibility, with its double intentionality, is a mode of being in the world, Heidegger's thought runs contrary to the modern impulse to de-psychologize the *Stimmung*, or attunement. In fact, attunements (for example, angst, boredom, fear, joy, astonishment) are the original modes of being of *Dasein*, wherein *Dasein* is open to itself prior to any knowing or willing. The attunement is, then, a mode of opening, a mode of transcendence. Without being able to develop here Heidegger's lengthy and complex analysis of *Stimmung*, this simple reminder is already helpful in reading the aforementioned passage of Paul's letter by making clear that humility, gentleness, and patience are ways of receiving the world, of perceiving it, before any knowledge [*connaissance*] and before any decision of the will.[5] Of course, pride, boorishness, and impatience are also modes of transcendence, modes of being in the world, but befitting a closure to the world, which is the most quotidian and habitual form of existence.

Phenomenological understanding attempts to go back to that which is original in Christian experience. For that reason, in humility, gentleness, and patience, phenomenology is able to see an original Christian religiosity, having to do with the "how" of hearing God's call and the "how" of vocation as a religious phenomenon. The concrete life of Christ manifests humility, gentleness, and patience, which constitute the means by which man is capable of receiving the Spirit. Original Christian experience, therefore, has nothing to do with interior sentiments, but with the way man is present to the Spirit through his sensibility. There is truly a Christian mode of being-thrown in the world that is not a simple variant of the pagan world but is its total reversal, for it is not primarily concerned with one's comportment toward other objects; rather, it transfigures one's very mode of existing. There is, for example, no continuity, no common essence, between pagan patience, which consists only in endurance [*endurcissement*], and Christian patience, which is constituted by hope. In patience, Christians do not try to escape suffering, but thanks to the gift of the Spirit, neither do they assign the same meaning to suffering. Patience may thus become the individuating principle of man, for he finds himself, he understands himself in his response to the call, in his capacity to support others with charity, in the act of preserving the unity of the Spirit. It is, therefore, possible to show that humility, gentleness, and patience are not primarily acts of reflection but, as modes of exposure to the world, constitute an opening to the world [*un pâtir*] prior to all objective intentionality, before all constituting activity.

From this point of view, humility, gentleness, and patience are not virtues properly speaking; rather, they are the conditions of any virtue. It is through them that strength, for example, can become a virtue. In fact, before the constitution of the other, as friend or foe, as fellow man or subordinate, as a member of the human community or a resource to be exploited, the other is first encountered either in an attunement consisting in mutual adherence to humility, gentleness, and patience or in the more natural attunement constituted by brutality and domination. Here again, humility and brutality are not a means of encounter, but the place, the ground that decides the sense of the encounter. Moreover, in humility, gentleness, and patience, the other is not simply encountered according to the modality of knowledge [*connaissance*], which requires only calm, availability, and astonishment; rather, the three active affects, which make charity possible, are equally affects of action, for they have to do with making peace, and without them there is no other possibility than social dispersion and violence.

Put differently, humility, gentleness, and patience are not accidents of character, they are not naturally possessed by some men and lacking in others; rather, they are gifts from God that allow man to go beyond his nature: being-in-the-world in the mode of being beyond the world. The Christian life is oriented toward the future; it is hope that determines its meaning. The Christian life is thus a mode of comprehension as an ability to face a situation, as a capacity to work for peace despite the reality of violence. Beginning with God's call, man opens himself to his own possibilities by being able to bring about peace. From this gracious gift, humility, gentleness, and patience lead man beyond the a priori horizon of purely human possibilities, for love can do all things. In effect, the Christian cannot be understood within the singular horizon of death, but within the hope of "bearing with one another in love [*charité*]." That hope drives man to grow in humility, gentleness, and patience—qualities that can be had only to the extent that they grow continually. As such, humility, gentleness, and patience are acts of comprehension, for in encountering the other, humility perceives grandeur, gentleness perceives sensibility, and patience perceives its appropriate duration.

As Heidegger has shown, there is no existence without attunement, and existence involves a constant passage from one attunement to another. The text of Ephesians 4 presents a fundamental alternative between the attunements of pride and humility. This goes along with the issue of access to the original phenomenon of life as spiritual life: in humility, gentleness, and patience, the world gives itself as full of life, as having a future. In each case, these attunements do not consist in seeing things in a naïve way, but in watching over the world and ourselves, while knowing that the spiritual life is beyond the measures of the world. Every action has its own place within an attunement, and it is only possible to achieve peace through humility, gentleness, and patience, for peace is not achieved as a spectator, but as one busy with hope. Thus a phenomenological reading of this passage shows that the peace in question is something other than a formal exhortation to unity—a far cry from an empty and meaningless affirmation of the "togetherness" of occasional fraternization. The text leads back to the original phenomenon of spiritual life, which is primarily a form of self-dispossession through humility, gentleness, and patience, for dispossession is the condition of willing and acting. Indeed, the will to peace has its source in the tangible proof of the other in the horizon of hope and not in reflection alone. From this perspective, being a self is tantamount to being in exile, being away from home, away from the exigencies of the world, in order that the self might be reassembled in the Spirit. If the ethical subject is a being who stays in the world and gets involved there, then the text of Ephesians 4:1–4 leads us beyond the ethical by describing an existence delivered from preoccupation with the self and worldly standards—that is, an existence governed by love and presided over by the unity of the Spirit that is beyond our categories. The man who exists in a vocation arising from grace and who finds his verticality in response to the call of the Spirit is a peacemaker.

The Call Received

By highlighting the affects of unity, reflection on Christian ethics—that is, reflection on the universal norms of action as they are presented in Christianity—becomes possible. Yet the fact remains that the commandment to bear with one another in charity, humility, gentleness, and patience leads to a life beyond ethics inasmuch as the path of humility, gentleness, and patience begins with Christ and proceeds from him. But what are humility, gentleness, and patience? What are love, peace, and unity? Christ alone can teach us and bring us out of our darkness, for he alone has fulfilled them perfectly. Christ alone shows us an accord that is not coerced by a play of the passions and that is not the simple result of reasoned reflection, for it is an accord without any condition wherein we unite ourselves to the other at the risk of our own lives. Put differently, in the text of Ephesians, humility, gentleness, patience, love, unity, and peace are not simply understood as values of a moral tradition aimed at assuring social coherence. The hope that comes from Christ's incarnation not only modifies the meaning of these values, which are certainly championed equally outside Christianity, but also calls into question their very status as values in order to show them in a new light as principles of individuation, which open up the possibility of an interpersonal life. Here we find ourselves beyond the traditional distinction between an ethic of wisdom and an ethic of freedom, for we hit upon the idea of vocation, which consists in living for the sake of unity and not for the sake of self. The central question, then, is not so much about finding universal values to guide our lives in order to be happy or to act freely; rather, it is a question of being worthy of the call received by occupying oneself with the response. This text of St. Paul thus frees us from an ethics based on maxims, which require the measurement of human decisions against ideal and irrevocable decisions, in order to lead back to the path of humility, gentleness, and patience, where the indeterminacy of a resolution is not an imperfection, but its properly human form, for it remains the resolution of an individual on the path. Thus reading St. Paul leads us beyond contemporary ethics, which ideally require the conformation of our will to absolute values established by evidence. In this view, the distinction between an ethics of responsibility and an ethics of conviction, while foundational for a philosophy of action, does not truly modify the status of ethical norms, but serves only as an important system of classification [*aménagement*]. The Bible proposes something altogether different as a principal of self-determination, for it demonstrates the essential humanity of a path formed by trial and error.

In effect, humility, gentleness, and patience show that the meaning of charity has yet to be settled and that human freedom is situational. Christ teaches us rightly that love cannot be measured by an ideal norm apart from the world and that love is mindful of singularity. Love is not a call to take up ideal values, but a call by the very person of Christ, not to be this or that, but to *be*, to become a person. Here we find ourselves beyond ethics, for the call does not prescribe particular standards for acting, but for loving, for bearing with one another in love. The difficulty consists in elucidating the philosophical sense of this proposition, which ought not be interpreted trivially—as it often is—by claiming that love replaces all ethical reflection. It has never been a question of replacing the rational analysis of just action with the unbearable pathos of a life intertwined [*fusionnelle*], which is always profoundly unjust. Leading a life worthy of the call does not demand that we stop reflecting; on the contrary, it requires a surfeit of reflection, for it is a life that cannot but seek the meaning of that call in each concrete situation. It is, therefore, crucial to study the nature of the call not as a call to adopt certain values, but as a call that invites man to know love, to achieve his utmost possibilities as one who is loved [*elú*]. Leading a life worthy of the call necessitates, then, a life spent continually questioning the meaning of that call in relation to humility, gentleness, and patience, resulting in an understanding of man as not simply a subset of mankind, but a neighbor who requires my action. In this new form of living-together [*vivre-ensemble*], I respect the dignity of the other, I know what to do for the other, not only by reflecting on myself and then proceeding from self-reflection to absolute values, but primarily by learning what is good for the other from the other himself. This is the chiaroscuro of a vocation that goes beyond the self-evidence of values: it consists in accepting a neighbor who is never given in full transparency, who reveals himself little by little at the time of his choosing. Such finitude is not an imperfection; on the contrary, it is the concrete form of being with others.

The Courage of Humility

Christian thought offers an entirely new understanding of humility, especially in relation to the Greek conception, where humility oscillates between a negative signification—consciousness of one's own baseness—and a positive signification—renunciation of excess pride.[6] While the pagans recognized humility as a virtue, inasmuch as it encourages modest and measured action, in the New Testament, humility becomes a force opposed to that of the powerful, arrogant, and wealthy. It has to do not with voluntary abasement, which is a way of masking pride, but with a certain ease in welcoming the events of the world: a sense of reserve, deference to manifestation. Thus, as Philo of Alexandria says, humility is a creature's consciousness of its own nothingness, through which it has access to the phenomenality of divine transcendence: "Therefore God becomes at once propitious, and propitious too, even without any supplications being addressed to him, to those who abase and humble themselves, and who are not puffed up with vain arrogance and self-opinion."[7] In Ephesians, humility never renounces resignation [*l'humilité n'est en rien le renoncement de la resignation*], but it lets the Spirit live in man; it allows the soul to hold more than it can properly contain. Humility is not, then, a simple recognition of inferiority; it acts in at least two ways: it protests against the world's injustices, and it opens us up to that which is greater than ourselves. This confirms that humility is not a simple affective state; it is simultaneously the power to know and the power to act. Humility reveals the presence of God in us inasmuch as it is always already the act of moving toward him. Consequently, humility is not exclusively reflexive; its original nature is responsive.

Humility is a condition of charity, and it is possible to demonstrate an eidetic link between them: in humility, an individual receives the other just as the other manifests himself, beyond all designs he may have on the other. He receives the other while conscious of his own finitude: he is neither able to comprehend the other completely nor to substitute himself for the other or to do everything for the other. Charity is the renunciation of omnipotence; it therefore requires patience. Yet this dream of omnipotence in still present in the contemporary idea of a pure and perfect responsibility for everyone and everything—an "omni-responsibility" beyond all finitude. Such a universalization of responsibility, which denies finitude, empties responsibility of all content and renders it powerless. The unity of the church is not an abstract gathering of wills united by a rational vision oriented toward the same telos, nor is it a muddle of good feelings, masking the unsubstitutable character of individuals; rather, it begins with the affective disposition of humility, without which it is impossible to respond to the other based on both the other's self-manifestation and our own finitude. Admittedly, humility does not suffice for knowing what one ought to do or what it is possible to do, though it is a condition for such knowledge: no one enters into the knowledge of what he should do without humility. So humility does not provide apodictic evidence for what must be done. Nonetheless, it provides evidence that a rule for my actions cannot be found outside the other. Moreover, humility provides the impetus for prayerful meditation, attentive to a light that comes not from within. In effect, it is not the *alter ego* that we support with charity, but the other's unique story, on which we pass no judgment.

Humility is, then, something altogether different from the simple psychological quality of reserve, and it has nothing to do with "knowing one's place" (to put it colloquially), for true humility renounces every worldly affirmation. Indeed, humility falls under a very particular form of withdrawal, which consists in living in ignorance of one's place, agreeing to receive one's place by encountering alterity. One may conclude that humility is the component of any action that causes it to be good, and, in that sense, humility is the cause of all goodness.[8] Without humility, patience could not become hope, and love could not become charity. From this point of view, humility is not a voluntary abasement, which would be a sophisticated form of pride; rather, humility is the grace to be free vis-à-vis oneself and free for the other. Humility gives self-knowledge its full meaning: it consists in knowing oneself in order to apply oneself to the task of peacemaking. Moreover, humility does not come from me; it is not something I possess, since it comes from an encounter with God. For that reason, it illuminates a goal beyond my possibilities. Humility is, then, the origin of all spiritual life and not just its beginning, for through humility one achieves that which is unhoped for: peace and the unity of the Spirit. There is a grandeur to humility—the only true grandeur—inasmuch as the proper task of each person consists in giving dignity to others by persisting in charity. Humility is, therefore, spiritual life itself, which does not allow itself to objectify others, as it is primarily a mode of care that frees the other to take up the task of peacemaking.

Humility is not servility, but the power to discern and to act, and thus it is joyful and loving, not resigned and bitter. To be sure, the sort of resigned humility that man accomplishes by himself is not nothing; it can free us from self-love blinded by pride. Nonetheless, the humility of which Christ alone is the master is alone capable of saving us from pride, for it does more than transform the humiliation suffered on those occasions when we learn our limitations; it transfigures the ordeal of humiliation into self-sacrifice [*don de soi*]. As St. Augustine puts it, Christ did not come to be served but to serve (Matt. 11:29), and the humility that Christ teaches is the "humility of patience."[9] Thus humility is that which gives a Christian meaning to every other virtue, and so where there is humility, there is charity. Humility is the very essence [*vie*] of charity.

The Force of Gentleness

The proper sense of gentleness is difficult to discern, and here again Ephesians invites us to highlight the ways in which gentleness is a gateway to love, peace, and unity. In other words, it is important to point out that gentleness is not a simple psychological quality, but a mode of being open to the world. It is true that gentleness is already a virtue in Greek thought, where it is understood as a sort of moderation that makes reconciliation and thus sociality possible. It is also a political virtue, as moderation is required in applying laws. Moreover, according to the Greek conception, gentleness is the quality of a good individual, who does not give into anger and revenge and who is prone to forgiveness.[10] We see again that the link between gentleness and patience is essential, for one who is gentle endures the misfortunes that befall him with calmness and patience. In other words, gentleness is at once a mastery of the passions and a capacity for acting with flexibility and moderation in determining how to follow a rule.[11]

The biblical concern for an amiable demeanor and gentle voice is not primarily aimed at self-mastery or a lack of excess; gentleness receives a new meaning as a disposition of the soul: restraint and modesty are the modes of being of a creature that is conscious of existing before [*devant*] the creator. Gentleness is no longer simply a virtue in the present, but it also portends a future unity of the human community, for it ought to apply to everyone.[12] According to this new meaning, the gentleness that comes from the Holy Spirit is more than a mastery of our anger. It is a manner of acting that makes unity between men possible. By opening us up to the grandeur of others, gentleness is much more than a victory over self. Rather, from this perspective, gentleness is a capacity of perception, for only gentleness can perceive the gentleness of the other—that is, only gentleness can perceive how the other carries within himself the promise of union. It is therefore possible to discern in gentleness the prospect of an existence spent caring for others—an existence that not only receives the other with attention and caution but also gives the other the capacity to manifest himself. Gentleness never requires anything, and it also refuses to force the other to respond to its questions; in this way, gentleness receives a word of truth. Nakedness enables nakedness, truth invites truth.

Humility and gentleness are not thinkable without each other; the two together provide apodictic evidence for phenomenological ethics. Gentleness is neither weakness nor feebleness. It is not saccharine. Rather, it is a steadfast strength that does not brutalize that which it encounters [*interroge*]. A virtuous man is not some oppressive individual who remains unwavering in his principles; the truly righteous individual is one who exercises restraint and flexibility when faced with the singularity of any given situation. Gentleness has nothing to with relativizing principles, but with learning to adjust to the world instead of making the world adjust to us. In effect, there is no love without gentleness, for in gentleness an individual is not the measure of love, but love is the measure of an individual. Christian charity is not the simple reciprocity of friendship, but a different way of opening up to the other, a mode of union totally different from that which takes place in the world. In love, we demand nothing, we do not set preconditions for the relationship, we do not determine a priori what is acceptable; rather, we take responsibility for that which overwhelms our defenses [*propres forces*] by receiving the other as pure gift. The strength of gentleness is altogether different from an unwavering affirmation of self, for it is the flexibility to receive all things. Gentleness can also be interpreted as poverty: it is a way of acting that does not consist in self-abasement, but that tries to empty itself in order to bear all things. Whether we call it humble gentleness or gentle humility, "the Spirit of gentleness" is an expression for the humility that manifests itself in anticipation of the neighbor.[13] Christ, who is "gentle and humble of heart" and who "neither disputes nor cries out," teaches by his compassion that God desires mercy, not sacrifice.[14]

Patience in Hope

Analyses of humility and gentleness prefigure an analysis of patience, which takes on a very novel meaning and which truly becomes the condition for all virtues. In order to highlight the essential characteristics of patience it is necessary to let go of a purely psychological understanding, which would reduce patience to a simple way of relating to oneself. In fact, patience, in the enlarged sense it receives in Ephesians, is primarily a manner of being in the world that is as suitable for contemplation as it is for action. More generally, patience is a way of bearing the world, others, and oneself. From this perspective, patience is not passive, for it contemplates and acts. True patience, a patience that truly endures, is not a "hardness of heart"—proper to, say, a miser—that suffers all things with an eye toward a particular goal we set for ourselves. Rather, true perseverance, which is eager to encounter the world and which experiences the ordeal of the other face-to-face (precisely as an ordeal, as destabilizing) is radically opposed to an obsessive existence blinded to the world, an existence that is inauthentically patient to the extent that it is insensitive. One who is truly patient allows himself to be affected [touché]; he questions his place in the world, for he does not experience the ordeal of the other as an aggression, nor does he respond by desperately clinging to the identity that he has given himself. Thus patience, in accordance with its own essential features, would be a patience that not only seeks the good but also knows how to wait and does not set conditions, for patience is founded on humility. That which opposes this sort of patience is not impatience, but patience founded on pride, for in its rigidity, it does not know how to receive or await anything and is thus unable to give anything. Such is the paradoxical distinction between a patience capable of anything because it asks nothing and a patience capable of nothing because it asks too much.

It is thus possible to find in the Bible a new understanding of sensibility and the pathetic (in the proper sense of that word) inasmuch as the Bible demonstrates that miserly patience is not virtuous, never realizing true patience inasmuch as it is closed-minded [elle manifeste une fermeture d'espirit]. In fact, hard-hearted patience has no capacity to feel and is thus an abyss into which our humanity falls in a deluded attempt to gain stability. Hardened and prideful patience is a prison that never recognizes itself as such. Yet in order to understand the true essence of patience, it is important not to get caught up in a simple dualism of hardness and sensibility. For it is altogether possible to envision a good sort of "armor" that resists blows without being enclosed in an impregnable fortress: such patience is necessarily linked to hope. In a remarkable way, it is necessary to harden oneself in order to become sensitive to that which is not immediately manifest, that which holds itself back, that which is no longer there. Between the Stoic conception of patience and the Christian conception (as presented by the church fathers), there is no common essence: the former is built on pride, while the latter finds its strength in humility and hope.

These two fundamentally different types of patience are irreconcilable. Patience outside of faith and hope has no common ground with patience inside faith and hope, and that which definitively separates these two "patiences" is the meaning of affectivity in existence.

Christian patience does not hold onto the inhuman ideal of a life without affect, but asks us to silence certain affects so that we might be touched by God's call. It has nothing to do with the patience of a man without God, which is a sort of illusory constancy bordering on despair, nor does it consist in bearing oneself. Every conversion of patience consists in transforming a patience of endurance into a patience of hope. The issue is very delicate: removing the impatience of suffering [*douleur*], in which one risks losing oneself, does not mean that one tries not to feel suffering. The entire task consists in giving a new sense to suffering. Minimizing the importance of affectivity in human life would be tantamount to philosophizing against experience. On the contrary, Ephesians indicates the importance of affectivity, which receives a new meaning. In effect, God's call frees us from a type of patience that would be ours alone, that would be a mode of rising above the world, and that would only be an affirmation of strength against the world. As has been shown, patience must become a form of humility inasmuch as it learns to receive and to be aware of its follies.

The text of Ephesians 4 prompts us, then, to highlight the original phenomenon of patience by distinguishing two very different types of patience: on the one hand, there is a closed-off sort of patience, which is pure self-affirmation and which desires not to be affected [*touché*] by anything. On the other hand, there is an open patience, in the sense of a constant and joyous fidelity. Open patience does not consist in momentarily "keeping a stiff upper lip" in hopes of a better future; rather, patience is a mode of waiting, full of uncertainty, in which man receives a future beyond his projections. The father's patience in the parable of the prodigal son does not rest on certitude or on probability (when he gets hungry, he will probably return); it is essentially hope. Such patience is so foreign to the rational calculation of probability (after the rain comes sunshine), which would provide a reason for waiting patiently; rather, true patience is suffused with love, which is alone capable of awaiting the improbable. Thus patience does not attenuate the pain of loss by rationalizing it or by giving a reason for hope, but it transfigures the pain of loss, giving it another meaning through that which can only be folly for human wisdom—namely, faith in God, faith in the unimaginable.

No man can become God, who exists without passion while full of compassion. Even so, Christ teaches the transfiguration of sensibility by compassion. In effect, patience, which is founded on faith in God, is simultaneously active in the world and lived collectively. Thus, "patience in hope,"[15] as St. Paul says, is the fruit of charity and the proper effect of love.[16] *Agape* alone bears all, not because it is a Herculean power, but because it is a totally new way of bearing—an assertive and enthusiastic form of patience that is confidant in God's promise. Yet, by this patience in hope, man does not find stability within himself, but in the beloved. Patience is neither the anesthesia of resignation nor the void [*vide*] of utopia, but a striving for the future, which is both anxious (because it constitutes an exposure to the world) and serene (because it is confident in the realization of the kingdom of God, which delivers existence from the all-too-human horizon of death). As Luke 8:15 states, "But as for that in the good soil, these are the ones who, when they hear the word, hold it fast in an honest and good heart, and bear fruit with patient endurance." Those who are patient are happy, like Tertullian in his treatise on patience, not because they do not suffer, but because they can decide the meaning of their suffering, because they can make their suffering into a capacity to perceive that which can be perceived only through suffering. It has to do with learning to suffer with Christ, for man is a being who, through suffering—and especially grief—can lose his very being by losing every interior possibility and thereby becoming a prisoner of exteriority. Thus every exercise of patience may be thought of as a tentative restoration of interiority. Those who are incapable of bearing anything are an unhappy lot, for they are totally dependent on exteriority; this applies equally to those who develop a vicious endurance based on worldly desire [*la convoitise du monde*]. Moreover, bracketing our self-concern allows us to see that true patience comes from charity, for in charity, we are patient for something other than ourselves; we become capable of suffering for the sake of justice, not for the sake of self. Humility, gentleness, and patience reveal that the capacity to love something other than ourselves cannot come from the self; it is a gift. These three virtues are not, however, simple prerequisites for preserving the unity of the Spirit; rather, they constitute the very act of seeking unity, for unity is impossible without these virtues, which alone provide an understanding of unity and the will to achieve it. The goal of true patience, which patience alone can envision, is unity and peace and not the self-preservation of an autonomous subject. Thus, because Christian patience is not tantamount to desire [*convoitise*], it is the very act by which love becomes a power [*dynamism*] of the will; it is therefore a continuing engagement, a task, a struggle for peace.

The difficulty, here, consists in providing rational evidence that the serenity of hope has nothing in common with the illusory security of endurance [*endurcissement*], for hope comes from trust in a promise. As

St. Augustine shows, "Behold the reason why we are in safety amid so great temptations, until there come the end of the world, and ages everlasting receive us; namely, because we are covered up in the veiling of His Wings."[17] This is a totally new understanding of human identity: the constancy and strength of our being are inseparable from charity—from charity's constancy—for only the patience of the poor never perishes.[18] Similarly, Kierkegaard, that thinker of suffering, has shown how patience, which is not resignation, is a human response to suffering: "L'impossibilité de se libérer extérieurement de la souffrance n'empêche pas la possibilité de se libérer intérieurement dans la souffrance, de s'en charger volontairement, lorsque par la patience on *veut* y consentir et accepter de s'y trouver."[19] Without going into a full Kierkegaardian analysis of patience, it suffices to show that Kierkegaard, in commenting on Luke 21:19 ("By [ἐv] your endurance [ὑπομονῇ] you will gain your souls"), points out that the text does not say "through" [*grâce à*] or "by" [*par*], but "in" [*dans*] endurance.[20] This signifies that patience is not an instrument to be utilized as impatience would be; rather, patience is the very act of taking possession of oneself. We acquire our souls "in" patience, and yet our souls do not belong to us. Certainly the temptation is always great to give in to impatience, in its many forms, or to resignation, for both attempt to abolish suffering, but man himself exists only *in* patience, for in patience man is faithful to himself. As Kierkegaard says, we do not first gain our souls and then preserve them [through patience], but we gain our souls precisely in preserving them.[21] Thus patience is not a means, but the act of a soul that has not gotten lost in the world, precisely because it is waiting.

To Unsettle, to Pacify, to Unify

The description of the three affects of humility, gentleness, and patience profoundly modifies the traditional understanding of Ephesians 4:1–4, which ultimately signifies something other than the abstract requirements of Christian unity. Indeed, these three affects manifest *agape*—that is, the love that constitutes a community, which, as the achievement of being together, presupposes welcome, approval, and acceptance. Put differently, humility, gentleness, and patience allow man not to "immobilize" love as a simple psychic state, but to give love its full verbal dimension: love does not have the character of a substance; it is not a psychological quality, but the proper way to move through the world. Humility, gentleness, and patience thus effect a sort of spontaneous phenomenological reduction, by which the phenomenon of love becomes manifest. This active love is joyous and may even be seen as a foretaste of the Beatitude. According to

Gal. 5:22, "the fruit of the Spirit is love [*charité*], joy, peace," inasmuch as charitable love is inseparable from knowing God and progressing toward him. Humility, gentleness, and patience are here understood in their active and cognitive capacities: they disclose and create desire for a form of unity, which cannot be seen or desired without them. For that reason, these three affects are the way to achieve love, unity, and peace. The affects therefore make possible a human community that is far more than a collection of autonomous subjects united by a common project. In effect, charity is both receptive and active, for it enables us to learn what we ought to do for the other. The unity of the Spirit makes possible a community that is not an assembly of subjectivities, where each is internally structured as an autonomous self, nor is it a simple outward assembly of individuals, for it is a community where the norms guiding my actions come from paying attention to the other as he is in himself.

Peace should not be understood naively as the state of a tranquil person who is never troubled or disturbed. On the contrary, we aspire to an inner spiritual peace, which prizes hope: "May the God of hope fill you with all joy and peace in believing, so that you may abound in hope by the power of the Holy Spirit" (Rom. 15:13). The Christian understanding of peace, which has its source in God's call, and which is a gift from God, is not the tranquility of a self at home with itself [*l'être auprès de soi*]; rather, peace transforms disciples into members of one and the same body where there is neither Jew nor Greek. Peace is itself an affect in which man is given to himself in a unity with other men. The man who feels at peace is not a tranquil man, but a man who knows that he exists in the unity of the Spirit. From this novel perspective, peace is not experienced as an absence of trouble by those sure of their place in the world, nor is it akin to the comfort of privileged individuals in a world made for them; on the contrary, peace is the ordeal of unity and thus a gift. Accordingly, humility, gentleness, and patience are the affects through which God's gift is sensed (that is to say, understood) and through which man responds to that gift with action: to receive God's peace, to love, and to make peace are one and the same act. Indeed, God's peace is not something one enjoys as a well-earned reward; it is received only in being a peacemaker. Affective experience has, then, an essentially responsive nature: the gift is received in one's active response to the gift that was sent. Unity is not an abstract ideal of essentially separate subjectivities, nor is it a fusion of sensibilities, but it is the task of acting together, of acting for others. The peace announced here is not the simple coexistence of a moral community founded on a common perception of duties and values; rather, it is a peace connected with recognizing one's neighbor as pure gift and responding to that gift. Here again, peace leads back to an affectivity that does not evaluate the other, an affectivity capable of knowledge and action—that is to say, love. The Bible thus demonstrates that peace is not a metaphysics of intersubjectivity, but is made possible by a passivity more original than the subject's intentional life.

While human peace in the historical world is always partial and provisional, the fact remains that the experience of peace always consists in making peace and spreading it as far as possible.[22] Consequently, the task of individuating human persons takes on the novel sense of an experience of pacification—that is, it becomes the tireless and daily task of realizing peace. Indeed, peace in the world is developed and maintained only by a continual search for peace. It therefore makes little sense to differentiate between peace with oneself, peace in God, and peace with others within the active process of making peace. It is clear in this passage of Ephesians that peace is the work of charity in humility, gentleness, and patience. From this perspective, the peacemaker is not a tranquil man, unconcerned with the miseries of the world, because peacemaking is first and foremost a struggle, a capacity for resisting evil. There is no abstract voluntarism involved, inasmuch as the reconciliation of men, which is also a reconciliation with oneself, is made possible by divine action: men become capable of making peace among themselves because God gives man peace.

Conclusion

Humility, gentleness, patience, love, and peace are the affects of unity through which man becomes unified in the always fragile and ongoing task of unifying all mankind. It is therefore possible, in interpreting Ephesians, to develop a true phenomenology of the passions, because it becomes possible to bracket the purely subjective character of sentiment—a notion of sentiment in keeping with Husserl's "natural attitude"—in order to demonstrate its transitive essence, its intentionality of encounter. In Christianity there is a philosophy in which the true meaning of sentiment is revealed not by purging that which is pathological in order to obtain a pure practical sentiment, but in the conversion of the pathetic dimension of existence that occurs in hearing God's call. Just as man never lacks passions, so his passions, by virtue of God's call, never lack compassion. Gentleness, humility, and patience are ways of opening up to my neighbor before I even become conscious of him and before I even desire him. Indeed, if sentiment is comprehended in a natural manner, by an examination of the self by the self—if it is only that—then it occasions a total loss of identity, as in the pain of grief, but if sentiment becomes a way of opening up to something other than oneself, it can be a true path to salvation. Humility, gentleness, and patience do not eliminate the suffering of grief—that would be absurd—but they give suffering a new meaning by showing that grief is also the consciousness of an interpersonal task.[23] This brief examination of grief indicates the possibility of distinguishing two mutually opposed senses of sentiment, which can be limited to the self-enclosure [fermeture] of pride, brutality, and impatience or can be a mode of being for the other. All phenomenology is a phenomenology of the unapparent, for it endeavors to make visible that which is not immediately visible. It is not a matter of claiming that there is a phenomenological project in the New Testament, but of showing that a phenomenological perspective is able to find in the New Testament a concern for finding out the true meaning of pathetic experience, which makes a phenomenology of passions possible.

Humility, gentleness, and patience in response to God's call and as the fruits of charity are the affects of unity, for these three affects not only allow one to enter into unity, but they *are* unification itself. Peace and unity are not possible without the serenity of trusting in God's call. From this perspective, humility, gentleness, and patience are not variable elements of one's personality, but they are affects in which man becomes open to his proper possibilities: to experience humility is to receive the truth; to experience gentleness is to perceive; to experience patience is to hope. Yet every man is first of all occupied with pride, callousness, and impatience, for such is his habitual mode of rapport with others. This most quotidian mode of existence is an inappropriate existence that gives itself over to the passions, including the false sense of mastery that comes from pride. Accordingly, the complete reversal in one's mode of being that Christianity offers consists not just in a purgation of self-concern, which ultimately maintains the contours of quotidian existence; rather, it consists in understanding that unity with oneself occurs only in the achievement of unity with the world. Consequently, the phenomena of humility, gentleness, and patience cannot be understood in the context of a definition of man, where they would be a priori possibilities. On the contrary, they are phenomena that open onto a new understanding of man, as one possessing the identity of exile and exodus.[24] God's call frees us from the singular project of the self, allowing us to temporarily suspend our desire to understand the world within a project of self-elucidation. It pushes us toward unfathomable possibilities, toward an unfathomable unity, which is not a simple assemblage of beings, but which is, on the contrary, a truly communal life. The exhortation of Ephesians 4 calls for an end to inauthentic life, wherein man loses himself by dint of his own will, in order to exist authentically in the light of God's gift, which is the true principle of individuation. The main refrain, to which Ephesians always returns, consists in showing that human-ity is inseparable from patience founded on hope. Kierkegaard himself thus ended one of his edifying discourses: "Praised be the God of patience. This is the end of this discourse."[25]

Translated by Adam Wells

Notes

1. See Jean-Noël Aletti, *Saint Paul Epître aux Ephésiens* (Paris: J. Gabalda, 2001). [Translator's note: The New Revised Standard Version of the Bible translates "ἀγάπη" as "love," whereas older English versions (for instance, the King James) and most contemporary French versions translate "ἀγάπη" as "charity [*charité*]." The latter translation reflects the social obligations inherent in "ἀγάπη."]

2. Emmanuel Levinas, *Totality and Infinity*, trans. Alphonso Lingis (Pitts-burgh: Duquesne University Press, 1969), 305.

3. See Jane Austen's romance *Sense and Sensibility*.

4. See Martin Heidegger, *Phänomenologie des religiösen Lebens*, Gesamtaus-gabe 60 (Frankfurt: Klostermann, 1995).

5. On the question of *Stimmung*, see Emmanuel Housset, *L'intelligence de la pitie: Phénoménologie de la communauté* (Paris: Cerf, 2003).

6. See Plato, *Laws* 4.716a.

7. Philo, *De congressu eruditionis gratia*, §107, in *The Works of Philo Judaeus*, trans. C. D. Yonge (London: Henry G. Bohn, 1854), 2:179.

8. See Jean-Louis Chrétien, *Le regard de l'amour* (Paris: Descleé de Brouwer, 2000).

9. Augustine, *City of God* 18.45.

10. See Aristotle, *Nicomachean Ethics* 4.11.1125b.

11. Jacqueline de Romilly offers a very nuanced view of this recognition of the virtue of gentleness [*douceur*]: "Et le fait est qu'on ne verra la douceur, le pardon, l'indulgence, la compréhension, devenir des vertus reconnues qu'au moment où s'affaiblissent le lien civique et le sens de la cite." [And the fact is that gentleness, forgiveness, indulgence, and comprehension only become recognized virtues at the moment when the civic connection and the sense of the city become weaker.] Jacqueline de Romilly, *La douceur dans la pensée grecque* (Paris: Belles Lettres, 1979), 36.

12. See Col. 3:12.

13. Gal. 6:1.

14. See Jacques Dupont, *Les beatitudes* (Paris: J. Gabalda, 1973), 2:544.

15. See 1 Thess. 1:3.

16. Rom. 8:25.

17. Augustine, *On the Psalms* 61.5.

18. Psalm 9:18.

19. Søren Kierkegaard, *Oevres completes*, vol. 13, *Discours édifiants* (Paris: Édition de l'Orante, 1966), 116.

20. Kierkegaard, *Eighteen Upbuilding Discourses*, trans. Howard V. Hong and Edna H. Hong (Princeton: Princeton University Press, 1990), 159. Translator's note: the NRSV translates Luke 21:19a ("ἐν τῇ ὑπομονῇ ὑμῶν") as "by your endurance." The English "by" implies an instrumentality that is not clear in the Greek. The French word "*dans*"—"in" in English—more accurately reflects the semantic range of the Greek preposition "ἐv." Additionally, "ὑπομονῇ" may be translated as "endurance" or "patience."

21. Ibid., 187.

22. See Jean-Louis Chrétien, *Pour reprendre et perdre haleine* (Paris: Bayard, 2009).

23. See my more developed analysis in Housset, "Deuil et transmission," in *Faut-il faire son deuil?*, ed. Pascal Dreyer (Paris: Editions Autrement, 2009), 51–69.

24. See my analyses in Housset, *La vocation de la personne: L'histoire du concept de personne de sa naissance augustinienne à sa redécouverte phenomenology* (Paris: PUF, 2007); see also my *L'intériorité d'exil: Le soi au risqué de l'altérité* (Paris: Cerf, 2008).

25. Kierkegaard, *Eighteen Upbuilding Discourses*, 202.

Response
Dwelling in the Thickness

WALTER BRUEGGEMANN

The interpretive methods of phenomenology are of course deeply elusive. They are not much spelled out in this volume, though Kevin Hart briefly suggests, after the reductions of Husserl, Heidegger, and Marion, that the proper aim is "disclosing givenness" that leads back to "transcendental consciousness" that leads "to the very margin of the world."[1] Hart usefully cites Lacoste, who advocates a "liturgical reduction" that "leads the one who prays back to the border of the world."[2] But such programmatic phrasing, with its rich nuance acquired in the history of this style of interpretation, does not help much with a particular text. As a result, perhaps more helpful is the resolve of Robyn Horner "to let the text speak for itself,"[3] to "show what is given there."[4] This phrasing is not so forbidding to an exegete and brings an exegete closer to familiar ground with a practice of what is readily termed "close reading." In fact, such close reading is a mainstay among many exegetes who have not been domesticated by more traditional notions of historical criticism. Because the theoretical formulations of phenomenology are not of much help or guidance to an exegete, I propose simply to probe what in fact these interpreters in these essays seem to be doing with the text. I propose to consider these acts of interpretation under the rubric "dwelling in the thickness" as an approach that refuses settlement and watches with attentiveness for interruption.

I

The notion of "thick description" has come to exegetical work from Gilbert Ryle via the anthropology of Clifford Geertz to the hermeneutics of George Lindbeck.[5] In his study of unfamiliar primitive cultures, Geertz contended that cultural articulations and performances were deeply coded and were not accessible to surface observation by an outsider but could be understood only by insiders who knew the codes. Lindbeck cites Geertz on thickness:

> The theologian, like the ethnographer, should approach "such broad interpretations and abstract analyses from the direction of exceedingly extended acquaintance with extremely small matters." . . . Only by detailed "familiarity with the imaginative universe in which . . . acts or signs" can one diagnose or specify the meaning of these acts for the adherence of a religion. What the theologian needs to explicate "is a multiplicity of complex conceptual structures, many of them superimposed or knotted into one another, which are at once strange, irregular, and inexplicit; and which he must contrive somehow first to grasp and then to render." In rendering the salient features, the essential task "is not to codify abstract regularities but to make thick description possible, not to generalize across cases but to generalize within them."[6]

Lindbeck adds:

> There is, indeed, no more demanding exercise of the inventive and imaginative powers than to explore how a language, culture, or religion may be employed to give meaning to new domains of thought, reality, and action. Theological description can be a highly constructive enterprise.[7]

The recognition of this semiotic density means that the narrative text is deeply ambiguous and indeterminate and eventually inexhaustible in meaning. I propose that these interpretive essays are exactly such probes of thickness that seek to go beyond the obvious meaning. The ambiguity is evident, for example, in the exposition of the Pauline "I" in Romans 7 by Jean-Louis Chrétien.[8] Such practice requires nerve to probe again and again, but also humility in a recognition that further exposition to further meanings still awaits us. The recognition of generative thickness is evident in the terse poetry of Amos Wilder concerning the "null point," with the accent on "breed." The text to which attention is paid breeds newness.

Accept no mitigation
But be instructed at the null point:
The zero
Breeds new algebra.[9]

It is exactly the generativity of newness that characteristically surprises the alert reader. As a result the text is most often not simply indeterminate and inexhaustible, but revolutionary in its break beyond all that we thought and assumed was there.

Such attentiveness requires dwelling in that thickness. That means that the reading cannot be rushed, summarized, or read off the surface. Rather, the reader must take up residence in the text and wait there because the text is not only a given in the phrase "what is given there" (as Horner); it is also a "giver" of what is not given until this particular reader waits there and then on occasion receives. What is received, moreover, is often other than what was expected, even though the reader dwells there with receptive anticipation. It is not, however, the case that the waiting reader is always "best friend" to the text so as to assume an easy intimacy; the text may indeed voice an interruption, even a contradiction to the receptive reader. Thus I suggest that these essays variously evidence and well exemplify such "dwelling in thickness." Such a practice is countercultural and revolutionary in our present context of belated capitalism. It is revolutionary because a technically oriented society does not want to acknowledge any thickness; it is countercultural because a hurried productive society does not want to dwell in any way that requires waiting or being directly addressed. Both the thickness of the text and the dwelling of the reader are acts of courage, patience, and humility that defy the ways of dominant culture.

II

The text and its reading constitute a welcome (and deeply unwelcome) act amid societal totalism that wants to monopolize imaginations and administer all possible meanings and so control all economic goods.[10] Wherever it can, such a totalism will also master the text so that meanings are limited and are in fact known ahead of time without dwelling in or attending to the text. Indeed, the management of the text and its interpretation is crucial for totalism. Phenomenology is a courageous response to European culture in which meanings were all known ahead of time, and now, as these essays attest, the text invites and offers standing ground outside the totalism in ways that may interrupt the totalism.

The first totalism that occupied the text to its own advantage is the totalism of church orthodoxy, a practice that still continues where the text must be bowdlerized, explained away, or omitted. Fresh reading of the biblical text that acknowledges thickness means that they do not yield the ready, packaged conclusions of church interpretation of any of the dominant interpretive church traditions. Thus the struggle for the emancipation of the text from the grip of church sanction, a move championed by Luther, is a continuing work of "dwelling."

A second, more formidable totalism that occupies the text is the totalism of Enlightenment rationality that has largely explained away what is interesting, compelling, and embarrassing in the text. The rise of "historical criticism" was designed precisely to wrest the biblical text out of the hands of church orthodoxy. But the text fell promptly into the thin rationality of modernity. Indeed, so-called historical criticism has functioned exactly to smooth away what has been objectionable to Enlightenment rationality, most notably "miracles" and "immortality," as though these mantras could engage the rich specificity of the text.

The third totalism, so powerful among us, is an impatient reduction of all of life to technical mastery. That reduction relies upon and promises quick technical fixes to all human problems and fosters a kind of bourgeois indifference or apathy. The result is that the biblical text in popular usage is readily received (not "heard") with a yawn of comfortable familiarity because it is a text already "known" before "hearing."

III

It strikes me that this fine collection of essays takes narrative as its primary genre. Thus we have commentary on:

The near killing of Isaac (Genesis 22)
The Father and Two Sons (Luke 15)
The Sermon on the Mount (Matthew 5–7)
Jesus and the Woman Taken in Adultery (John 8)
The ambiguous "I" of Paul (Romans 7)
Acknowledgment of unity (Ephesians 4).

The most poignant of these texts are narrative. And even the texts that are not narrative are turned back to the particularity of dispute and possibility that take narrative form. One cannot judge that narrative texts are the only ones that merit attention. But one can conclude that the opportunity to "dwell in thickness," as these phenomenologists are wont to do, pertains peculiarly and definitively to narrative. And that is because, I suggest, no totalism can rely on a narrative because narrative inescapably allows alternative readings and generates new possibility for the characters that may run well beyond totalizing control. The totalizers must always hurry to other genres:

The church has reduced narrative to *propositions* that could become a test of membership.

The Enlightenment reformulated narrative into *syllogism* that generated self-congratulatory control that could function as universal claim.

Late capitalism has reduced narrative to a *medical prescription* with the proper dosage that will numb enough to tolerate a predatory economy.

But *proposition* or *syllogism* or *medical prescription* is no adequate script for the maintenance and nurture of humanness, because these genres close off all possibility.

The interpretive insistences of Geertz have been mirrored by the way in which W. B. Gallie, in his remarkable essay "The Historical Understanding," has focused on the peculiar practice of narrative interpretation.[11] Gallie contrasts the freedom of narrative with conventional scientific/philosophical ways of thought:

We follow a story through or across contingencies,—accidents, coincidences, unpredictable events of all kinds; yet the story's general direction and continuous advance towards its final conclusion somehow succeed in rendering these contingencies acceptable. Yet to traditional philosophical ways of thinking, there is something paradoxical about the juxtaposition of the terms: contingent and acceptable. . . . Somehow or other, therefore, or so traditional ways of thinking suggest, we must transform this appearance of "acceptable contingencies" into something more intellectually respectable.[12]

It strikes me that the combination of "contingent and acceptable" is precisely what we are offered in these essays. The contingent occurs when these alert readers make a move beyond any conventional expectation. These contingencies, in our context of reading, are "acceptable." They are acceptable only in the world of thickness where we seek to dwell. They are clearly not acceptable in any of the totalisms that I have enumerated. In my own discipline of Old Testament study, there is much current interest and dispute about "the violence of God" in the text.[13] The common strategy of commentators, whether in the service of the church or of modernity, is to explain away the violence. But the violence clearly belongs in the narrative and song and is irreducible when we take the narratives (and their lead character) as given to us.

Gallie famously insists on "following the story" rather than explaining it away. He observes of such following:

> In following a story we must always keep our minds open and receptive to new possibilities of development, new hints, clues and leads, up to the very last line. . . . There is probably no better way of suggesting the general structure of the act of following a story than to recall the kind of intelligence, the kind of person, who excels in following (and perhaps also in creating) stories, and by contrasting this kind of intelligence with that which excels in systemic studies, but is slow or insensitive in appreciating stories or histories of any subtlety or complexity.[14]

Gallie becomes lyrical in his readiness for narrative. In commenting on Bougainville's narrative report on Tahiti, he writes:

> The scenes are so brilliant, the incidents so compelling, the passion involved so inevitable, and yet so unheard of, the whole story bathed in a freshness such as we associate with dream or imagination, but which here is due to a kind of irresponsibility that attached to the circumstances. . . . Let the critical, doubting, questioning, assessing attitude of mind lapse—or rise—into the sheer joy of following an absorbing narrative, and the historical mind has passed into the land of story, and is heading hard towards the land of dreams.[15]

Jeffrey Bloechl follows Agamben in speaking of "messianic" time:

> Agamben takes particular interest in the conception of time as messianic, which he defines by a futurity that would transcend the worldly future that is never more than not-yet-now. The way of life that is oriented to such a futurity is not, at root, restricted by any worldly order.[16]

Bloechl suggests that such messianic time "is essentially decentered" and, following Badiou, has an interest in liberating us from totalization.[17] The notion of messianic time is a recognition that in narrative imagination the present tense authorized by any totalism is not a settled state and that our reading of the text is not a settled reading but is always open to new possibility. While that may be true of any and many narratives, it is, as our culture experience attests, peculiarly true of the biblical text with its capacity always again to breed new revolutionary possibility.[18]

The texts of new possibility that are studied here keep refusing old explanations and dramatizing new possibility: the "coming kingdom" is like a man with two sons, like the woman who is sent away "to sin no more," like the almost slain son who becomes the heir, like the wretched "I" of Romans 7 who becomes the buoyant self of Romans 8 who is never separated. The narratives present human agents who have their lives opened to new possibility that can only be termed "messianic." Such a usage calls to mind the exposition of Enriqué Dussel, who looks for a way and time in which the victim can erupt in insistent social possibility:

> The victim who becomes conscious, who erupts with a revolutionary praxis, produces a rupture of "continuous time." He or she erupts "remembering (the liberatory anamnesis)" "commemorating" other liberatory-messianic moments of past history.[19]

Dussel appeals to Gramsci, who dared to judge that such a move by the victim was "the small door through which the Messiah might enter."[20] These several usages of the term "messianic" suggest that while Gallie's notion of following surely pertains to all narratives, the biblical narrative is peculiarly occupied with messianic potential that is re-performed, each time freshly, when it is taken seriously on its own without totalizing domestication. It is perhaps unfortunate that these essays do not reflect more on the proper context that will permit reading and receiving outside the totalism. It is the "elsewhere" as the venue for reading that may be decisive. "Elsewhere" from totalism is to be without power or wealth or leverage, but not without narrative imagination that conjures new historical possibility.

IV

A final thought about where we read. I suggest an analogue and metaphor from Ray Oldenburg. In two books, Oldenburg has characterized and identified specific "third places," specifically a library, a book store, a coffee house, a church, a pub.[21] Not just any of these but particular ones. Oldenburg's notion of "third places" is apart from the "first place" of work and the "second place" of family and home. The first place of work is a venue for coercive, endless production and performance. The second place is the intimacy of home with all of its tacit rules and orders of power in which all members are cast in firm and expected roles according to unexpressed codes. But a third place is a place outside coercive production or familial codes. It is a place of freedom, play, imagination, and possibility. It is most exactly a place of *permitted transgression* of social boundaries, roles, and expectations. Such transgression, of course, opens up all kinds of new possibilities.

Mutatis mutandis, it occurred to me that readings offered by these phenomenologists in this volume are readings from and in a third place. The first place of reading in such a taxonomy would be the church, with its long practice of reading. Such reading is particularly championed as canonical by Brevard Childs and Christopher Seitz and is contained in the service of the community that perforce brackets out any excessively venturesome reading in the interest of church certitude.[22] Thus resonance with the creed and the confessing tradition is paramount and is reflected in the new commentary series that holds to such a doctrinal discipline. Obviously there is a long reading in this trajectory that fails to observe the cost of resisting readings that depart from the canonical.

The second place of reading in such an analogy is the critical academy that historically has lived in tension with church reading. This reading transposes the "outrages" of the text according to modernist categories that regularly feature supersessionism so that the preferred reading always supersedes the objectionable reading. While the first place of church reading contains the character of God through a canonical filter and the rule of faith, the second place of reading turns the character of God into a human socio-psychological projection.

It is evident that neither of these approaches can afford to take the text seriously on its own terms so as to "let the text speak for itself," to "show what is given there." And indeed, that latter may be an impossibility for any of us as interpreters, because we do not come to the text innocently. But we have to try, and these essays model such an attempt. Reading in the third place "from elsewhere" permits the text to be transgressive about what is possible and invites the reader well beyond the familiar to new awarenesses and new possibilities. It is not likely that such a reading can be sustained for very long, because it will either succumb to some totalism in which the reader is engaged or it will become a new totalism on its own. And that means, of course, that yet another reading from elsewhere must always be again undertaken.

I am appreciative of the fresh interpretations offered in this volume. But I also want to assert, in finishing, that this is no new venture here undertaken by the phenomenologists. I notice that the citations in these essays are largely lacking in any awareness of the work that is going on in the field of these texts. Without having the technical nomenclature of the style of phenomenologists, current close reading of the text is much practiced by many exegetes who live in tension with both church authority and modernist rationality. Such a lively unauthorized practice includes a cloud of witnesses who consistently dwell in the thickness. Among them is my teacher James Muilenburg, who refused the dominant scholarly model of his day.[23] It is a welcome recognition on my part that we exegetes have such formidable companions in the enterprise. The continuing task is an important one, as the contemporary totalism of too much orthodoxy allied with predatory economics seeks to slow and impede the coming of the Messiah who is and will be attentive to the cries of those left behind—that is, those who are required to live "elsewhere."

Notes

1. See, in this volume, Kevin Hart, "The Manifestation of the Father: On Luke 15:11–32."

2. Ibid.

3. Robyn Horner, "Phenomenology as *Lectio Divina*: Jesus and the Woman Caught in Adultery," in this volume.

4. Ibid.

5. George A. Lindbeck, *The Nature of Doctrine: Religion and Theology in a Postliberal Age* (Philadelphia: Westminster Press, 1984), 115.

6. Ibid.

7. Ibid.

8. Jean-Louis Chrétien, "Split Interpretations of a Split I: Romans 7:7–5," in this volume.

9. Amos Wilder, "A Hard Death," *Poetry* 107 (1965–66): 168–69.

10. See Emmanuel Levinas, *Totality and Infinity: An Essay on Exteriority* (Pittsburgh: Duquesne University Press, 1969), and, with more historical concreteness, Robert Jay Lifton, *Witness to an Extreme Century: A Memoir* (New York: Free Press, 2011).

11. W. B. Gallie, "The Historical Understanding," in *History and Theory*, ed. George H. Waddell (Middletown, Conn.: Wesleyan University Press, 1977), 149–202.

12. Ibid., 155.

13. Representative volumes include Jerome F. S. Creach, *Violence in Scripture*, Interpretation (Louisville: Westminster John Knox Press, 2013), and Eric A. Seibert, *The Violence of Scripture: Overcoming the Old Testament's Troubling Legacy* (Minneapolis: Fortress, 2012).

14. Gallie, "Historical Understanding," 164.

15. Ibid., 173–74.

16. Jeffrey Bloechl, "Love and Law according to Paul and Some Philosophers," in this volume.

17. Ibid.

18. On the continuing generativity of social possibility in the text, see Michael Walzer, *Exodus and Revolution* (New York: Basic Books, 1985).

19. Enriqué Dussel, *Ethics of Liberation in the Age of Globalization and Exclusion* (Durham: Duke University Press, 2013), 242–43.

20. Ibid., 243.

21. Ray Oldenburg, *Celebrating the Third Place: Inspiring Stories about the "Great Good Places" at the Heart of Our Communities* (New York: Marlowe, 2001), and Oldenburg, *The Great Good Places: Cafes, Coffee Shops, Bookstores, Bars, Hair Salons, and Other Hangouts at the Heart of a Community* (New York: Marlowe, 1999).

22. Brevard S. Childs, *Biblical Theology of the Old and New Testaments: Theological Reflection* (Minneapolis: Fortress Press, 1992); Christopher R. Seitz, *The Old Testament as Abiding Theological Witness* (Grand Rapids: Eerdmans, 1998).

23. James Muilenburg, "Form Criticism and Beyond," *JBL* 88 (1969): 10–18; see also Phyllis Trible, *Rhetorical Criticism: Context, Method, and the Book of Jonah*, Overtures to Biblical Theology (Minneapolis: Fortress, 1984).

Response
Interpretation and Agency

DALE B. MARTIN

The essays in this collection are rich in variety and deep in theological insight. They offer fresh readings of scripture that, though informed by modern historical criticism, go beyond that ascetic, and sometimes dry and narrow, discipline. They often read more as meditations on passages of scripture than strictly historical-critical exegesis. They are thus a pleasure to read. In general, my response is one of appreciation. Yet after commenting on several of the essays of the collection, I shall respond to others with a quibble over some of the epistemological and methodological rhetoric framing some of the essays—and the entire collection because of the introduction to the volume by Adam Wells. Because I group the different essays with regard to their method of interpretation and degree of acknowledgment of the activities of the interpreter, I will be dealing with the articles not in the sequential order of their appearance in the volume, but according to my own way of responding to them.

In "To Exist without Enemies," Jean-Yves Lacoste meditates on the seemingly impossible command of Jesus ("the foolish commandment par excellence") to love one's enemies, meaning precisely the enemy who attempts to do us *personal* harm rather than an enemy of one's country ("the *inimicus* and not the *hostis*"), the latter of whom may be easier to love simply because more distant from us and less personal in the threat. In the first place, we may imagine fulfilling the command by an act of will rather than affection. If I can sincerely pray for my enemy, for my enemy's good, perhaps that means I love the enemy.

But Lacoste argues that if we love as God loves, we will end up imitating the affection of God, even toward our enemies. In a complex theological discussion, Lacoste links this to the doctrines of divine simplicity and *theōsis*, the possibility of our participation in God's divinity in some mysterious way. "Love of enemy is to be heard as word and way of beatitude or blessedness." It should be noted that Lacoste gives no explicit attention to the rationale for his claims or reasons for them. What he says he states as something like common sense: this is just the way things are. May I take it that this is how the essay is phenomenological?[1]

In a similar way, Kevin Hart's essay, "The Manifestation of the Father: On Luke 15:11–32," is not an exegesis but rather a retelling of the parable of the prodigal son, but with the father—not the son—as the central character. By reading the story very slowly, expanding on its details in imaginative speculation, Hart leads us to identify with the story and its different characters: the father, the younger son, and his elder brother. Hart does not offer the meaning of the parable. Rather, he invites his readers to let themselves down into the story in order to see that, by moving within the narrative, readers may experience the move from worldly logic to divine logic, from world to *basileia* (kingdom). The movement, moreover, comprises two moments: *kenōsis*, in which I empty myself of "the worldly logic that has controlled" my life, and then *epektasis*, "stretching" myself "into the kingdom of God, that is, into the embedded relations of unconditional love that are already available." Ultimately, the parable teaches us something about the nature of God, a God we can never fully know to be sure: God is like a human father and yet "*unlike* any human father we know." What I have offered here is of course only an inadequate summary of the retelling and its interpretation. Experiencing the meaning of Hart's sensitive essay, like the parable, requires a slow reading—and rereading.

Jeffrey Bloechl's essay, "Love and Law according to Paul and Some Philosophers," is not a retelling of a biblical text or a meditation on a passage of scripture. It is rather something like a combination of two different dialogues, first with the secular and political readings of Paul promoted by Giorgio Agamben and Alain Badiou, and second with the writings of Paul on community and love. Both dialogues are fair to Bloechl's interlocutors and complex in philosophy and theology. One of Bloechl's important points, and one with which I completely agree, is that the appropriations of Paul by both Agamben and Badiou is in terms of the structure of Paul's Gospel, not its content.[2] Bloechl is certainly correct to point out that by having only a secularized grace—that is, grace without God—Agamben and Badiou end up not having a robust (Pauline) context of unconditional love, which not only leaves out the most central ethic and promise of Paul's

Gospel, but also makes any emphasis on true community all but impossible, at least in Pauline terms. I also agree that whereas Badiou's Paul addresses only individual subjects, Paul himself was much more concerned about community and perhaps had almost no concern for what we moderns know as the individual. Bloechl shows what we miss when we take on Badiou's and Agamben's secularized Paul.

Some Reservations and Quibbles

So far, so good. I have briefly noted that the three essays thus far discussed provide valuable and creative readings of scripture within full-bodied theological and philosophical contexts. Another aspect the essays share that may be emphasized a bit more is that they betray little explicit attention themselves to the activities of interpretation. Indeed, they work with a rhetoric of implying that this is simply the way things are or wishing to hear Paul on his own terms. My unease with apparent assumptions about interpretation and the lack of acknowledgment of interpretive agency, though, is provoked more in my reading of certain of the other essays.

Jean-Luc Marion, on the phenomenon of sacrifice, begins by noting that a common understanding of sacrifice is the making sacred of something previously profane. Though people commonly may think of sacrifice as necessitating the destruction of the thing sacrificed, Marion notes an alternative: to consider sacrifice within the logic of exchange, which then leads him into a discussion of the various controversies surrounding the gift. But rather than ending up with the *aporia* caused by thinking that giving a gift thus deprives the giver of the thing given, Marion, returning to sacrifice, offers an alternative understanding: "Sacrifice does not return the given to the giver by depriving the recipient (*donataire*) of the gift: it renders givenness visible by re-giving the gift."

Marion then illustrates what he means by an analysis of Genesis 22:1–19, the sacrifice of Isaac. Precisely because Isaac belongs to God and was given to Abraham only as a gift, Abraham is not deprived of something that is his when he offers Isaac back to God. "By sparing Isaac, . . . God re-gives Isaac to him, gives him a second time." Neither God nor Abraham is deprived of the gift. And the thing sacrificed is therefore not destroyed. The thing sacrificed, precisely because it was an *unconditional* gift, remains present to the giver and the recipient. Nothing is destroyed except the distance between the two.

As have the other essays thus far mentioned, Marion's reading usually presents itself as simply observing things as they are. He makes claims about sacrifice, gifts, and exchange, among other topics, with an air of common sense, as if he is simply describing what we all see and know. But the very fact that he is heavily involved in interpretation comes abruptly to the fore in his analysis of the sacrifice of Isaac. Why take this *as* a sacrifice? After all, Jewish tradition and interpretation reject the term "sacrifice" for the narrative at all, insisting that since Isaac was in the end not sacrificed, it should be called "the binding of Isaac." By *interpreting* the passage as about the sacrifice of Isaac, Marion has already to some extent predetermined the meaning of the passage in a way he need not do. In fact, calling the scene the "sacrifice" of Isaac already renders it a foreshadowing of the sacrifice of Jesus, God's son, for the world. This is not simply the way things are; it is a strong (Christian) interpretation of what was originally a Jewish text. I don't believe there is anything wrong with that. I just want to highlight its activity as an *interpretation* by a particular person—in this case the agent Marion.[3]

Robert Sokolowski's essay, "God's Word and Human Speech," is a thoughtful theological rumination on the problem of combining the doctrine of the radical transcendence of God in relation to the universe with the faith that we may trust the communication of God—through human authors or other media—to us.

But again, and even more so here, there is no attention to the very complex and active necessity of human *interpretation*. Sokolowski says that "words and pictures capture and carry the intelligibility of the things they represent." These inanimate objects do that themselves? He claims that "Phenomenology . . . deals with the manifestation of things." In his section entitled, "Allowing Words to Do Their Work," the agency of the interpreter is completely eclipsed by the supposed agency of words. "Words capture the intelligibility of things . . . the very words exercise a power on those who hear and use them. . . . The words do the work. What we need to do is to let them sink into us and shape our minds."

This may all work as persuading us to assume a certain stance or attitude to interpretation. We may tell ourselves, when we read scripture, that we should open our minds and be ready for unexpected thoughts or experiences. But if this kind of rhetoric masks the very activity of *human interpretation* and therefore the recognition of *our own agency* in the theological and ethical *use* we put scripture to, that is not only theologically insufficient; it is also immoral in its denial or ignorance of our responsibility as agents of interpretation. The words of the text simply do not do what Sokolowski says they do, unless his language is taken in a consciously metaphorical way. But all the way through Sokolowski's rhetoric, and that of many of the essays in this collection, phenomena and words and texts simply have their meaning in themselves and just present that to us. Readers are passive receptors, not agents in meaning-making.

This insistence that texts provide meaning and that readers simply receive that meaning is not surprising, since it appears first in the Introduction by Adam Wells.[4] Wells says that "a true science of scripture must draw its methods from a concrete engagement with scripture." Phenomenology, at least as proposed by Husserl and described by Wells, demands a "return to the things themselves." It should "draw its method *from* its objects of inquiry." Its scientific method "must be derived" from "the things themselves" (emphasis in Wells).

But how is that supposed to happen? Do we use historical criticism to note that Jesus interpreted scripture by rejecting a clear command concerning divorce, by which Moses permitted it and turning instead to a text that says nothing at all about divorce in order to forbid divorce completely (Mark 10:1–12; Matt. 19:1–12; Deut. 24:1, 3, Gen. 1:27; 5:2)? Jesus's interpretive method here goes against both ancient and modern hermeneutical rules that one should interpret the obscure by the clear rather than the clear by the obscure.[5] If we reject that old hermeneutical rule and follow Jesus's hermeneutical example, we have after all made a *decision* to do so. Do we follow Paul's method of reading scripture by insisting that Deuteronomy 25:4 must not have anything to do with actually muzzling an ox while it treads out grain, since we know, with Paul, that God doesn't really care about oxen? The text must be about preachers being paid (1 Cor. 9:8–10). Or perhaps we should practice allegory, as Paul does in his interpretation of Sarah and Hagar in Galatians 4:21–5:1. I am not saying we should *not* use these methods of interpretation for ourselves. I'm just insisting that the text of scripture itself did not tell us to do that, nor is the text of scripture constraining our interpretations in any way. The very taking of these texts to be about methods of interpretation is our activity. And it would be *our choice* to use them as models of interpretation, not something we just were told to do by the text.

Repeatedly in the first half of Wells's essay, phenomena or texts are spoken of as the agents of their own meaning-making. Phenomenological methods just "allow scripture to give itself fully." "Everything that gives itself to be perceived (in whatever way it gives itself) ought to be accepted as being just what it is." A phenomenon simply manifests itself. But how is that possible? Things, whether objects of nature, of art, of society, or, yes, the things that are texts, do not speak. They cannot simply deliver their meaning to us as if we merely passively observe or listen to them. Texts simply cannot do that, as is even empirically demonstrated (no text has ever meant anything apart from some kind of interpretation).[6]

Later in the Introduction, Wells seems to realize this. He eventually asks, "Aren't presuppositions and assumptions insidious and inescapable?" To which the proper answer must be, "Yes, inescapable; but of course they are not necessarily insidious. They may be perfectly open, benign, or even generous." Wells ends up adding, "Objects do not simply exist 'out there.' They are constituted as particular objects . . . by experiencing subjects." Yes, they are for us *as* they are *interpreted* by us and other human beings. But then why all this talk about letting texts speak for themselves, supplying for us the methods of interpretation we are then supposed to use to interpret them? Why not put the agency where it belongs, with us human beings, rather than where true agency can never reside: in things themselves? My discomfort with much of the rhetoric of many of the essays in this collection springs from this: what I consider rather confused language about agency and interpretation.[7]

The nature of my frustration may be finally illustrated by my reading of Emmanuel Housset's essay, "The Affects of Unity," on Ephesians 4:1–4. Housset's essay is, in my opinion, more a meditation than pure historical-critical exegesis, and it suffers nothing because of that. Indeed, I find it an inspiring Christian theological meditation on humility, gentleness, patience, love, and peace. But the value of Housset's edifying reading comes not from some property of the text itself, but from Housset's own expert, learned, and sensitive interpretation.

Housset frames his practice in the same objectivist rhetoric of (what we are told in many of these essays is) phenomenology. "Thus phenomenological theology exists only in the context of a radicalization of the requirement to return to the 'things themselves' beyond all mental constructions." The goal of phenomenology "is to understand everything according to its own standard of knowledge." According to Housset, "phenomenology requires humble submission to the phenomena as they give themselves, endeavoring with the most possible rigor to avoid all theoretical or speculative bias." But an analysis of Housset's analysis shows how that is not at all what he has done. He has, rather, been a very active agent promoting one particular interpretation of Ephesians.

First, Housset takes Ephesians to be by Paul himself, though most of us critical biblical scholars and historians nowadays would say that the letter was written by a later disciple of Paul, who was himself using the Letter to the Colossians as his model, which was itself written not by Paul but by *another* of his admirers. Whether one takes Ephesians to be authentically Pauline will have something to do with how one reads it. In other words, because Housset reads Ephesians as by Paul, he and I are not going to read the text in the same way. We can't just take the text on its own terms. Housset *brings to the text* one of the terms: Pauline authorship. I *bring to the text* my assumption that Paul is not the author. Reading as changes meaning. Because I *cannot* (any longer) read Ephesians as actually by Paul, I will necessarily not see the same meaning in the text as does Housset, who *does* take Paul to be the author.

The inescapable meaning-making done by the interpreter may be further illustrated in Housset's interpretation by noting the several lenses through which Housset reads Ephesians 1:1–4: Philo of Alexandria; the conception of patience "presented by the church fathers"; Augustine; Kierkegaard; and not coincidentally Emmanuel Levinas and Heidegger himself. Without these lenses, or interpretive strategies, one will not see the phenomenon of the text here seen by Housset.

Recognizing Agency

My reader may have noticed that I have yet to mention two essays, those by Robyn Horner and Jean-Louis Chrétien. I have saved those for last because they illustrate precisely the kind of recognition of interpretive activity I have been urging. They both recognize the activity of agency and even play with it in their essays.

Horner begins "Phenomenology as *Lectio Divina*: Jesus and the Woman Caught in Adultery" by resisting Adam Wells's brief "just to let the text speak for itself, without interfering in that speech." In her words, "we cannot ignore the way in which hermeneutics plays its part." This was where I noticed for the first time in the book attention to the agency of the interpreter *as interpreter* and maker of meaning. In her reading of John 8:2–11, Horner plays around (if I may describe her very serious interpretation with a playful verb) with the notion that she can't see Jesus in the scene very well at all, no matter how hard she tries: "we can do no more than guess at his appearance . . . we cannot even begin to imagine who he is, not just how he appears." Horner here acts out her self-conciousness in interpretation. What follows, then, in the rest of her essay is an imaginative *lectio divina*, a devotional reading of the story of the woman taken in adultery. When Horner finally gets to the end of the story, where Jesus asks the woman if any of her accusers remain on the scene, Horner notes, "She cannot make this assessment with her eyes downcast (have they been downcast?)." Note how this is again a gentle, but clever, nod to Horner's own interpretive agency.

In his delightful *tour-de-force* of the manifold interpretations throughout history of Romans 7:7–25, "Split Interpretations of a Split I," Jean-Louis Chrétien illustrates the necessity of interpretation (even without saying so explicitly), with all its uncertainties, choices, exclusions, and inclusions of meanings. Precisely in his emphasizing that readers over the centuries have debated who is meant by the "I" in Romans 7:7–25, Chrétien demonstrates that the meaning of the text ends up only with the interpretive activities of readers. Is the "I" an autobiographical reference to Paul's own experiences? And if so, is Paul referring to himself before baptism, and thus outside the grace of Christ? Or does Paul indicate the present: does Paul still, even after baptism and justification, experience the struggle of will and evil? Or is Paul here practicing *prosopopoiea* (or *ethopoiea*), "speech-in-character," that he almost certainly would have learned in rather elementary rhetorical education? Is the character of the *psosopopoiea* Man universal? Or only gentiles, who do not sufficiently have the law as guide? Or does the character represent both Jews and gentiles but before the justification and knowledge that comes with Christ? Chrétien admits that recently most critical scholars accept the "speech-in-character" interpretation, but not all.

Chrétien proceeds to bring in "certain modern, post-Romantic interpretations of *Paradise Lost*." He describes the importance of the passage for "Luther's doctrine of the law," but then admits, "but the text itself does not impose his [Luther's] interpretation." Chrétien's essay is a demonstration and proof of "surplus of meaning," and surely that is true not just for Romans 7, but for all texts.

As an historical critic, I would argue that the "I" in Romans 7 must be speech-in-character for the human being without Christ (constructing, that is, what I would take to be Paul's intention for the passage). Yet as a (postmodern) theologian (of an amateur sort), I would suggest that we allow both readings of the passage: one that identifies the meaning of Romans 7 in Paul's own historical situation and the context of the complete Letter to the Romans, but also one in which we find scriptural illumination of our own struggles with the will and our inability always to do the good we want to do. In a postmodern theological context, we still use historical criticism, in all its ascetic narrowing down of the meaning of the text, but we are not limited to that method or that meaning. We can have different meanings of the text, and many of them, all at the same time, interpreting differently for different ends and needs.[8]

I happily conclude with these last two essays because they illustrate well the kind of attention to our agency as readers of texts—rather than the rhetoric of listening to the text, or acting as if the text itself will tell us how to interpret it—that I missed in some of the other essays. That quibble aside, I close by commending all these essays as rich in theology, even poetry of a sort, and meditations. They model the art of Christian reading. They provide valuable examples of invested Christian use of scripture.

Notes

1. As an aside, I mention my puzzlement at Lacoste's statement: "In the strictest sense, Jesus never receives a messianic mantle in the gospels." What, then, would he do with Mark 8:29, Matt. 16:16, or many other passages, including just about all of the Gospel of John? Perhaps I just don't understand what he means by "the strictest sense."

2. Perhaps this is at least similar to a point I once made about the lack of content of the event in the philosophies of Badiou and Žižek; see Dale B. Martin, "The Promise of Teleology, the Constraints of Epistemology, and Universal Vision in Paul," in *St. Paul Among the Philosophers*, ed. John D. Caputo and Linda Martin Alcoff (Bloomington: Indiana University Press, 2009), 91–108.

3. Some obvious problems with Marion's interpretation also jump out. Marion takes Isaac to be the one and only son of Abraham. What about Ishmael? Marion takes the sacrifice of Isaac to be related to God's command that the Israelites offer their "first-born sons" to him (Exod. 22:29–30, 13:2). But, of course, Abraham's first-born son is Ishmael, not Isaac. Much could be made (though I will not here) of Marion's erasure of Ishmael (and his descendants?) in Marion's very creative and active *interpretation*.

4. Perhaps I should point out that I previously read an earlier version of the Introduction. This second, revised version emphasizes less than the earlier one the insistence on letting phenomena or texts speak for themselves or tell us how to interpret them.

5. See, for example, Augustine, *De doctrina christiana* 3.83 (26.37); Duncan S. Ferguson, *Biblical Hermeneutics: An Introduction* (Atlanta: John Knox, 1986), 161.

6. I have spent a good deal of my career trying to battle against the notion that texts speak or just give us their meaning and that we should just be passive listeners of texts. I have argued many times that that notion of reading is not only theoretically erroneous but morally questionable, as it hides the actual interpretive agency of interpreters; see Dale B. Martin, *Sex and the Single Savior: Gender and Sexuality in Biblical Interpretation* (Louisville: Westminster John Knox, 2006), and Martin, *Pedagogy of the Bible: An Analysis and Proposal* (Louisville: Westminster John Knox, 2008).

7. Reading much of this kind of rhetoric, as if things simply have meaning in themselves and are capable of communicating that to us, I could not push out of my mind Ludwig Wittgenstein's "duck-rabbit"; see Wittgenstein, *Philosophical Investigations*, trans. G. E. M. Anscombe, 3rd ed. (New York: Macmillan, 1953), Part II, xi, 194e.

8. For a (rather long) illustration of this kind of postmodern, antifoundationalist, Christian theological reading of scripture, see Martin, *In a Sense: Theology WITH the New Testament* (New Haven, Conn.: Yale University Press, forthcoming).

Acknowledgments

Many thanks to the contributors and translators for their excellent work and patience throughout the process of putting this volume together. I am also grateful to everyone who offered encouragement and advice on this project—particularly the late Helen Tartar, Kevin Hart, and the excellent staff at Fordham University Press. Thanks are also due to the University of Virginia Press, Indiana University Press, St. Paul Center for Biblical Theology, Brill, and the National Gallery of Scotland for permission to reprint material. Last, I thank my family for their unflagging support.

Contributors

Jeffrey Bloechl is Associate Professor of Philosophy at Boston College and Honorary Professor at Australian Catholic University. His publications include *Christianity and Secular Reason: Classical Conceptions and Modern Problems* (University of Notre Dame Press, 2012); *Religious Experience and the End of Metaphysics* (Indiana University Press, 2003); and *Liturgy of the Neighbor: Emmanuel Levinas and the Religion of Responsibility* (Duquesne University Press, 2000). He is also the founding editor of *Levinas Studies: An Annual Review* (Duquesne University Press) and, with Kevin Hart, *Thresholds in Philosophy and Theology* (University of Notre Dame Press).

Walter Brueggemann is Professor Emeritus at Columbia Theological Seminary. A world-renowned theologian and scholar of the Hebrew Bible, his recent works include *The Creative Word: Canon as a Model for Biblical Education* (Fortress Press, 2015); *Chosen? Reading the Bible amid the Israeli-Palestinian Conflict* (Westminster John Knox, 2015); and *Truth Speaks to Power: The Countercultural Nature of Scripture* (Westminster John Knox, 2013).

Jean-Louis Chrétien, Professor of Philosophy at the University of Paris-Sorbonne, is the author of a number of works on philosophy and theology. Many of his works are available in English translation, including *Under the Gaze of the Bible* (Fordham University Press, 2014); *The Call and the Response* (Fordham University Press, 2004); *The Ark of Speech* (Routledge,

2004); *Hand to Hand* (Fordham University Press, 2003); and *The Unforgettable and the Unhoped For* (Fordham University Press, 2002).

Kevin Hart is the Edwin B. Kyle Professor of Christian Studies at the University of Virginia and Edwin D'Arcy Professor of Philosophy at Australian Catholic University. An acclaimed poet and theologian, his recent publications include *Wild Track: New and Selected Poems* (University of Notre Dame Press, 2015); *Kingdoms of God* (Indiana University Press, 2014); *Clandestine Encounters: Philosophy in the Narratives of Maurice Blanchot* (University of Notre Dame Press, 2010); and, co-edited with Michael A. Signer, *The Exorbitant: Emmanuel Levinas between Jews and Christians* (Fordham University Press, 2010). He has received multiple awards for his poetry, including the Christopher Brennan Award and the Grace Leven Prize for Poetry.

Robyn Horner is Associate Professor and Associate Dean (Learning and Teaching) in the Faculty of Theology and Philosophy at Australian Catholic University. Her publications include *Rethinking God as Gift: Marion, Derrida, and the Limits of Phenomenology* (Fordham University Press, 2001) and *Jean-Luc Marion: A Theo-logical Introduction* (Ashgate, 2005), as well as numerous book chapters and journal articles engaging the thought of Jean-Luc Marion, Emmanuel Levinas, and Jacques Derrida with theological concerns.

Emmanuel Housset is Professor of Philosophy at the University of Caen Basse-Normandie and Director of the Identity and Subjectivity research group. He has written many works in the phenomenological tradition on Husserl and ethics, including *Husserl et l'idée de Dieu* (Cerf, 2010); *L'intériorité d'exil* (Cerf, 2008); *La vocation de la personne* (Presses Universitaires de France, 2007); and *L'intelligence de la pitié* (Cerf, 2003).

Jean-Yves Lacoste is a Life Fellow of Clare Hall, Cambridge. A philosopher and theologian who works in Paris and Cambridge, his recent publications include *L'intuition sacramentelle* (As Solem, 2015); *Être en danger* (Cerf, 2011); and *Experience and the Absolute* (Fordham University Press, 2004).

Jean-Luc Marion, member of the Académie Française, is The Andrew Greeley and Grace McNichols Greeley Professor at the University of Chicago Divinity School, Department of Philosophy, and Committee on Social Thought; Dominique Dubarle Chair of Philosophy at L'Institut Catholique de Paris; and Professor Emeritus at the University of Paris-Sorbonne. He is the author of many books, including *Negative Certainties* (University of

Chicago Press, 2015); *In the Self's Place: The Approach of Saint Augustine* (Fordham University Press, 2012); *Being Given: Toward a Phenomenology of Givenness* (Stanford University Press, 2002); and *God without Being* (University of Chicago Press, 1991; 2nd ed., 2012).

Dale B. Martin is Woolsey Professor of Religious Studies at Yale University. He specializes in New Testament and Christian Origins. His books include *New Testament History and Literature* (Yale University Press, 2012); *Pedagogy of the Bible: An Analysis and Proposal* (Westminster John Knox, 2008); *Sex and the Single Savior: Gender and Sexuality in Biblical Interpretation* (Westminster John Knox, 2006); *Inventing Superstition: From the Hippocratics to the Christians* (Harvard University Press, 2004); *The Corinthian Body* (Yale University Press, 1995); and *Slavery as Salvation: The Metaphor of Slavery in Pauline Christianity* (Yale University Press, 1990).

Robert Sokolowski is the Elizabeth Breckenridge Caldwell Professor of Philosophy at The Catholic University of America, where he has taught since 1963. He has been a visiting professor at the Graduate Faculty of the New School and the University of Texas at Austin, Villanova, and Yale. His recent publications include *Phenomenology of the Human Person* (Cambridge University Press, 2008) and *Christian Faith and Human Understanding* (The Catholic University of America Press, 2006).

Adam Y. Wells is an Assistant Professor of Religion at Emory & Henry College. He received his Ph.D. from the University of Virginia in Comparative Scripture, Interpretation, and Practice. His research focuses on phenomenological approaches to scripture in the Abrahamic traditions.

Index

Perspectives in Continental Philosophy
John D. Caputo, series editor

Recent titles:

Françoise Dastur, *Questions of Phenomenology: Language, Alterity, Temporality, Finitude*. Translated by Robert Vallier.

Jean-Luc Marion, *Believing in Order to See: On the Rationality of Revelation and the Irrationality of Some Believers*. Translated by Christina M. Gschwandtner.

Adam Y. Wells, ed., *Phenomenologies of Scripture*.

An Yountae, *The Decolonial Abyss: Mysticism and Cosmopolitics from the Ruins*.

Jean Wahl, *Transcendence and the Concrete: Selected Writings*. Edited and with an Introduction by Alan D. Schrift and Ian Alexander Moore.

Colby Dickinson, *Words Fail: Theology, Poetry, and the Challenge of Representation*.

Emmanuel Falque, *The Wedding Feast of the Lamb: Eros, the Body, and the Eucharist*. Translated by George Hughes.

Emmanuel Falque, *Crossing the Rubicon: The Borderlands of Philosophy and Theology*. Translated by Reuben Shank. Introduction by Matthew Farley.

Colby Dickinson and Stéphane Symons (eds.), *Walter Benjamin and Theology*.

Don Ihde, *Husserl's Missing Technologies*.

William S. Allen, *Aesthetics of Negativity: Blanchot, Adorno, and Autonomy*.

Jeremy Biles and Kent L. Brintnall, eds., *Georges Bataille and the Study of Religion*.

Tarek R. Dika and W. Chris Hackett, *Quiet Powers of the Possible: Interviews in Contemporary French Phenomenology*. Foreword by Richard Kearney.

Richard Kearney and Brian Treanor, eds., *Carnal Hermeneutics*.

Aaron T. Looney, *Vladimir Jankélévitch: The Time of Forgiveness.*

Vanessa Lemm, ed., *Nietzsche and the Becoming of Life.*

Edward Baring and Peter E. Gordon, eds., *The Trace of God: Derrida and Religion.*

Jean-Louis Chrétien, *Under the Gaze of the Bible.* Translated by John Marson Dunaway.

Michael Naas, *The End of the World and Other Teachable Moments: Jacques Derrida's Final Seminar.*

Noëlle Vahanian, *The Rebellious No: Variations on a Secular Theology of Language.*

A complete list of titles is available at http://fordhampress.com.